THE SHIP MODEL BUILDER'S HANDBOOK

FITTINGS & SUPERSTRUCTURES FOR THE SMALL SHIP

By Tom Gorman

Nexus Special Interests Ltd
Nexus House
Azalea Drive
Swanley
Kent BR8 8HU
England

© Tom Gorman 2000

The right of Tom Gorman to be identified as the Author of this work has been asserted by him in accordance with the Copyright, Designs and Patents Rights Act of 1988.

All rights reserved. No part of this book may be reproduced in any form by print, photography, microfilm or any other means without written permission from the publisher.

ISBN 1-85486-206-5

CONTENTS

Acknowledgements		5
Introduction		6
Ship Models and Types		7

Chapter 1	Aerials		1
Chapter 2	Anchors		4
Chapter 3	Anchor Cranes and Davits		7
Chapter 4	Binnacles		9
Chapter 5	Bitts		10
Chapter 6	Bollards		12
Chapter 7	Bows		15
Chapter 8	Bulwarks		17
Chapter 9	Cable Stoppers		21
Chapter 10	Capstans		24
Chapter 11	Chain Cable		27
Chapter 12	Cleats		28
Chapter 13	Cranes		29
Chapter 14	Davits		33
Chapter 15	Decks and Deck Plating		39
Chapter 16	Fairleads		43
Chapter 17	Fire Fighting Equipment		47
Chapter 18	Funnels		51
Chapter 19	Hatches		55
Chapter 20	Hawsepipes		59
Chapter 21	Hull Construction		60
Chapter 22	Ladders and Companions		69
Chapter 23	Lifeboats		73
Chapter 24	Lifebuoys		79
Chapter 25	Liferafts		81
Chapter 26	Lights		83
Chapter 27	Masts and Derricks		89
Chapter 28	Mooring Pipes		95

INTRODUCTION

This volume is designed to help the model ship builder to readily find data and pictures of the many fittings that can be found on the decks of small ships such as tugs, fishing boats, coasters and short sea traders and similar vessels that measure under 250 feet (75m) in length. Many keen ship modellers live and work many miles inland and far from the large ports and estuaries where ships can be seen and readily photographed. I have been fortunate enough to have lived almost my entire life close to or connected with ships and their ports, berths and building yards. Having been brought up the son of a seagoing marine engineer, a great deal of my youth was spent on cargo ships and my early working life was in the offices of a marine engine works. From an early age I used a camera quite extensively but failed to keep pictures taken until after the late 70s. I often wish I had kept many of the films I shot, as some would be a source of invaluable information today. Since about 1976 I have kept my photographs carefully and it is from these and from pictures taken in recent months that this volume is produced.

It is hoped that the information, pictures and sketches included will be of value and assistance to the ship modeller. Some of the photographs were taken with a marked rod positioned against the fitting; this rod is marked in 100mm wide bands and this banding allows the viewer to measure the equipment quite accurately. Regretfully not all the pictures incorporate the measuring rod. Wherever possible tables of sizes have been provided and these will, in most cases, provide the correct sizes of the fittings for the given sizes of ships.

It must be remembered that almost every fitting, piece of machinery, boat or superstructure is subject to the controls and rules laid down by the appropriate classification society i.e., Lloyds, Bureau Veritas, etc. There are, of course, some items that are installed to suit the owner of the particular ship and such items may well be in excess of the requirements of the classification society.

Fig. 1 ACADEMUS a scallop dredging fishing vessel built in 1998.

ACKNOWLEGEMENTS.

I must acknowledge the invaluable assistance rendered to me by the following who gave of their time and knowledge so freely. Messrs Tim and John Rix and their staff at J.R.Rix & Sons Ltd., Hull who allowed me free and easy access to their fleet of ships and to their masters who showed me the finer points of their vessels and answered never-ending questions. My thanks, too, to Eric Hallam senior naval architect of I.M.T. Marine Consultants who provided a great deal of data and help. Also to Jan and John Noble who provided a great deal of information on fishing vessels, navigation lights etc. Lastly but by no means least my thanks must go to my associate of more than 28 years for his assistance and forbearance in our endeavours over the years. To all those others who have helped in many ways I also offer my sincere thanks, for a work of this kind cannot be done without a fair degree of research and assistance.

Tom Gorman, Walkeringham 2000.

Chapter 29	Portholes	97
Chapter 30	Propulsion	98
Chapter 31	Pumps	110
Chapter 32	Radar Equipment	111
Chapter 33	Rails and Stanchions	112
Chapter 34	Rigging	116
Chapter 35	Rivets	120
Chapter 36	Rope Reels	122
Chapter 37	Rudders	125
Chapter 38	Sails	129
Chapter 39	Shafts	131
Chapter 40	Skylights	134
Chapter 41	Steering Gear	137
Chapter 42	Superstructures and Deckhouses	140
Chapter 43	Tanks	147
Chapter 44	Tankers	148
Chapter 45	Towing	149
Chapter 46	Tow Hooks	151
Chapter 47	Vents and Ventilation	155
Chapter 48	Winches	163
Chapter 49	Windlasses	168

Appendices

Sources and reference	175
Specialist suppliers - kits and bits	175
Magazines and Plans	177
List of Illustrations	178

Note that there is very little information and/or data applicable to warships (the grey fleet), as there are many notable books on such ships with a huge store of suitable photographs. Some fittings can be seen on ships much larger than those catered for here but that is purely down to the fact that they are well designed and easily scaled to suit a given vessel's size.

The great majority of model ship kits available in the model shops today are very comprehensive and contain a host of fittings with which to enhance the projected model. Some even contain additional parts in case of loss or to cater for a modified version of the box-pictured ship. Some of the kit makers also make their range of ship's fittings, lifeboats etc available to the modeller who merely wishes to use them on a model of his/her own design. It is necessary for the scale ship modeller to ensure that the fittings used are of correct size and pattern for the ship model under construction and for him/her to verify that such parts were actually fitted to the ship at the time at which the model is depicted.

Fig. II Model of the scallop dredger ACADEMUS built for presentation to the owner.

Fig. III Working model of the stern trawler GLENROSE I.

Many ships are modified structurally during their service lives for many different reasons. Some are lengthened to increase their cargo carrying capacity, some are fitted with different engines leading to removal of a funnel or a similar detail visible above the waterline, while others have alterations made to their superstructure to facilitate better navigation or increase accommodation. These all can affect the model that is to be built and it is essential that the modeller depict the ship at a given date particularly if the model is being entered in competition or for a specific display.

It is quite possible that the precise fitting needed by a modeller for a specific ship will not be found within these pages but there will certainly be an item very close to that required and from which a suitably altered fitting can be constructed. Obviously, too, between the production of this text and the printing of the book some new fittings or parts of ships can have been made. Under such conditions it will be necessary for the modeller to research the part individually. No good ship model is ever built without adequate research being spent on the project and good starting points for such research are the owners of the particular ship, the builders, Lloyds Register of Ships and the facilities of the maritime museums. Most will assist if polite requests in writing are sent complete with return postage or prior telephone calls are made from which the costs of the searches can be ascertained.

It is hoped that the information herein will be of value to ship modellers of all experiences. To ease searching for a particular fitting or detail the entries are listed alphabetically so that one only needs the name or type of part to find it. It must also be explained that the fittings depicted here are applicable, in the main, to ships of less than 250 feet in length and thus they may not always be seen to be correct for larger ships, which have heavier scantlings. Many of the fittings seen on the modern ship bear no resemblance to fittings of older vessels as, frequently, the modern ship carries items that relate to modern navigation, radio and satellite systems which are recent innovations. Many of the aerials seen on the modern ship have no place on the older ship and it would be incorrect to fit such items on a ship depicted to be sailing in the days between the wars. It is part of the research into the ship to ensure that all the items used are correctly depicted and researching into the history of a ship, even a fairly new one, can be very enjoyable and satisfying.

Fig. IV Steam driven model open steam launch MARVON QUEEN.

SHIP MODELS AND TYPES

Model ships fall into a number of categories and the ship model builder needs to be aware of these standard categories. The illustrations here show some models built in these standard forms.

Scale working models

These are usually divided into to two classes for exhibition purposes; models built to a scale of up to 1:24 and models built to a scale of over 1:24 (1:24 equals 1/2in to 1 foot in imperial measurement). The yardstick for metric measurements would read 1:25. Working models include those driven by electric motor, steam engine and internal combustion engine.

Static scale models

These are in the same vein as above except that the models are built without any propulsion and are usually built for display purposes. In general the same scale sizes prevail dividing the section into two classes.

Miniature models

These are generally models built to very small scales of smaller than 1:200 and most are built to 1:600 or 1:1200. They are almost invariably displayed housed in glass cases. Very few models in these small scales are produced with radio controls and electric drive although there are a few.

Dioramas and similar scenes

These are models built to depict a scene including a ship or shipbuilding yard etc. and are generally to a small scale.

Fig. V Model pilot cutter, steam driven. CHIMAERA.

Fig. VI Model of CHIMAERA completed and ready for testing.

When ship models are entered into competitions such as the International Model Show held each year in the London area they are usually divided into the classes shown above although those models built from kits are shown in a separate class devoted to kits only and they are not subdivided by scale. The fact that a model is built from a kit does not mean that the result is inferior to that built from scratch, some very fine models are made from kits by discerning modellers and there is quite often little to chose between them for quality workmanship.

Fig. VII Prize winning working model of the twin screw coaster ARRAN MAIL built by the author.

Some model ship builders work to produce models specifically for entry into competitions and they often elect to build models of ships they have visited or seen with the advantage of having had the chance to take photographs to assist with the project. Some modellers build purely for their own edification selecting drawings from the ranges of various plans services and enhancing their models without ever setting foot on a ship at all. Others build for the pleasure of sailing at the local model boat club and, often, to enter into local and regional sailing competitions. Some ship modellers build in their own workshops for themselves alone and

Fig. VIII Model of SEGUIN under way.

their models are rarely exhibited at all. All these model ship builders need access to data and information. Whether from the ship owners, builders or museum services, information is needed to complete a good-looking and serviceable ship model.

The photographs shown here illustrate some of the types of model that may be seen at venues round the country and are provided to assist the ship model builder. The models built by the author fall into the first two categories; about 50% are powered and radio-controlled and the balance are static and fitted into display cases. On occasion a model is built from a kit for review purposes and these afford a view of how some kit manufacturers overcome some of the problems of providing detail. The ability to research into and make some of the small fittings found scattered round the decks of modern ships is often quite a daunting task and it is hoped that the following pages will be of assistance.

Where there is a number of like fittings to be made and fitted to a model it is sensible to investigate the possibility of making a single, good quality master and from this to make a mould in silicon rubber and cast the required number of parts in white metal or resin. The process has been described in a number of publications and is fairly straightforward. A number of specialist suppliers can supply the necessary materials and also the instructions on how to make full use of the products. It should always be remembered that some materials can be hazardous and should be handled with care and strictly in accordance with the maker's instructions. White metal being a compound containing lead is one such product although there are some so called 'white metals' that are lead free. The making of a number of parts from a single master in no way prevents the model from being totally scratch built, it is only when such parts are produced commercially that the term 'scratch built' may not be used for a model.

It is also possible to make masters of lifeboats and produce a number for a model using a flexible rubber or silicon rubber mould and making the models in GRP (Glass Reinforced Plastic) or even in papier-maché. This, too, is a time saving when building a model ship having a number of like boats fitted. It is wise to research all aspects of the chosen vessel so that correctly made model fittings can be fitted or, at the very least, fittings that closely resemble the real thing are used. There are many ship's fittings that are of standard size and form and these are often used in many different locations on the ship, sometimes with slight alterations. It is important to site these correctly and to paint them so that they blend into the model as they do in full size.

Fig. IX Model of luxury sailing yacht INGA IV fitted with auxiliary electric motor and radio controls, shown here ready for first tests.

Wherever possible, in the following pages, there has been provided as much data as possible regarding the fitting or item and its use but the onus of verifying the correct fitting for a specific vessel remains with the model builder. The model ship builder will find some anomalies among the matters into which he/she researches, for example I have not been able to ascertain precisely when ships changed the colours of their side boards from red/green to black. I believe that this occurred in the early 1970s but it may have been earlier. Similarly at one time ship's depth marks were in Roman numerals on one side of the ship and in Arabic on the other and in imperial measurement. They are now in metric measurements and Arabic numerals on both sides of the ship. When this change came about is, again, uncertain but I believe that it, too, came in the early 1970s.

Today all lines and general arrangement drawings for ships are drawn in metric units and, obviously built to these measurements except in the USA where feet and inches still prevail. The model builder must thus be careful to ensure that he/she builds in the correct scales. It is easier to build a model in imperial measurements if the original ship was built to such measurements, as converting from imperial to metric scales will only lead to error. Obviously it is also sensible to build a model in metric measurements if the full size ship is in the same. Today, too, it is possible to have scale drawings enlarged or reduced very accurately at the premises of a specialist copier and at very reasonable charges. Even just three decades or so ago it was necessary for the modeller to enlarge or reduce a ship's drawings to the scale required by redrawing the plans or by employing a draughtsperson so to do. This was a time-consuming process or, at the very least, expensive.

It is not necessary today to own a comprehensive kit of tools as many fine models are made using but a few good quality hand tools. A good craft knife, a steel rule and a self-healing cutting mat will handle almost all the cutting of thin plywood or styrene sheet needed. A selection of small drill bits and a small hand drill will cater for most needs while a small pin hammer and a tenon saw will be useful. Most other tools needed will be found in the average home. Obviously the use of a lathe, a pedestal drill, a power drill and a power fretsaw will give advantages to the modeller but they are certainly not vital.

The object of this volume is, however, not to provide instruction in model building but to illustrate and list many ships' fittings and details to provide data for the modeller and to this end I hope it will prove of value. It must be pointed out that the drawings included within this volume are not usually drawn to a particular scale but to represent types of equipment. They should not, therefore, be copied for making the particular fitting unless there are dimensions given.

Fig. X Model of HM Customs & Excise cutter BADGER in rough water.   Photo courtesy of Ray Brigden

AERIALS

In the early years of radio communication, ships carried transmitters and receivers, which were very large, and which required aerials to be strung between masts - usually the main and fore masts, see sketches **Figs. 1 & 2**. These wire aerials were strung between porcelain insulators and had leads that ran into the radio room which was usually located aft of, but close to, the bridge of the ship. Ships were thus fitted from the early 1900s until after the last world war. Since the 1950s the radio communication industry has advanced in great leaps and bounds. Today all communication is by voice; no longer does the merchant ship carry a radio operator nor is it necessary for a crewman to have knowledge of Morse code. Aerials abound from the top of the modern ship as illustrated. They cover not only communications, but also satellite navigation of a number of types and many other functions such as computer-controlled information data. Radar is illustrated later.

Note from the photographs how aerials differ and, when researching a ship, ensure that the correct configuration of the range of aerials is logged for repetition on the model. Even quite small fishing vessels carry a sophisticated range of telecommunication and search equipment. Methods of producing aerials in model form are a matter for personal preferences but fine piano wire will adequately reproduce the whip-type aerial while small lengths of styrene tube will make up the casings. Short pieces of copper or aluminium tube will also make suitable rod aerials. For earlier ship's radio aerials it will be necessary to model the porcelain insulators and these can be simulated using the split lead shot used by anglers to weight their lines. Such shot can be bought from most fishing tackle shops in a variety of sizes and weights. The sketch **Fig. 6** illustrates the general shape of the porcelain insulator that was used on early ships.

Fig. 1   <u>**Single Wire Aerial**</u>

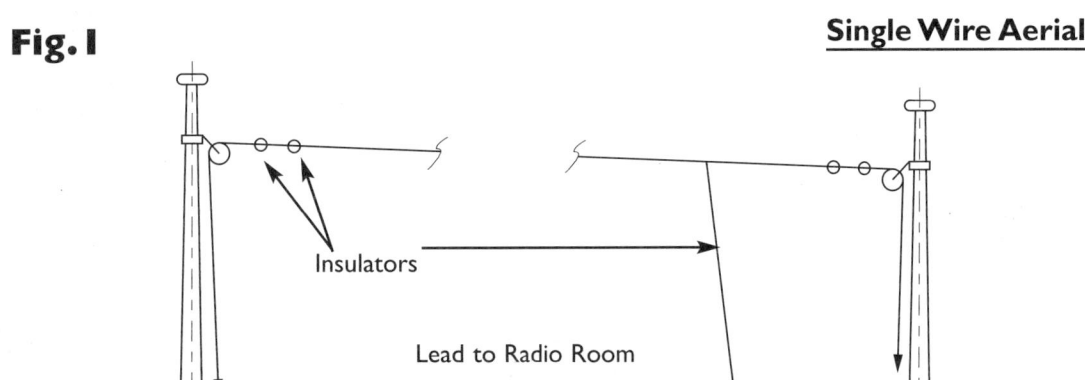

<u>**Twin Wire Aerial**</u>   **Fig. 2**

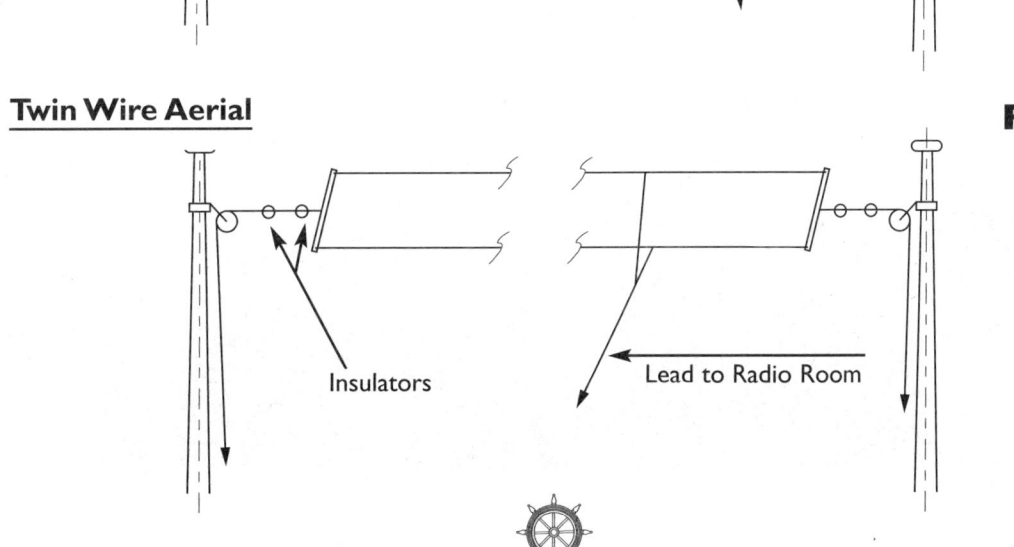

Fig. 3 Main mast of short sea trader showing aerials, radar etc.

Fig. 4 Mast and aerial detail on an inshore fishing vessel.

Fig. 5 Mast and detail of aerials on stern trawler GLENROSE I

Typical Porcelain Insulator

Fig.6

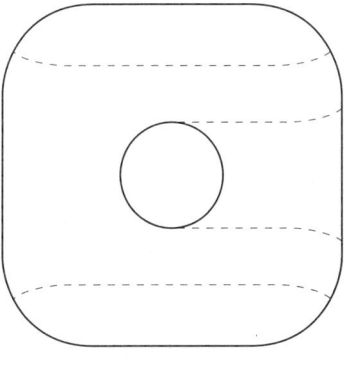
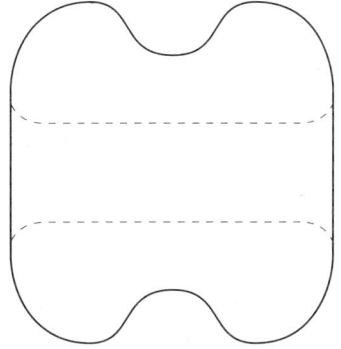
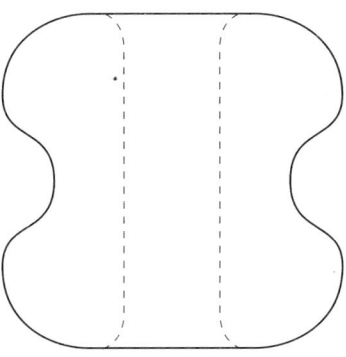

Fig. 7 Model of main mast for a small trawler.

Fig. 8 Model of main mast for an inshore fishing vessel

ANCHORS

Anchors on ships are made to comply with the classification society's requirements relative to the size and power of the ship. The number of anchors carried is also under the ruling of the classification society. Most merchant ships carrying general cargo, containers, etc., tankers and similar vessels will carry two anchors in ready-to-use form shackled to their respective chain cables and drawn up into the hawse pipes or hawse boxes near the bow of the ship. Almost invariably the ship will carry a spare anchor secured on the foredeck close to the anchor windlass. It is rare to find a ship carrying an anchor for duty at the stern and this practice is usually found only on very large vessels or large warships.

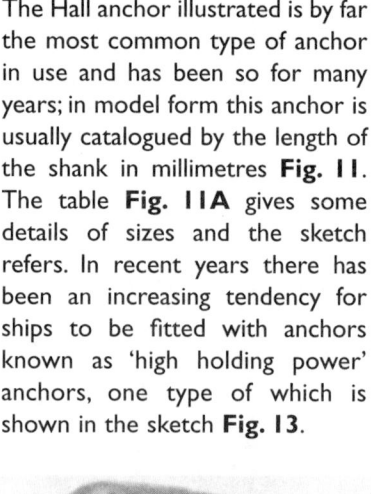

The Hall anchor illustrated is by far the most common type of anchor in use and has been so for many years; in model form this anchor is usually catalogued by the length of the shank in millimetres **Fig. 11**. The table **Fig. 11A** gives some details of sizes and the sketch refers. In recent years there has been an increasing tendency for ships to be fitted with anchors known as 'high holding power' anchors, one type of which is shown in the sketch **Fig. 13**.

Fig. 9 Hall anchor shown drawn snugly into hawse pipe of a cargo vessel.

Some smaller ships, particularly fishing vessels, carry only one anchor in ready-to-use form drawn up into the hawse pipe or box and generally on the port side of the bow. An example of this can be seen in the pictures of the Glenrose I that carried a second anchor mounted on a support on the starboard side of the foredeck in front of the bridge. Very early vessels and most sailing ships carried the common stocked anchor shown in sketch **Fig. 14** but rarely seen today.

Fig. 10 Spare anchor fitted behind substantial frame on foredeck of cargo ship - note measuring rod.

'Hall' Anchor

Fig.11

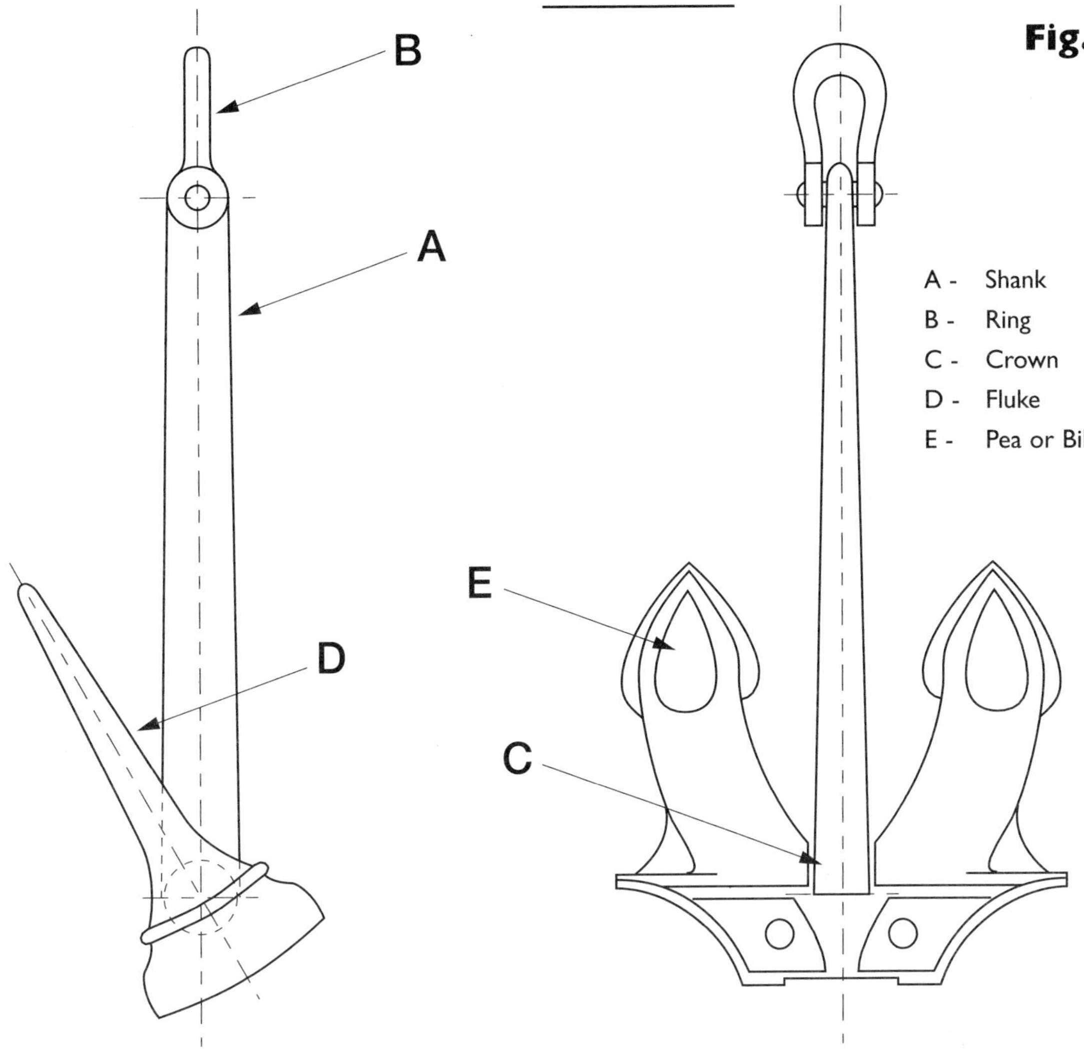

- A - Shank
- B - Ring
- C - Crown
- D - Fluke
- E - Pea or Bill

Fig.11A   Some Dimensions For 'Hall' Anchors

Weight of Anchor in pounds	Length of Shank		Length of Arm	
	Inches	Millimetres	Inches	Millimetres
220	32.50	825	16.25	412
440	40.00	1016	20.50	520
880	51.50	1308	25.75	654
1500	62.00	1575	31.00	787
2200	70.00	1778	35.00	889

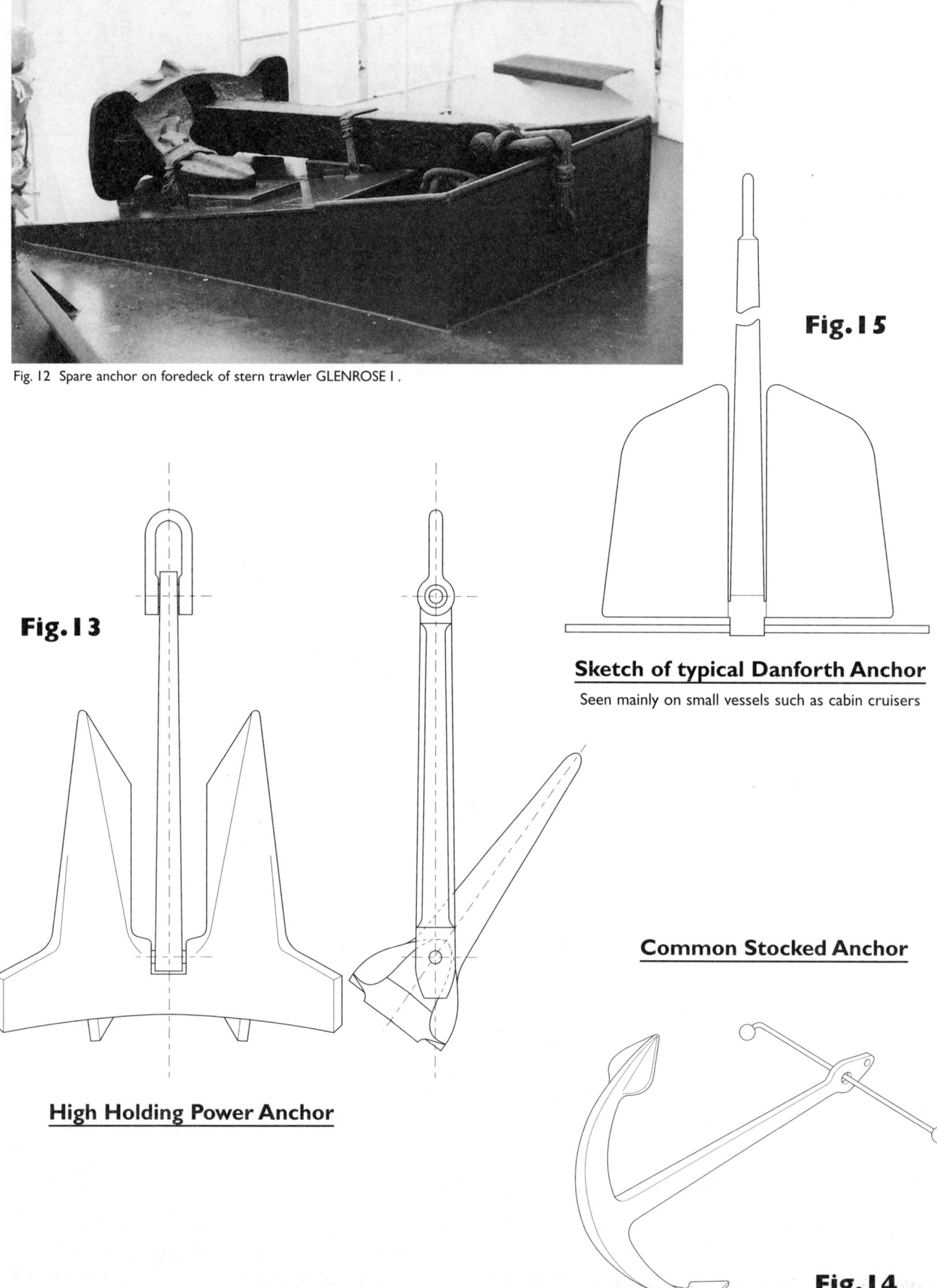

Fig. 12 Spare anchor on foredeck of stern trawler GLENROSE I.

Fig.15

Sketch of typical Danforth Anchor
Seen mainly on small vessels such as cabin cruisers

Fig.13

High Holding Power Anchor

Common Stocked Anchor

Fig.14

ANCHOR CRANES AND DAVITS

On some of the early ships such as the herring drifters and steam trawlers, there were no hawse pipes extending from the foredeck to the sides of the ship's bows. A hole cut through the bulwarks on both sides of the ship was heavily reinforced with hardwood and the anchor cables were fed through these holes. The anchors were lifted over the bulwarks by means of a small davit similar to those used for lifeboats and stowed securely on the deck until needed.

The sketches illustrate both davits **Fig.16** and anchor cranes **Fig.17**. Anchor cranes were less common on ships of up to 250 feet long, as they were needed for anchors of reasonably heavy weight. The crew used the warping drums of the windlass or the capstan to haul the ropes of the tackle and to lift the anchor clear of the ship's sides before it could be swung inboard and lowered into a suitable cradle. Models of both davit and crane can easily be constructed from brass rod and tube with few tools or they could be made from styrene rod and tube. The latter will be less robust but possibly easier to handle particularly for a small-scale model.

Typical Anchor Davit

Fig.16

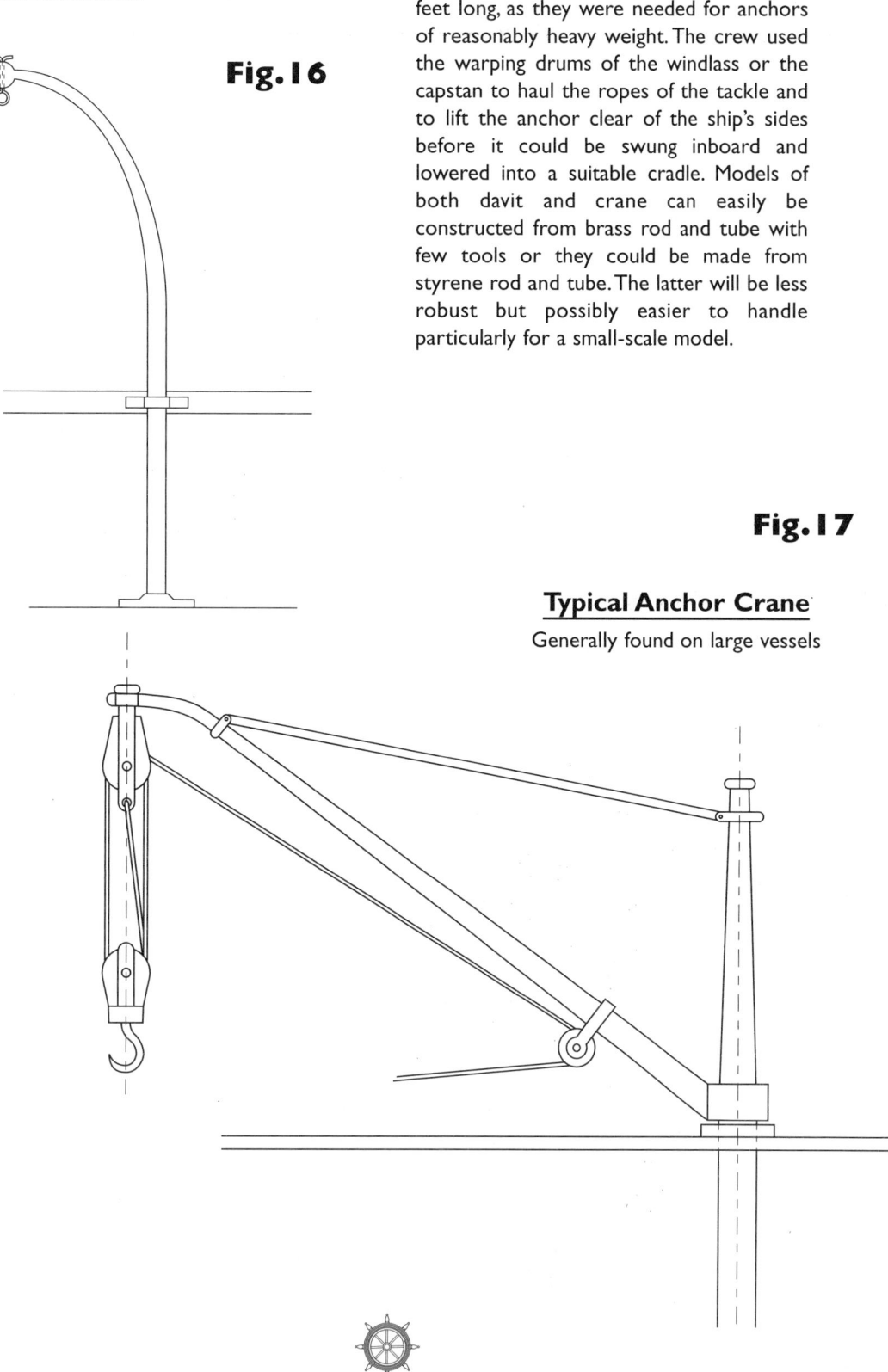

Fig.17

Typical Anchor Crane
Generally found on large vessels

Fig. 18 Anchor davit on bow of a model steam yacht.

BINNACLES

There have been almost no changes in the design of the binnacle over the years. It is a unit made to contain the ship's compass. It is made of non-magnetic material and wood with the compass mounted in a set of gimbal frames at the top. On either side near the top of the unit are angle frames carrying the correction spheres on slotted arms. Usually there is a form of illumination built in to light up the compass card and at the back will be found the tube of the flinders bar.

As will be seen from the photographs many ships carried binnacles both inside the wheelhouse and also on the wheelhouse roof. A highly decorative item, the binnacle has sadly slowly disappeared to be replaced by more modern gyro compasses and satellite navigation equipment. It was quite usual for many ports to have a turning circle within the navigable area of the port or river where, under the control of two tugs, a ship could be turned through 360 degrees to allow the compass to be adjusted. This was an essential task performed at regular intervals to ensure that the compass was always reading correctly. The steel or iron construction of the ship interfered with the swing of the compass and this was compensated for by the spheres which were moved and locked in place once the compass had been seen to read correctly. Generally the sphere on the port side of the binnacle was painted red and that on the starboard was painted green although some of iron were encased in brass which was kept highly polished as was the rest of the brasswork. A well-detailed model binnacle is an attractive feature for a well-made model. They varied little in size and height and were usually about 18in in diameter by about 48in tall (480 x 1200mm). The compass card was viewed through a glass window set at an angle at the top and the 'lubber's line' was clearly marked at the back of the casing. Suitable illumination of the compass card was provided.

The photographs show model binnacles produced from mini-kits that were part of model ship kits manufactured by Mount Fleet Models to a scale of 1:32 - see appendices.

Fig. 19 Binnacle on top of wheelhouse of a small model coaster illustrating weather cover open.

Fig. 20 Binnacle with voice pipe and telegraph for fitting into the wheelhouse of a coastal tug model

BITTS

These are very large bollards used for towing and fitted to tugs mainly of American pattern. The European and UK tug fleets largely use towing hooks. Until recently only very large ocean-going or salvage tugs were fitted with towing winches. Today the tendency in towing is to use towing winches specially designed for towing duty in all sizes of tugs. The bitts used mainly in the U.S.A. are illustrated here with the larger units **Fig. 21** mounted aft of the accommodation and athwartships and the smaller unit **Fig. 22** mounted ahead of the accommodation in line with the keel.

Fig. 21

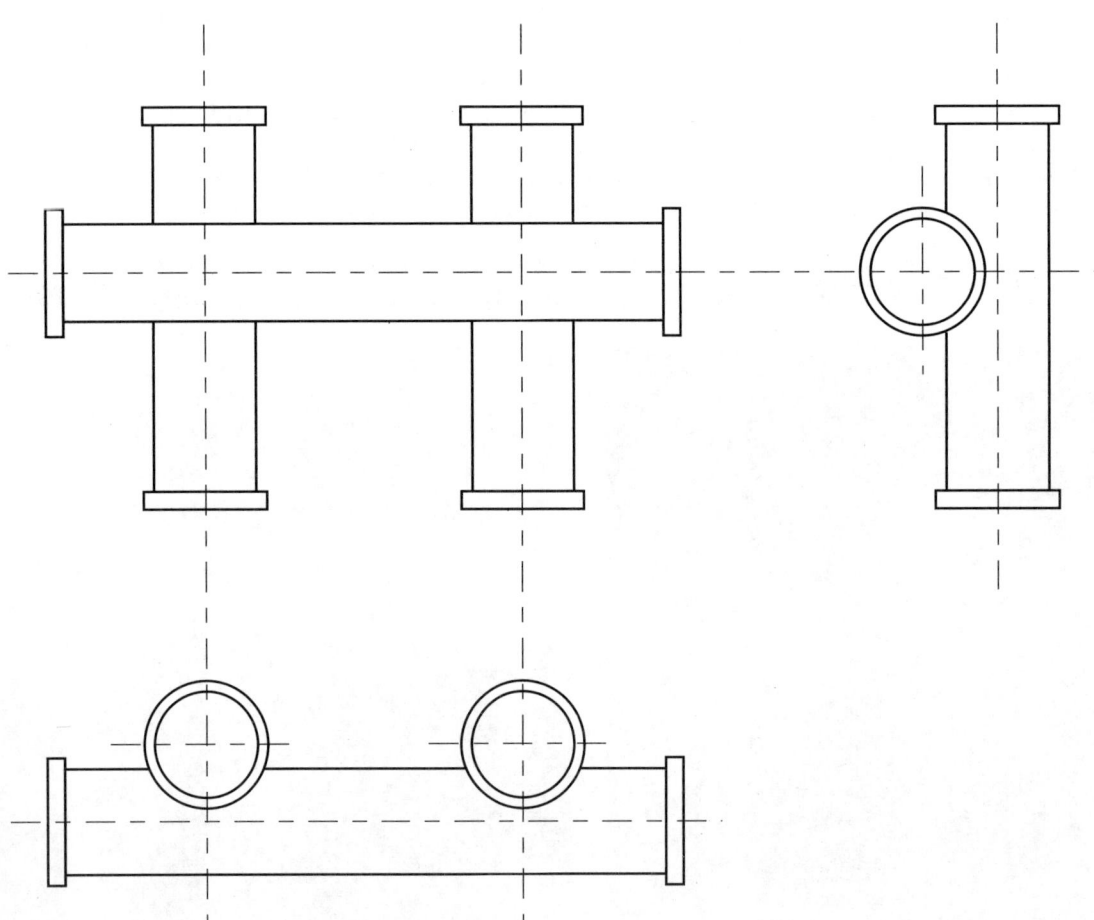

Main Towing Bitts (USA)

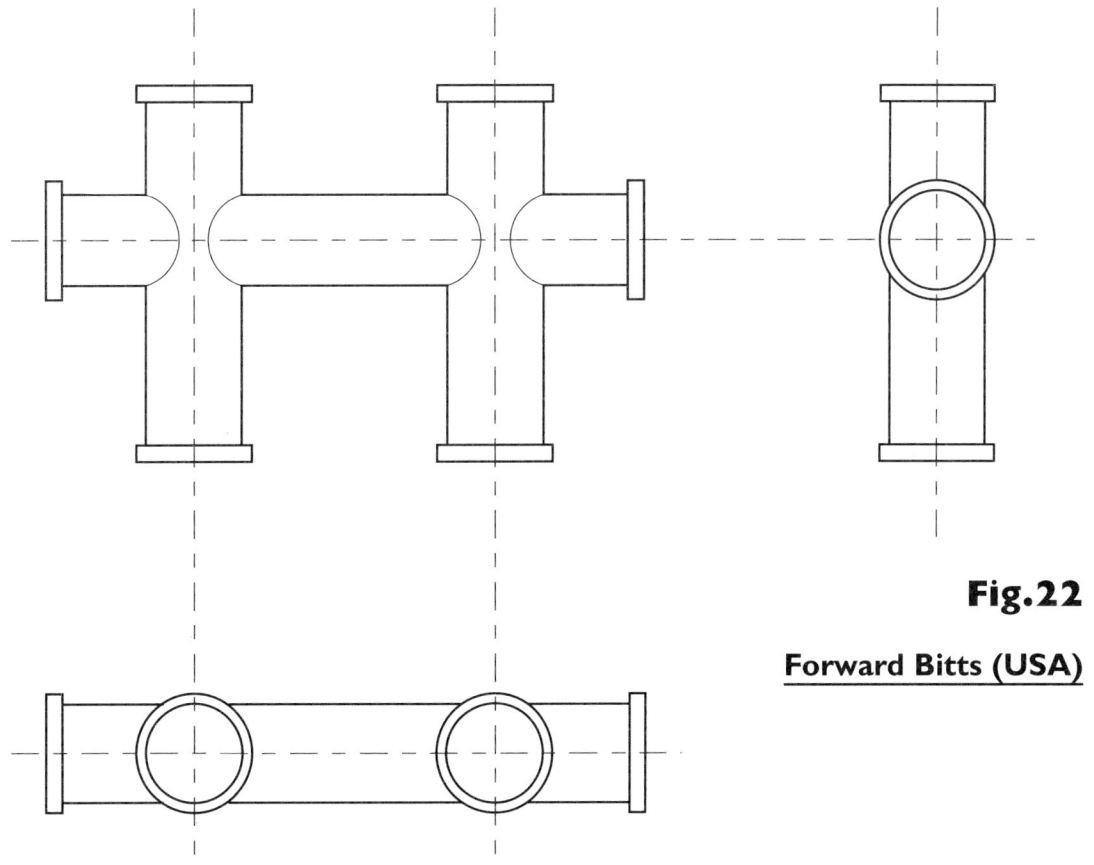

Fig.22

Forward Bitts (USA)

Fig. 23 Towing bitts on a model tug where the bitts were added for secure towing under competition conditions.

BOLLARDS

The size of the bollard, that is the diameter of the post, is commensurate with the size of the ship and where fitted. They are made to suit the requirements of the classification society and can be found in a variety of forms. The sketch **Fig. 24** illustrates a standard pattern bollard and the table **Fig. 25** gives an indication of sizes. Some ships would have more than one size of bollard although this is usually more common on large vessels. Not all bollards are mounted in pairs as some ships carried a number mounted singly although this is rare. The positioning and sizing of the bollards for a model ship is a matter of some importance; incorrect size and location of these important items have spoiled many models. To assist the modeller a number of photographs is included here showing bollards on both full size ships and models. The earlier ship generally carried bollards which were prefabricated or of cast construction and bolted to the decks, whereas the more modern ship is likely to have the bollards made from tube and plate, welded in place.

Typical Arrangement of Double Bollards Fig.24

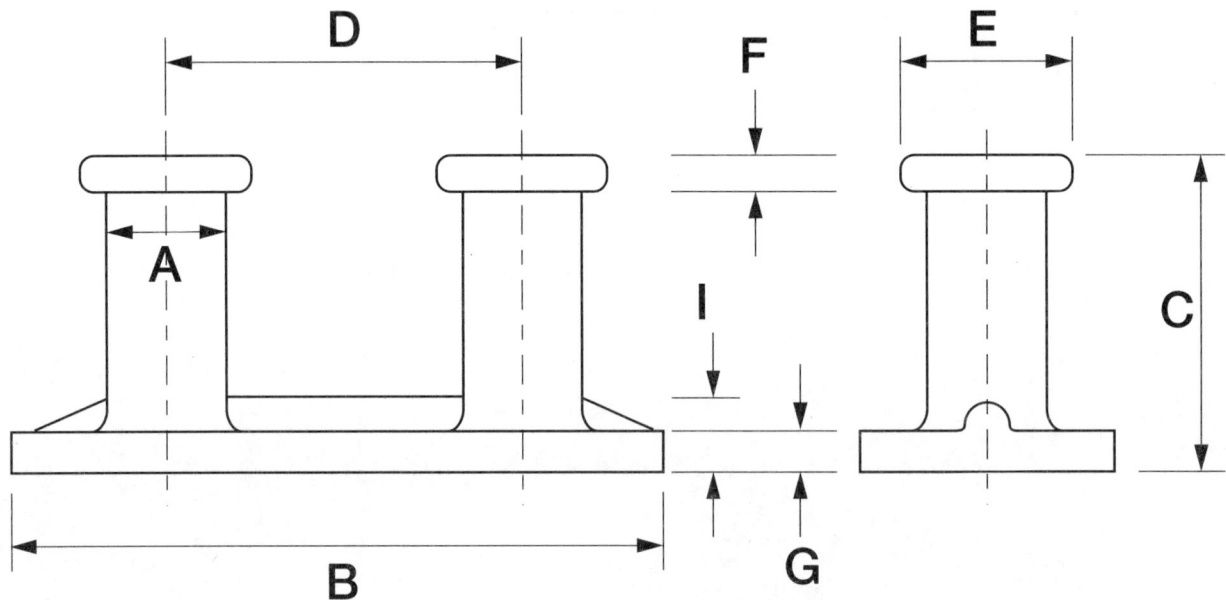

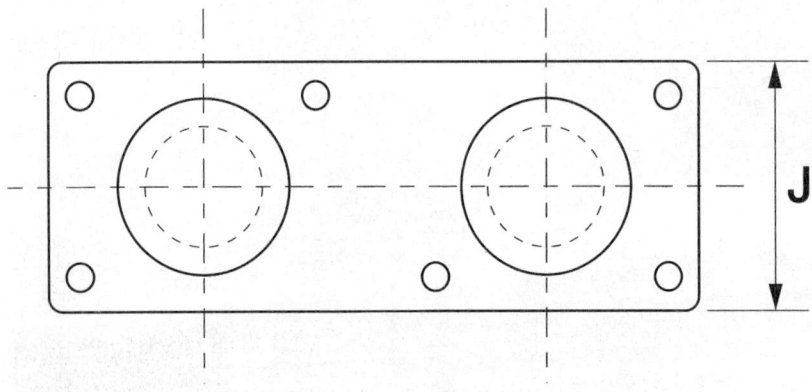

Fig.25

Typical Size Table for Double Bollards

Reference Fig. 24. All dimensions in millimetres.

Size	A	B	C	D	E	F	G	J
1	114	600	200	350	145	10	100	210
2	168	800	275	500	205	10	100	260
3	219	950	350	600	255	10	100	330
4	273	1150	400	750	320	10	110	370
5	324	1350	475	900	370	12	110	420
6	356	1500	535	1000	405	12	110	470
7	406	1650	600	1100	450	14	125	540

Bollards are not difficult to make; plastic knitting needles are an accurate source of rod in metric sizes and the mounting bases can readily be fashioned from sheet styrene. Frequently a model can be spoiled by the use of purchased bollards that are either too large or too small or of incorrect configuration. Researching into the chosen vessel should result in details of the mooring posts and bollards that would have been or are fitted. Mooring posts, single tall posts of steel tube, are more usually found on tugs and very small ships and, while they can be classed as bollards, they are mounted usually against the bulwarks and welded or bolted in place. Some are shown in the photographs of the model tug Cruiser.

Fig. 26 Quadruple bollards on the stern deck of a cargo

Fig. 27 Above: double bollard unit on a coastal motor ship.

Fig. 28 Left: double bollard on foredeck of short sea trader (Note measuring rod)

Fig. 29 Single bollards or mooring posts aft of windlass on model coaster ARRAN MAIL.

BOWS

The pointed forward end of the ship known as the bow or bows was formed from the front section of the keel and, except in the case of fine yachts, was quite blunt. The keel in those early days could measure anything from 9 to 24in wide according to the timber in use. It was usual for the shipwrights to choose the forefoot from a tree that had a shape close to that required. In the case of the iron or steel-built ship the fore section in earliest times was formed from a thick piece of plate to which the hull plates were riveted. The welded steel ship of today has plates shaped to the required form so that the bows are of a much more efficient shape. Many modern ships have a bulb-shaped extension forward below the waterline that, it is understood, gives increased speed and fuel economy, but it also gives increased buoyancy for fishing vessels that load in forward fish holds.

On either side of the bow there are figures denoting the depth of the hull from the keel upwards; these depth marks are also repeated at or near the stern. The depth marks are normally spaced at intervals of 200 millimetres and show clearly the depth of the ship below the water. They, together with the stern marks, allow the officers and crew of the ship to ensure that the loading is correctly distributed and that the ship is not going to sail head down which would be dangerous. Applied in Arabic script today, in earlier times the marks would be carried out at 6in intervals and would usually have been in Roman numerals on one side of the hull and Arabic on the other. Depth marks are illustrated in the photographs. Further marks that may be found just above the waterline near the bow indicate the presence of a bulbous bow and the installation of thrusters see **Fig. 33**.

Fig.33   <u>**Bow Markings**</u>

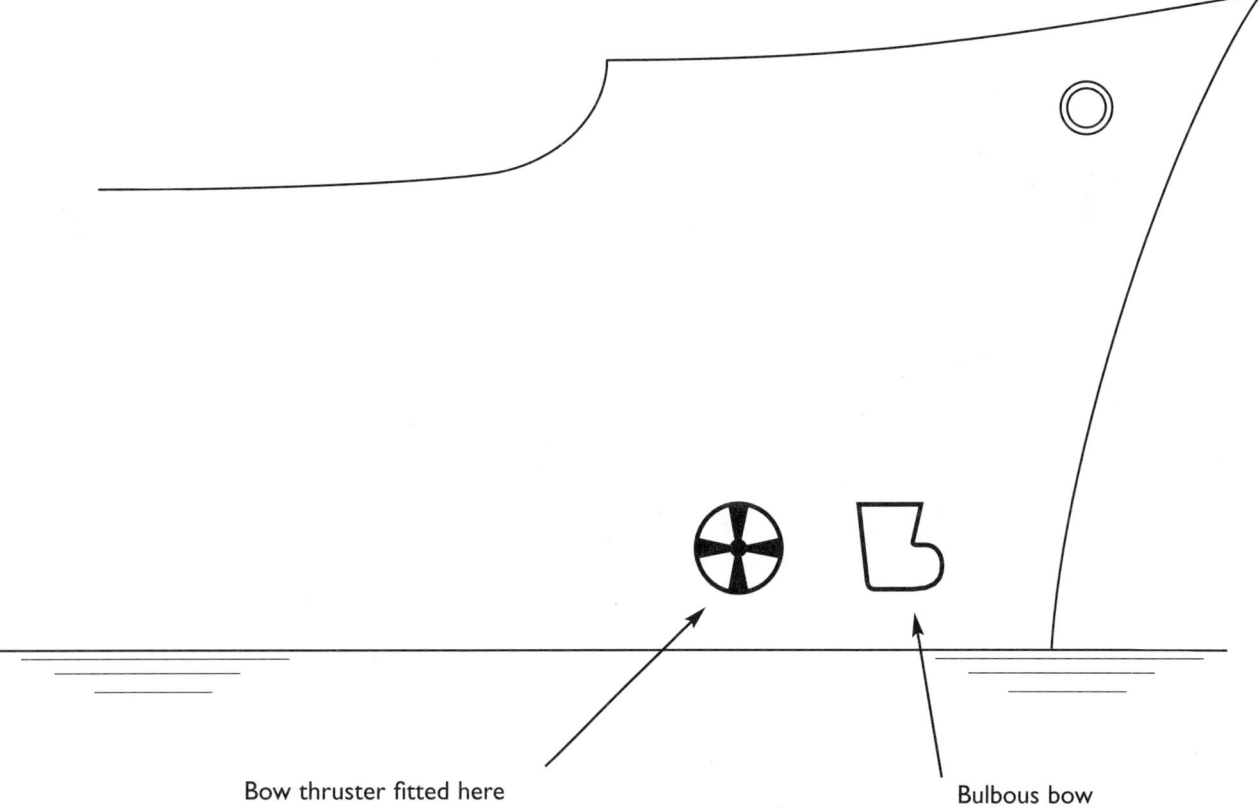

Bow thruster fitted here   Bulbous bow

Fig. 30 Bulbous bow showing on a fishing trawler.

Fig. 31 Fishing vessel under construction showing framing for bow bulb.

Fig. 32 Bow of coaster showing depth marks in metres and in Arabic script. (Photo courtesy of D.Milton)

BULWARKS

On wooden ships the bulwarks form extensions to the planking of the hull sides as shown in the sketch **Fig.34**. There were variants to the form and shape often down to the designer at the building yard. Almost all timber bulwarks were supported by 'timber heads'; square-section timbers extending from the frames below or set into the deck beam system. The bulwarks were invariably surmounted by a timber rail which could be as wide as 9in (225mm) and usually of 2 to 3in thick (50 to 75mm). The fitting of wash ports through the bulwarks of the timber-built ship varied with the duty of the ship and the degree of sheer imparted to the deck. Some wash ports were simply slots left in the bulwarks between specific timber heads, others were large openings with iron bars fitted to prevent other than small objects from being washed through. The herring drifters and steam trawlers had large wash ports with bars to allow the water to run through freely but to prevent fish from being lost; such ships gutted and prepared their catches on the open decks. Modern fishing vessels usually treat the catch below decks in rooms specially built for the purpose. The photographs show some wash port detail on wooden ships.

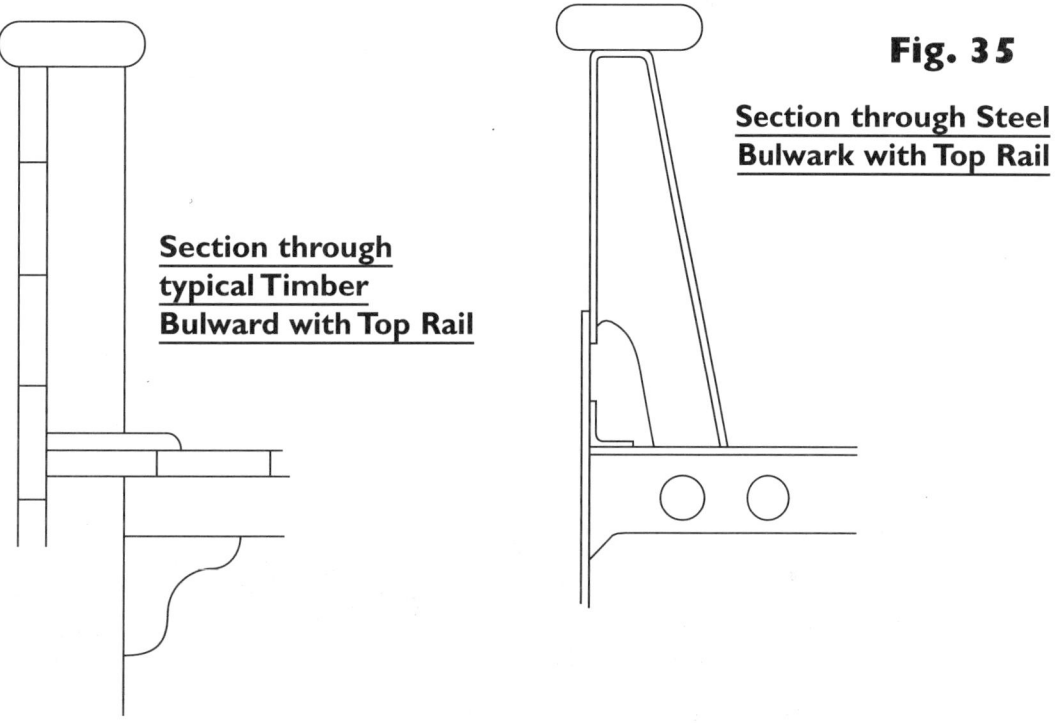

Fig. 34

Section through typical Timber Bulward with Top Rail

Fig. 35

Section through Steel Bulwark with Top Rail

General arrangement of Self-Closing Wash Port

Fig. 36

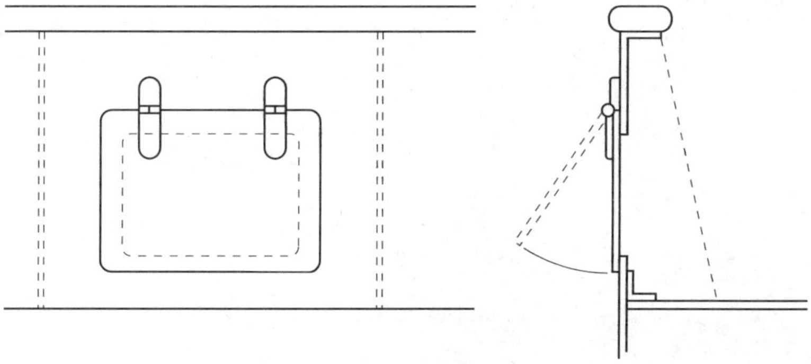

On the steel ship the bulwarks formed an extension to the sheerstrake plating and were usually attached to the sheerstrake as shown in the sketch **Fig. 35**. In recent times most ships have been built with the plating of the bulwark for most of its length fitted above the sheerstrake, leaving a long slot. This long slot serves as a wash port and is usually but 3 to 6in (75 To 150mm) deep. As will be seen from the sketches, the bulwark plating is attached to stays or brackets. In some cases the bulwark plating is turned inward to form a small flange. It is rare to find a ship in the size range covered herein, where the sheerstrake is curved in to a rounded section between deck and ship's side; this is generally found on the large bulk carriers and tankers of all-welded construction. As will be seen on most arrangement drawings of steel-built ships the bulwarks were almost always swept up to meet the vertical sides of the forecastle or other superstructure. Such curves were invariably gentle and reached to the top of the house or next run of bulwark.

Wash ports or freeing ports in many steel ships were of rectangular form and fitted with covers that were balanced to open and allow water to be released but closed to prevent water from entering. The Classification Societies laid down rules and schedules for the total area of freeing ports on each side of well-deck bulwark for a given length of well. The rules governing how the wash port or freeing port is made is also laid down by the Classification Societies. One type of wash port is shown in the sketch **Fig. 36**.

Fig. 38 Starboard side of the LIZRIX showing continuous wash port opening through which can be seen the bulwark support stays at regular intervals

Fig. 37 Bulwarks on a steel ship showing stays, cleats and tank vents.

Fig. 40 Model of American all wood steam tug showing timberheads and bulwark rails.

Fig. 41 Timberheads fitted round bulwarks of a model herring drifter prior to fitting timber rail.

Fig. 42 Timberheads on the bulwarks of a model herring drifter.

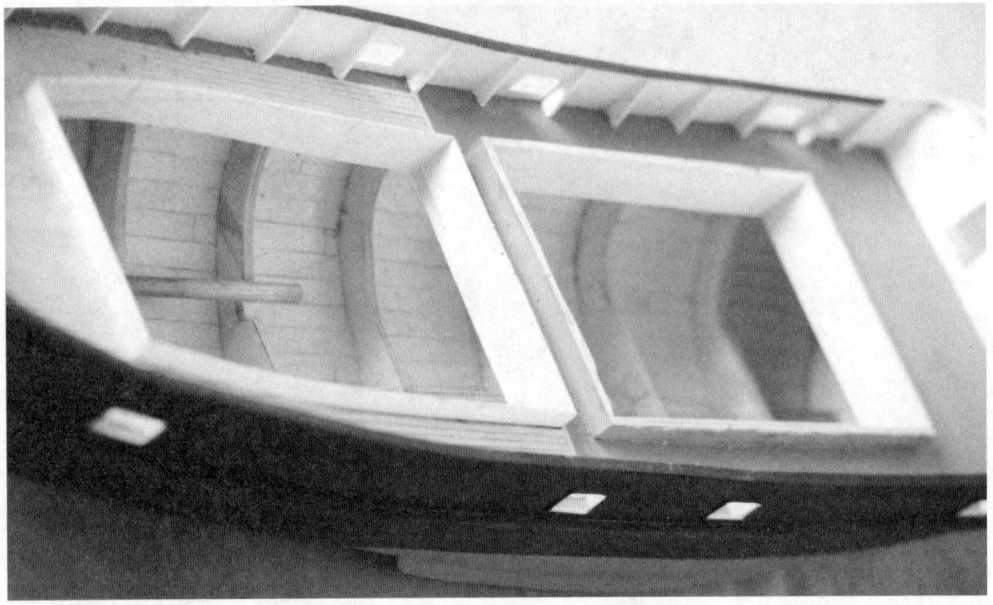

Fig. 43 Model of coaster under construction showing bulwark stays and wash ports.

CABLE STOPPERS

The anchor windlass is not designed to hold the ship against the anchor but only to lift the anchor when required. To prevent strain on the windlass, cable stoppers are used both when the ship is lying at anchor and when the anchor is in its stowed position. The cable stopper is fitted between the windlass and the top of the hawse pipe and there is a stopper for each anchor cable. They are comparatively simple pieces of equipment where the anchor cable is trapped by a bar or screw system so that the loading on the cable is transmitted to the structure of the ship and not to the windlass. Some cable stoppers take the form of a pivoted heavy bar operating over two heavy cheeks through which the anchor cable passes; as each link passes the bar lifts in the manner of a ratchet. This system prevents strain on the windlass when lifting the anchor under heavy weather conditions as the bar prevents the cable from being drawn backwards. Once the cable is fully wound in and the anchor is in its stowed position, the bar is secured at the loose end and thus traps the cable. This method of trapping the cable is also brought into play when the ship lies to the anchor. See sketch Fig. 43.

The screw pattern cable stopper does not have the ratchet-type action but relies upon the action of a screw to compress the cable and prevent further movement. Both types are shown in the photographs. In all cases the cable stoppers are mounted on substantial bases angled to suit the run of the anchor cable.

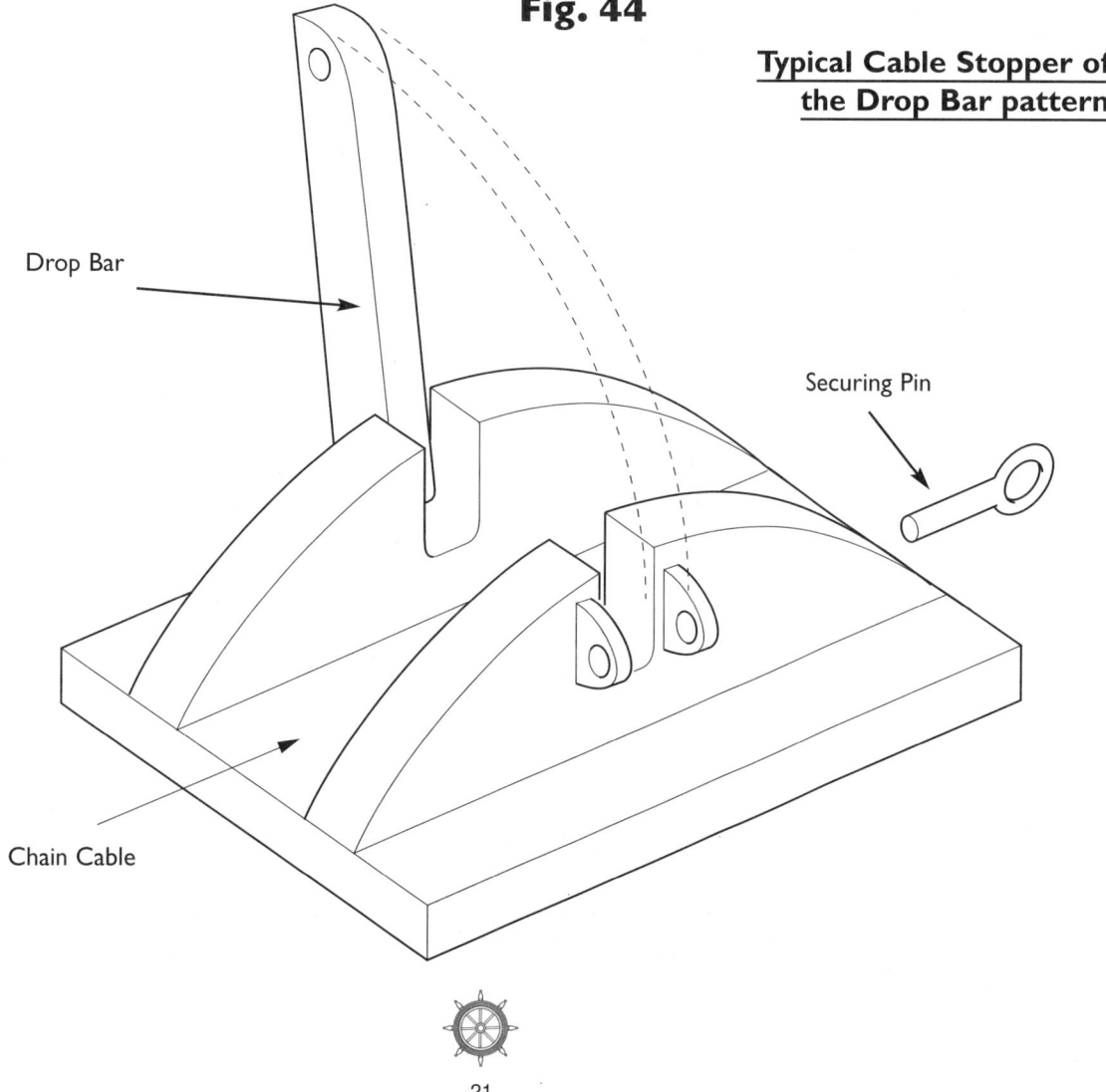

Fig. 44

Typical Cable Stopper of the Drop Bar pattern

Drop Bar

Securing Pin

Chain Cable

Fig. 45 Screw pattern cable stopper on a modern coaster - port side.

Fig. 46 Screw pattern cable stopper on a modern coaster - starboard side.

Fig. 47 Screw pattern cable stopper closed on cable on the stern trawler GLENROSE I. Note roller guides, fairleads, bulwark stays and pipes to hydraulic windlass.

CAPSTANS

There are few ships that are not fitted with a capstan. In the days of the sailing ship capstans were manually operated using sturdy posts or bars that fitted into the head of the unit and which were pushed by the required number of crewmen. The bars were stowed close to the capstan. The capstan was prevented from running backwards by a series of pawls at the base of the capstan and which engaged in a ring of teeth.

In the more modern ship the capstan was first steam driven and one of the photographs illustrates a steam capstan in model form. More recently capstans are either electrically or hydraulically driven and capable of working with remarkably heavy loads. On some small ships the capstan located on the foredeck has the facility of hauling the anchor stud link chain cable which is mounted beneath the warping drum Fig. 48. On the steam drifter, however, and peculiar to steam drifters, was the steam capstan built by Elliott & Garoods and other makers. In this the steam engine sat on top of the capstan and was fed with steam through the centre from below decks with the drum and other working parts revolving round the fixed central support. The photographs show one such in model form.

The most common use for the capstan today is the hauling of the mooring ropes and it is usually sited near the stern of the ship and surrounded by bollards. The picture of the coaster here shows a mooring capstan. Handling of the mooring ropes at the forward part of the ship was generally carried out using the warping drums of the windlass. A mooring capstan of the electrically-driven type can be seen in the photograph of the stern deck of an oilrig support ship.

Typical Capstan with Cable Gypsy
(Electric / Hydraulic motor inside the drum)

Fig. 48

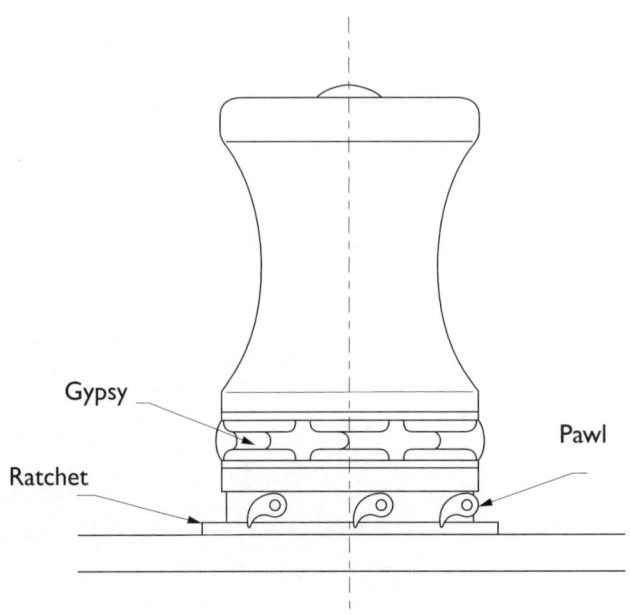

Fig. 50 Model of a steam capstan for a model herring drifter.

Fig. 52 MV TIMRIX in dry dock showing 'Hall' anchor and bow depth marks.

Fig. 49 Electric capstan on the stern of a motor coaster.

Fig. 51 Capstan on the stern of an oil rig support ship.

CHAIN CABLE

The type of chain correctly known as anchor cable used on all ships today is of the barred type and known as stud-link chain shown in the sketch **Fig. 53** and illustrated in the photographs. Such cable is made specifically for the purpose and in the sizes laid down by the classification society concerned to suit the weight and type of anchors designed for a specific ship. Each ship will carry a specified length of cable for each size of anchor - some ships carry two sizes although this is rare on a ship of less than 250 feet length overall. Obviously the size of anchor and anchor cable will dictate the size (diameter) of the hawse pipe and box (where fitted) and, of course, the size and power of the windlass. At the time of writing only a few ship model shops carry the correct pattern stud link chain. Two kit makers are able to provide such chain: Jotika have a range of sizes while Mount Fleet can supply it as separate links in cast white metal. So many models can be spoiled by the incorrect use of chain that is of plain oval-link pattern.

Barred Chain Cable

Size of link varies with size and weight of anchor

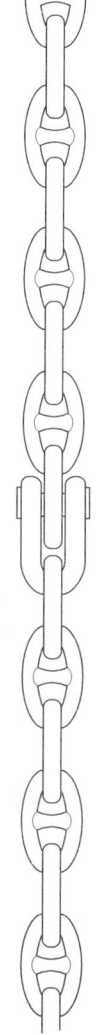

Fig.53

Fig. 54 Anchor cable on a vehicular ferry.

CLEATS

Cleats, used for tying off or 'belaying' ropes, come in many sizes and a number of different types. On the wooden ship, such as the herring drifters and early trawlers, wooden cleats called 'cavils' were fitted inside the bulwarks and generally fitted with belaying pins of round rod to which ropes could be tied off. One of the photographs shows a model fitted with cavils on the bulwarks. The larger belaying cleats which were securely bolted to the ship's structure are shown in the diagram **Fig. 56** and the smaller 'horn' cleat is also illustrated **Fig. 55**. These sketches are drawn to scale and can be re-measured to suit the size and duty when necessary. Some model kit makers provide cleats in scale sizes, notably Billings who produce them in hard plastic in a number of sizes. There are other makers, too, and the model ship shop should be able to assist when necessary.

Fig. 55

Fig. 56

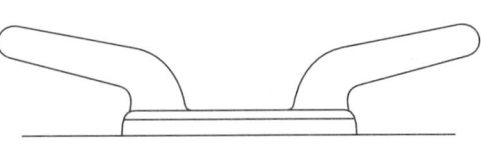

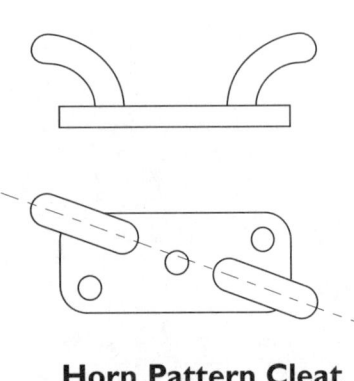

Belaying Cleat

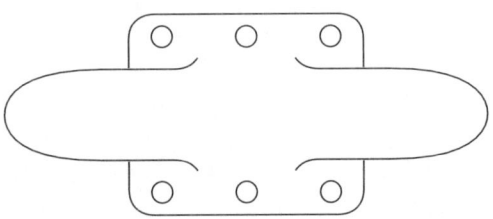

Horn Pattern Cleat

Fig. 57 Bulwarks of a model herring drifter showing Cavils.

CRANES

Small cranes for cargo handling have been fitted to ships for more than 100 years but it is only in the last two decades or so that they have been specifically built for the purpose. In fact the modern small ship within the size range encompassed by this volume is more likely to have a small crane purely for the purpose of handling the rigid inflatable boat for life-saving duty than for cargo-handling. Many modern coasters and short sea traders carry no cargo handling equipment at all and rely upon the port facilities for loading and unloading. The photographs show a small crane on a model used for R.I.B. handling together with some hydraulic cranes used for cargo and net handling on fishing vessels.

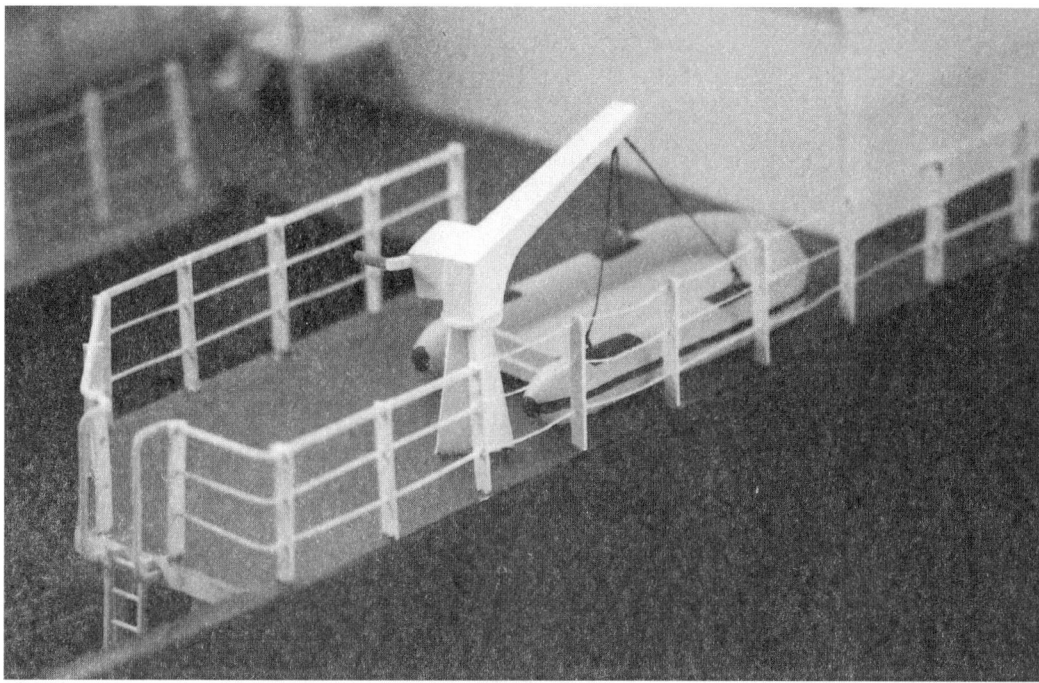

Fig. 58 Model of a small crane for handling a rigid inflatable boat (RIB)

Fig. 59 Hydraulic crane with net haul on a seine net boat.

Fig. 60 Small cargo crane for handling stores etc. on a merchant vessel.

Fig. 61 Base of hydraulic crane for handling fish boxes and baskets on a stern trawler.

Fig. 62 Top section of the fish handling crane.

Fig. 63 Middle section of the same crane.

DAVITS

Basically davits are used to handle the lifeboats of a ship but there are other small davits that are used for anchor handling and for handling large fenders. The small davits used for anchor-handling and for other duties are illustrated and are little more than small cranes with rope blocks as can be seen. Lifeboat davits were originally similar to the anchor handling units and called radial davits. More modern types as illustrated have progressively superseded these. The lifeboat davit has been the subject of development over many years until, today, many ships have no davits at all. Some have their lifeboat mounted on a slipway at the stern of the vessel while others rely upon a rigid inflatable boat that is placed in the water by a small manually-operated crane.

In recent years there have been developments that have resulted in a davit system that can place a lifeboat or other small boat in the water safely in adverse weather conditions. The standard gravity-type davits can place a lifeboat in the water but severe wave patterns can cause the boat to be swamped before it is released. While lifeboats are fitted with buoyancy tanks this will not prevent the boat from being filled with water when lowered into heavy seas. The Caley davit illustrated can place a boat safely in the water under its control system in all weathers.

Fig. 64 Radial davits on a model of the American tug SEGUIN.

Fig. 65 Radial pattern davits for the lifeboats on the model of ARRAN MAIL.

Fig. 66 Quadrant davits on the model steam coaster ROVUMA.

Fig. 68 'Caley' davit on the oilrig support ship SCOTT GUARDIAN.

It is probable that the radial davit is the type most likely to be seen by model ship builders on the older vessels. The general arrangement drawings of the chosen ship will usually give all the details needed for such davits but there is a simple formula for calculating the maximum diameter (d) in inches of a radial davit: -

$$D/C = L \times B \times D (H + 4S)$$

Where L, B & D are the length breadth and depth of the ship, H is the height of the davit head and S is the outreach or span. When all these dimensions are in feet the diameter d will be in inches. C is a constant of 144 for wrought iron or 174 for wrought ingot steel. In each case the constant allows for enough men to launch the boat. The values become 82 and 99 respectively if the boats are launched with a full complement on board. The Welin Davit & Engineering Co. has produced most of the davits for ships built world-wide or designed the davits built under licence by many engineering companies. Some types are shown in the sketches **Figs. 67 & 70**. The latest pattern lifeboat slip and crane system is illustrated in **Fig. 71**.

Fig. 67   <u>Early Types of Davits</u>

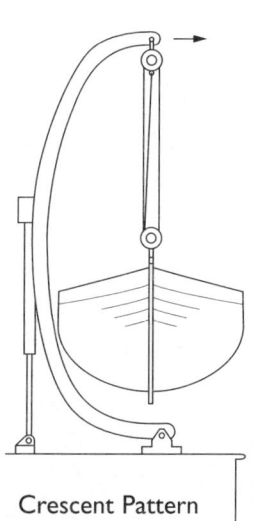

Crescent Pattern

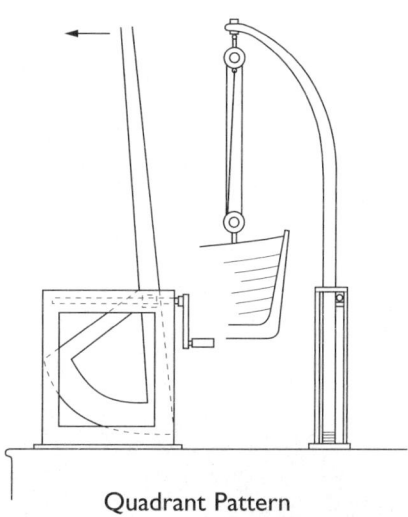

Quadrant Pattern

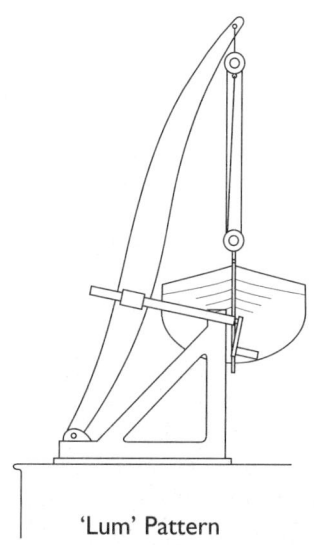

'Lum' Pattern

Fig. 70 Typical Arrangement of a Gravity Davit

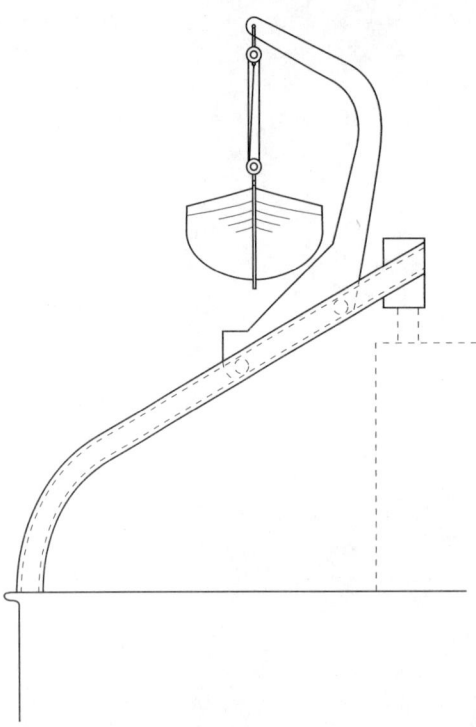

Fig. 69 `Caley' davit on the oilrig ship shown prior to loading the rescue boat.

The type of davits fitted to the modern ship is very diverse; the type and size of davit and the construction of the cradle and mounting varies from installation to installation. In the past the types of davits used were those described and illustrated in the sketches **Figs. 67 to 70** and these could be found on a great variety of ships. This is not the case today and the ship model builder really needs to research his/her vessel very carefully. Even two ships built to the same designs can have different davits and lifeboats.

Fig. 71 Totally enclosed lifeboat stowed on slip of large coaster.

Fig. 72

Arrangement of Slip and Crane for Free-fall Lifeboat

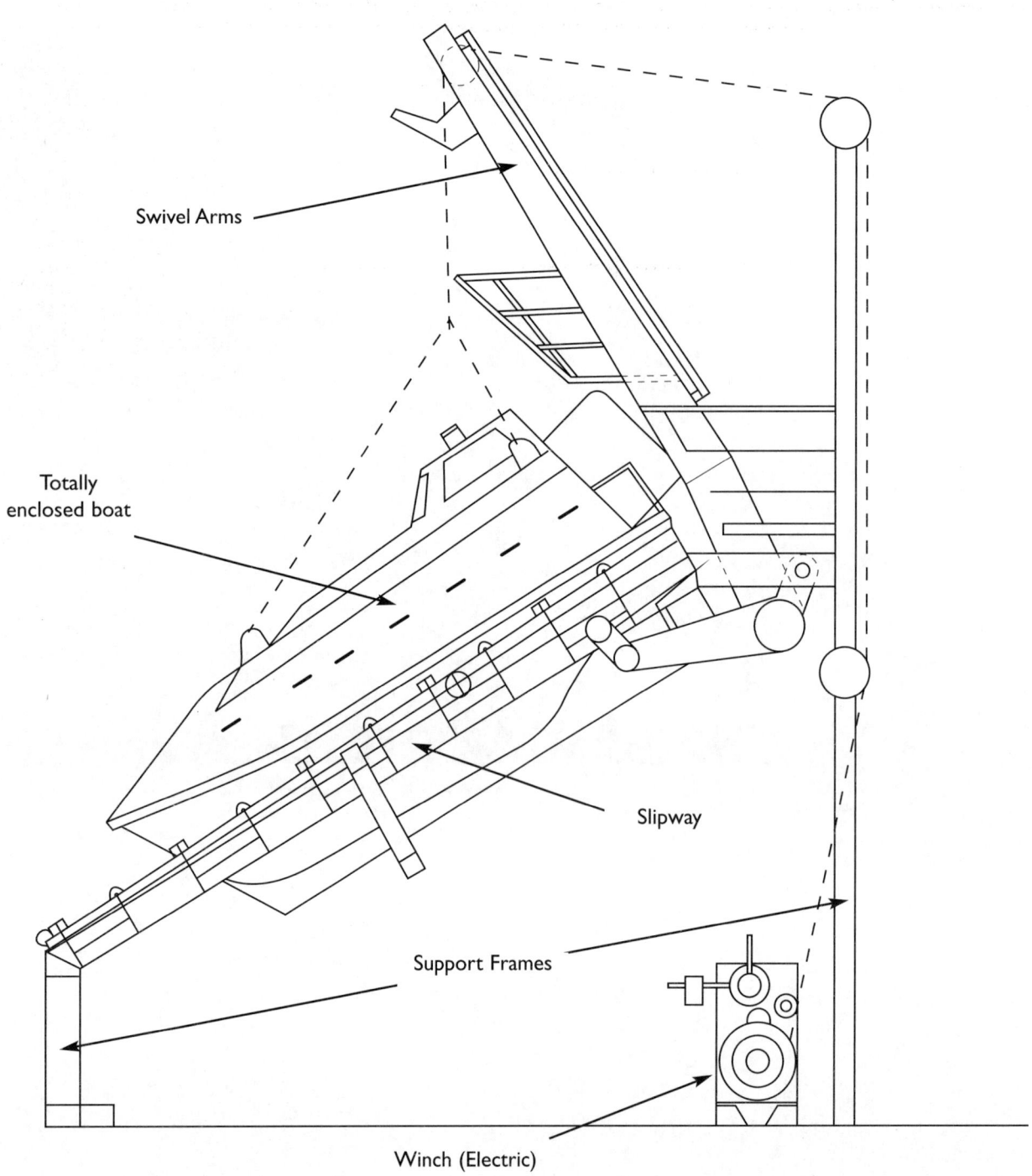

DECKS & DECK PLATING

The early herring drifters, trawlers, tugs and small ships were built of timber and had timber decks. The early iron and, later, steel ships continued to have their decks made of timber for some time. Working ships of more recent times tend to have their decks made of steel plates although some have parts of the decks finished with timber planks laid over the steel plating. As with almost every part of the ship, the classification society concerned with the survey during building has rules covering decks, deck plating and timber with associated caulking. The ship model builder would have considerable problems trying to interpret all the rules so that he/she must rely upon data provided on the general arrangement drawings etc.

Fig. 73 Planked decks of a model pilot cutter showing waterways.

Fig. 74 Forecastle deck of a model coaster showing smooth plate finish, windlass, cable stoppers etc.

In general the laying of timber decks was carried out using teak planks of 3in (75mm) thickness x 5 or 6in wide (125 x 150mm) with the possible exception of a central 'king' plank of greater width **Fig. 75**. The deck planks were bolted to the supporting beams through holes bored with an auger and counter bored so that plugs of timber dowel could seal the holes after the bolts had been tightened down. Between the planks the joiner or shipwright laid caulking of teased out hemp, driven into the gaps between the planks using tools known as caulking irons followed by sealing with hot pitch. This provided a waterproof deck that weathered to an almost white colour due to frequent scrubbing and the action of the weather. The planks were supplied to the shipyard in random lengths that could vary from 15 to 28 feet. Rules demand that butt joints in the deck planking must not occur on the same beam within a minimum of three runs and preferably a minimum of four runs. (See sketch **Fig. 76**.) The shipwrights thus selected planks, to use the random lengths as sensibly as possible with minimum waste.

Fig. 75

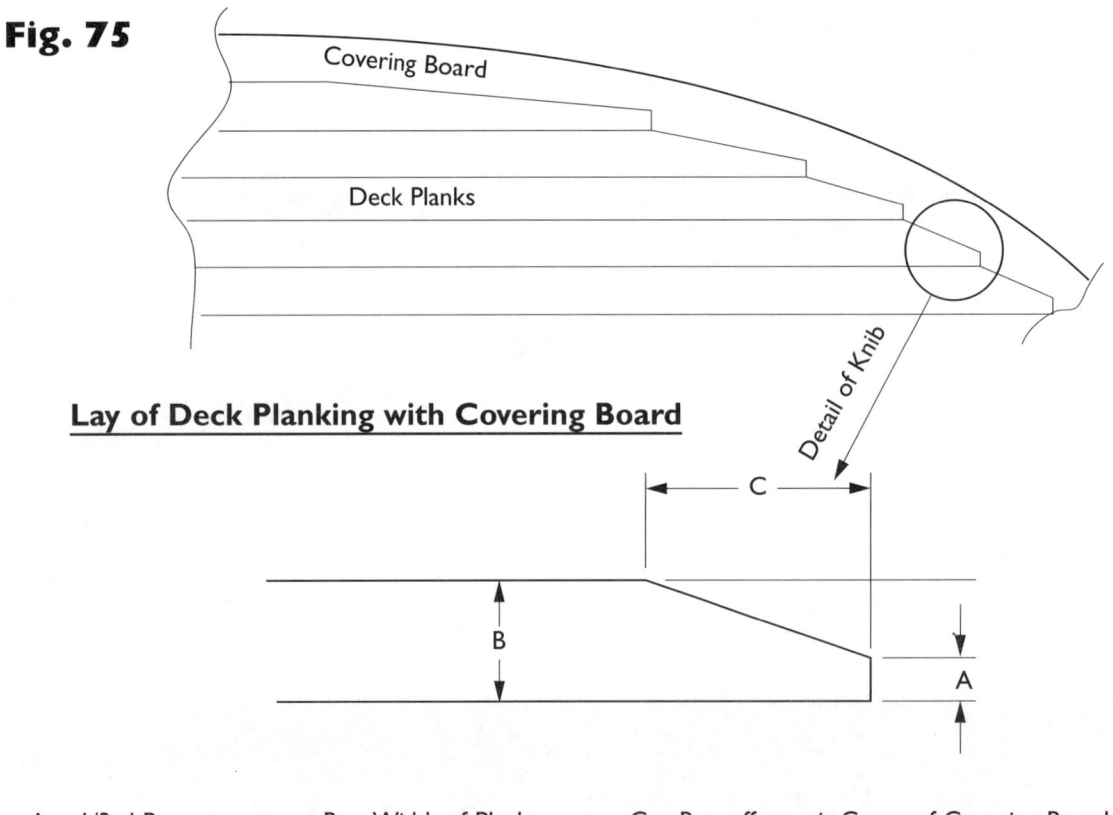

Lay of Deck Planking with Covering Board

A = 1/3rd B   B = Width of Plank   C = Run-off to suit Curve of Covering Board

Lay of Deck Planks and Butt Joints

Fig. 76

Round the perimeter of the decks on timber-planked ships there would be a waterway left and completed with concrete or, more often, of a shaped-timber system known as a covering board. The fore-and-aft running planks would be knibbed to fit the covering board and this is illustrated in the sketch **Fig. 75** and photographs. The rule for cutting the fore-and-aft running planks was that the cut section at right angles to the plank would extend one third of the width of the plank while the taper would be cut to suit the location.

Steel decks in the earlier ships were riveted and followed the rivet lines and so forth of the shell plating fairly closely. Parts of the decks of some ships were coated with a mastic compound similar to tarmacadam where the area might be subject to heavy working. Other parts of the decks would be planked with timber in the same manner as were wooden ships. As recently as 1998 I watched a joiner laying deck planking over a steel deck for a small fishing vessel. This planking was laid in exactly the same way as were the decks of yesterday using caulking irons of the same kind; the only difference today was that the pitch used was of modern composition and poured cold. The planks used were not of teak but of deal and they were 3in thick by 6in wide. When asked why the deck should be planked thus on a fishing vessel the answer given was that the planks insulated the space beneath and were better for working on.

It is usual for passenger-carrying vessels to have planked decks particularly in those areas used by the passengers, the timber being more comfortable and safe to walk upon than bare steel which can be slippery even when dry. Some of this planking would be laid over the steel deck but in other areas the planks could be laid over the deck beams that run athwartships and without the additional support of steel plates.

Fig. 77 Detail of tank deck on a model coastal bunkering tanker showing array of pipes, valves etc.

FAIRLEADS

Fairleads are, in effect, rope guides fitted to the sides of ships and frequently on top of the bulwark rails **Fig. 84**. They come in a variety of forms and sizes and some are illustrated here. As can be seen some are open at the top, some are closed, some have roller guides and some are plain. The more complex forms that are fitted into openings in the bulwark plating have both horizontal and vertical rollers for guiding the ropes. A portable fairlead known as a molgogger can be found on the herring drifter where it was used to guide the net haul rope. The molgogger was a portable form of the type fitted with vertical and horizontal rollers. It was fitted through a bracket on one or other side of the hull and was secured with a lanyard when in use. The Panama port is another type of fairlead, which is sometimes fitted into the plating of the bulwarks or that can be deck mounted as seen in the photographs. The sheaved fairlead is more commonly used where wire ropes would be used in preference to the coir or nylon types **Fig. 85**.

Fig. 84

Standard Pattern Open Fairlead
Typical Measurements

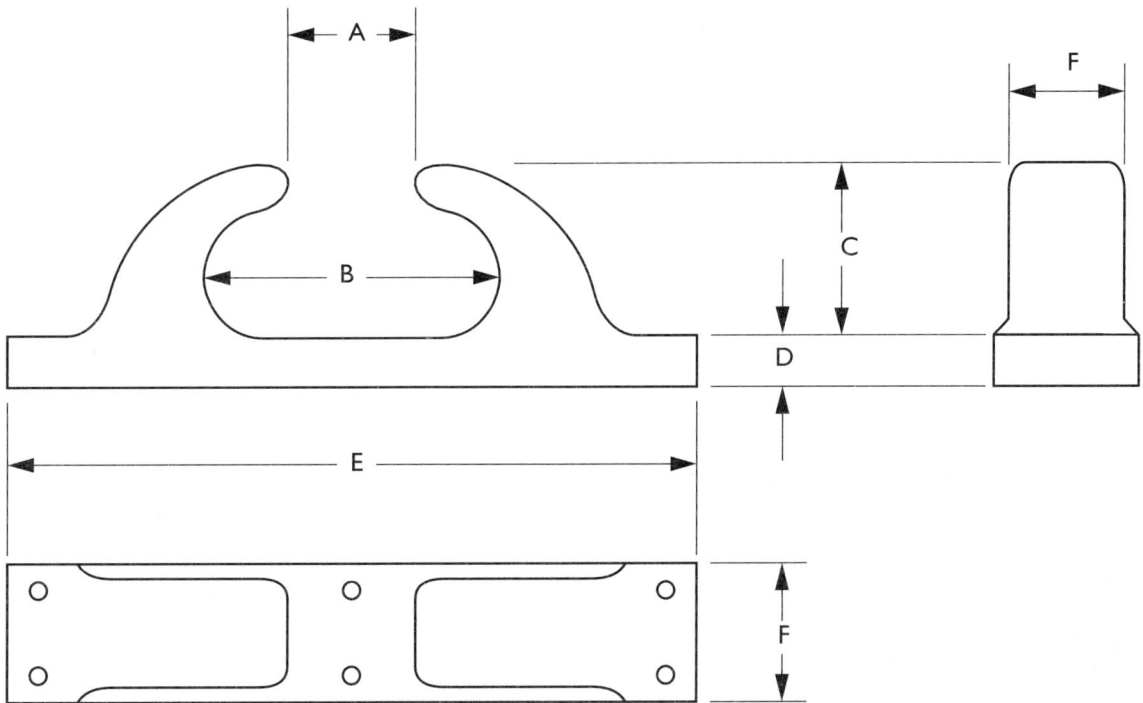

A = 178mm   B = 380 mm   C = 220mm   D = 65 mm   E = 910 mm   F = 150 mm

Fig. 85 **Typical Double Sheaved Fairlead**

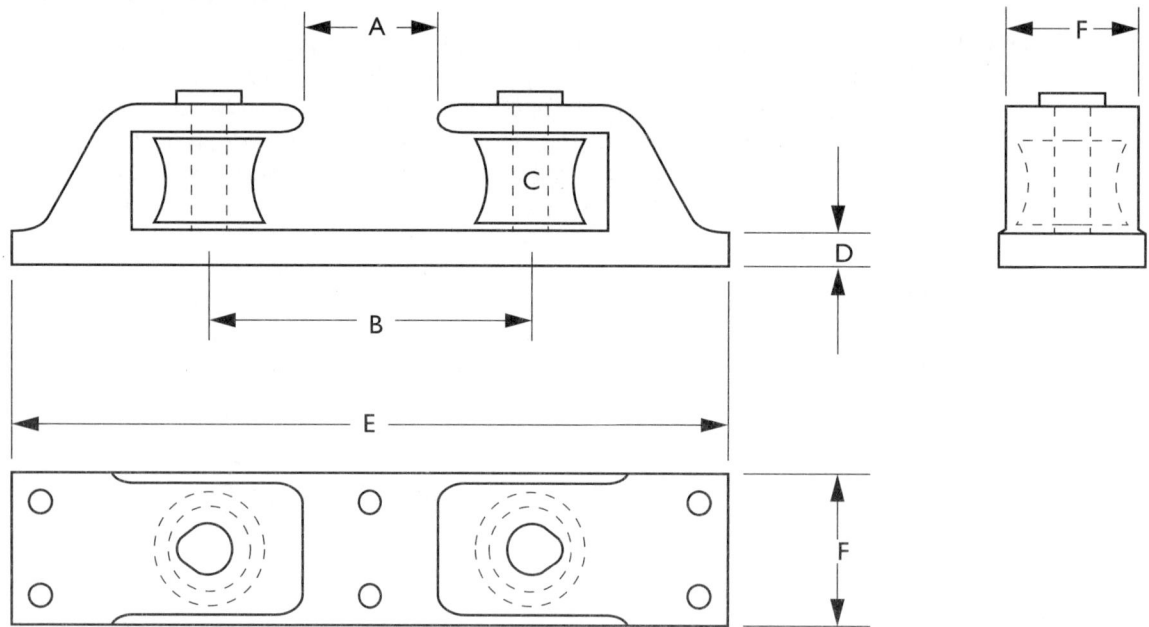

A = 200 mm   B = 460 mm   C = 115mm   D = 32 mm   E = 990 mm   F = 190 mm

Fig. 78 Twin sheaved fairlead fitted on a platform in the bulwarks of a motor coaster.

Fig. 79 Fairleads on the foredeck of a model stern trawler.

Fig. 80 Roller fairlead built into the bulwarks of the motor vessel JONRIX.

Fig. 81 Panama pattern fairlead built into the bulwarks of a ferry.

Fig. 82 Panama pattern fairlead on a model steam coaster.

Fig. 83 Open fairleads on a model of a steam coaster.

FIRE-FIGHTING EQUIPMENT

All ships carry some form of fire-fighting or prevention equipment. On the dry-cargo ship, small tug and fishing vessel this can be fairly basic with suitable fire extinguishers positioned at strategic locations. Most will also have a system of pipes and valves through which water or foam can be pumped to smother fires; such pipes and valves will be painted red and be highly visible. The oil tanker does, of course, have a sophisticated system of pipework and valves for feeding foam to locations round the ship and a set of pumps for this duty. The photographs illustrate some of the pipes and valves installed on ships for this duty.

Fig. 86 Fire valve and tank vent on a small motor ship.

Fig. 87 Range of three fire valves on a short sea trader.

Many large tugs and most oilrig support vessels carry fire monitors and pumps specifically for the purposes of attending fires as do land-based fire engines and crews. Fire monitors are specialised items of equipment capable usually of operation locally and remotely. They are generally mounted upon the bridge wings of tugs and other ships but some tugs have platforms specially built at high level to carry the monitors. They are capable of spraying huge quantities of water to quite long distances. Some are shown in the accompanying pictures and sketch **Fig. 88**.

Arrangement of Fire Monitor for Remote Control

Fig. 88

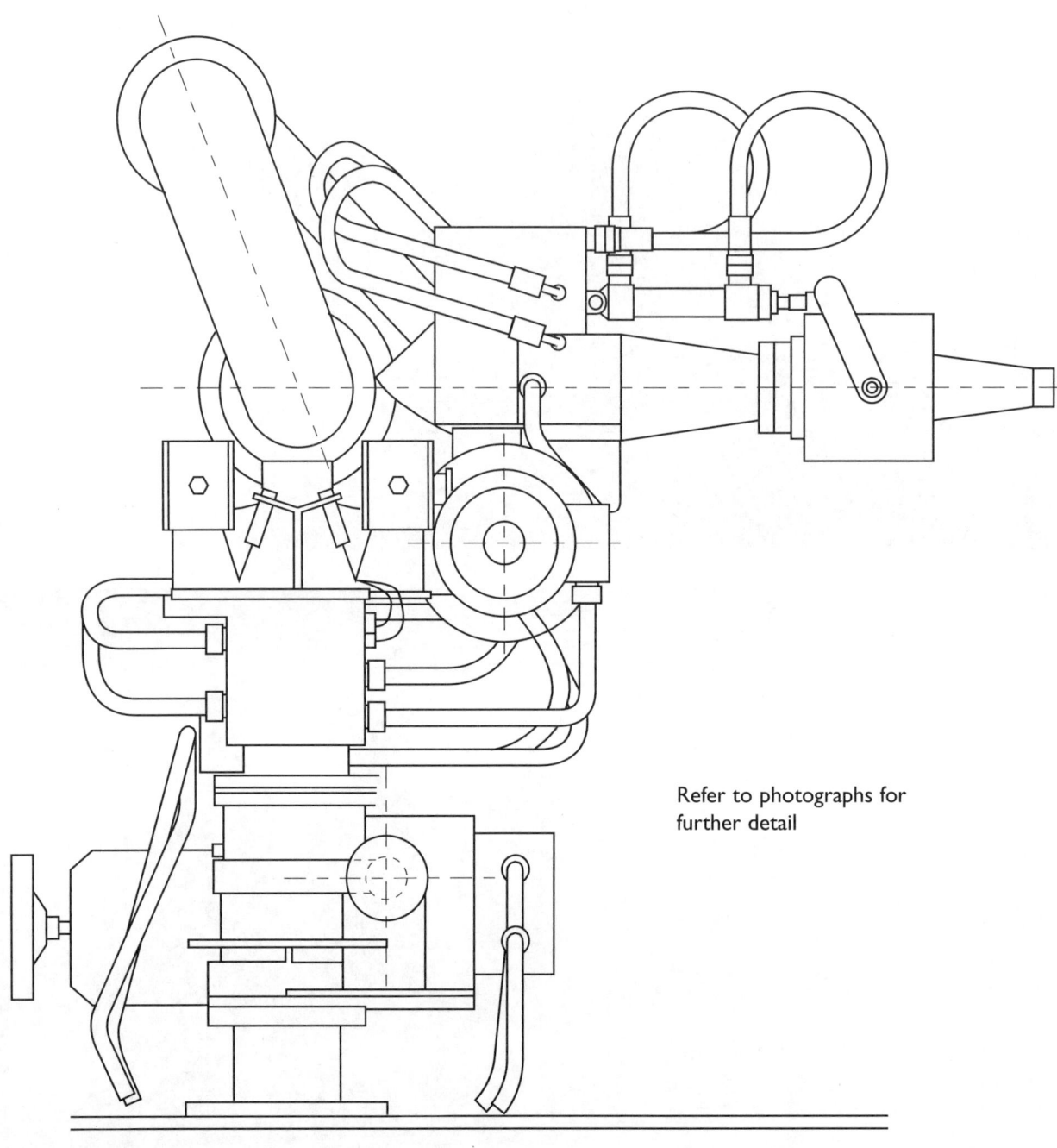

Refer to photographs for further detail

Fig. 89 Fire monitor on the bridge top of an oilrig support ship.

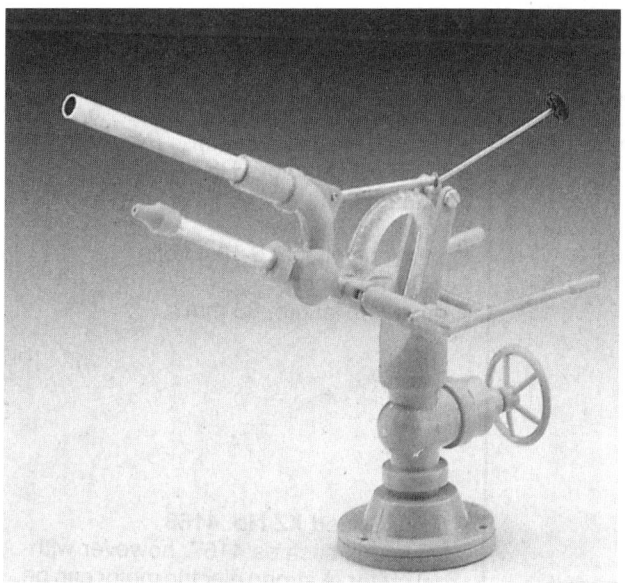

Fig. 90 Working model fire monitor (photograph courtesy Graupner)

Fig. 91 Fire pipeline and valve on bunkering tanker RIX HARRIER.

Fig. 92 Fire monitor on the oilrig support ship SCOTT GUARDIAN.

FUNNELS

There are very few modern ships that do not have at least one funnel. I believe that a number of motor ships built in the early 1950s used hollow masts for the exhaust and thus dispensed with the traditional funnel. Such experiments were, however, short lived. The funnel of the powered ship can be found in a multitude of forms, shapes and sizes. The early steam-powered ship had tall slender funnels, being tall to create adequate draught for the fires. Later they were fitted with outer casings that insulated the inner flue and allowed the hot gases to be evacuated more easily. Later still, with the advent of forced draught, the funnel became shorter.

The motor ship has virtually always had a fairly short funnel; high enough to exhaust the gases well above the decks. Most of such funnels carry, within the casing, a silencer of one kind or another to reduce the noise level of the oil engine. Some of the larger vessels use a vertical boiler as a silencer and then heat from the exhaust gases generates the steam needed to condition the oil for the engines and for other services.

Some funnels, on those ships that carry two funnels, are purely cosmetic and are fitted at the owner's whim. Some carry the fans and ducting for the ship's ventilation system. The photographs and sketches **Figs. 96 & 97** depict a number of funnels but the model builder should research his/her model carefully in respect of the funnel and its use. On the very small fishing vessel and service launches the exhaust can be taken through the stern transom and thus a funnel would not be used. Such vessels are generally less than 50 feet in length.

Fig. 93 Funnel on model of steam pilot cutter, note open steering position and detail.

Fig. 94 Funnel for model of steam tug CRUISER.

Fig. 95 The very prominent and almost square funnel of the motor ship LIZRIX.

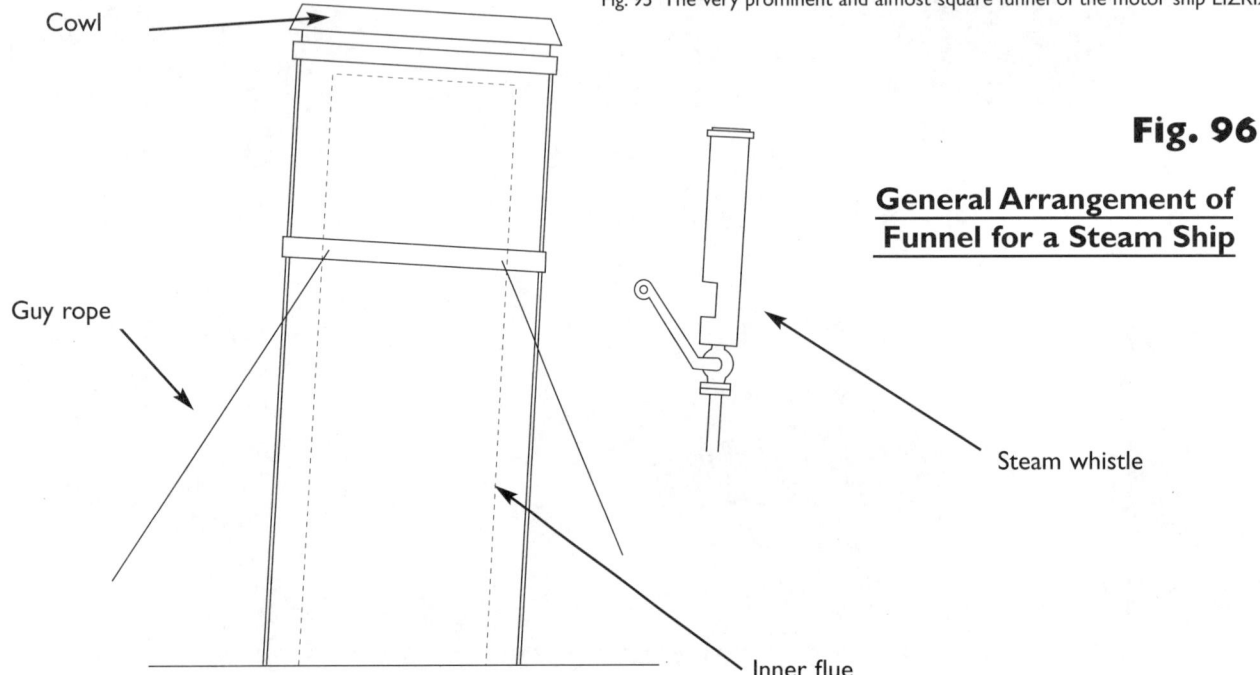

Fig. 96

General Arrangement of Funnel for a Steam Ship

Cowl

Guy rope

Inner flue

Steam whistle

Arrangement of Funnel for a Motorship

Fig.97

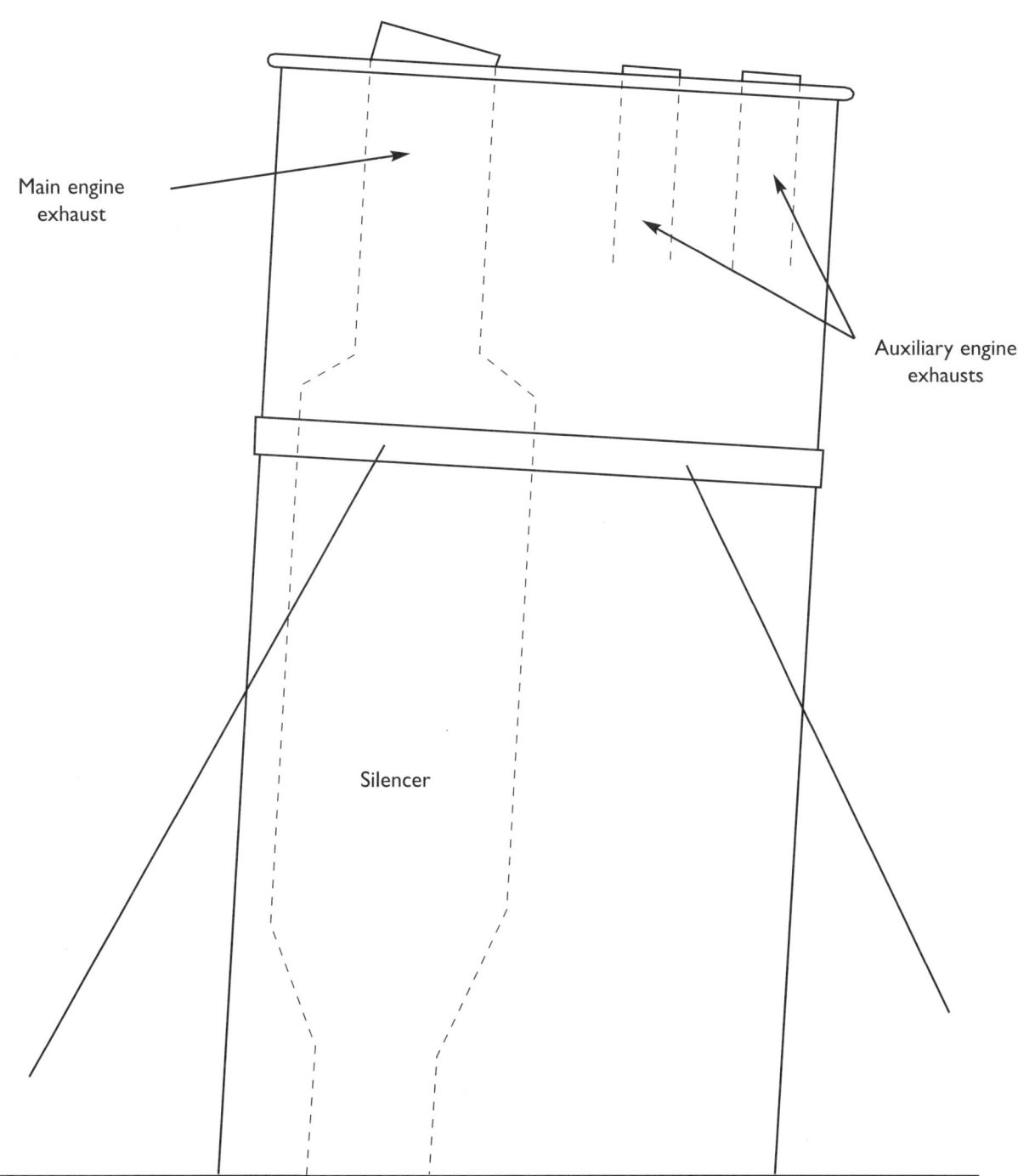

HATCHES

Hatches, as far as the ship model builder is concerned, have the useful function of giving access to the inside of the hull. On full size ships they were developed over the years, as were many other parts of the ship. Small hatches to give access to machinery spaces and tanks etc. have a variety of covers as illustrated in some of the photographs. Hatches that give access to cargo holds are very different. Initially on the early wooden and iron ships the openings in the decks for access to the holds were small openings covered with tarpaulin sheets supported centrally by a beam fitted over the centre of the opening. Later hatch openings were built up with coamings, supports to accept wooden covers and the tarpaulins for waterproofing were secured round the hatch by steel bars with wedges driven in place to hold the bars tightly. This arrangement lasted well into the 1960s on the small cargo ship. The sketch **Fig. 106** illustrates the coaming and brackets that carry the securing bars and wedges on a small coaster.

Fig. 106   <u>**Typical Early Pattern Hatch, Coaming etc.**</u>

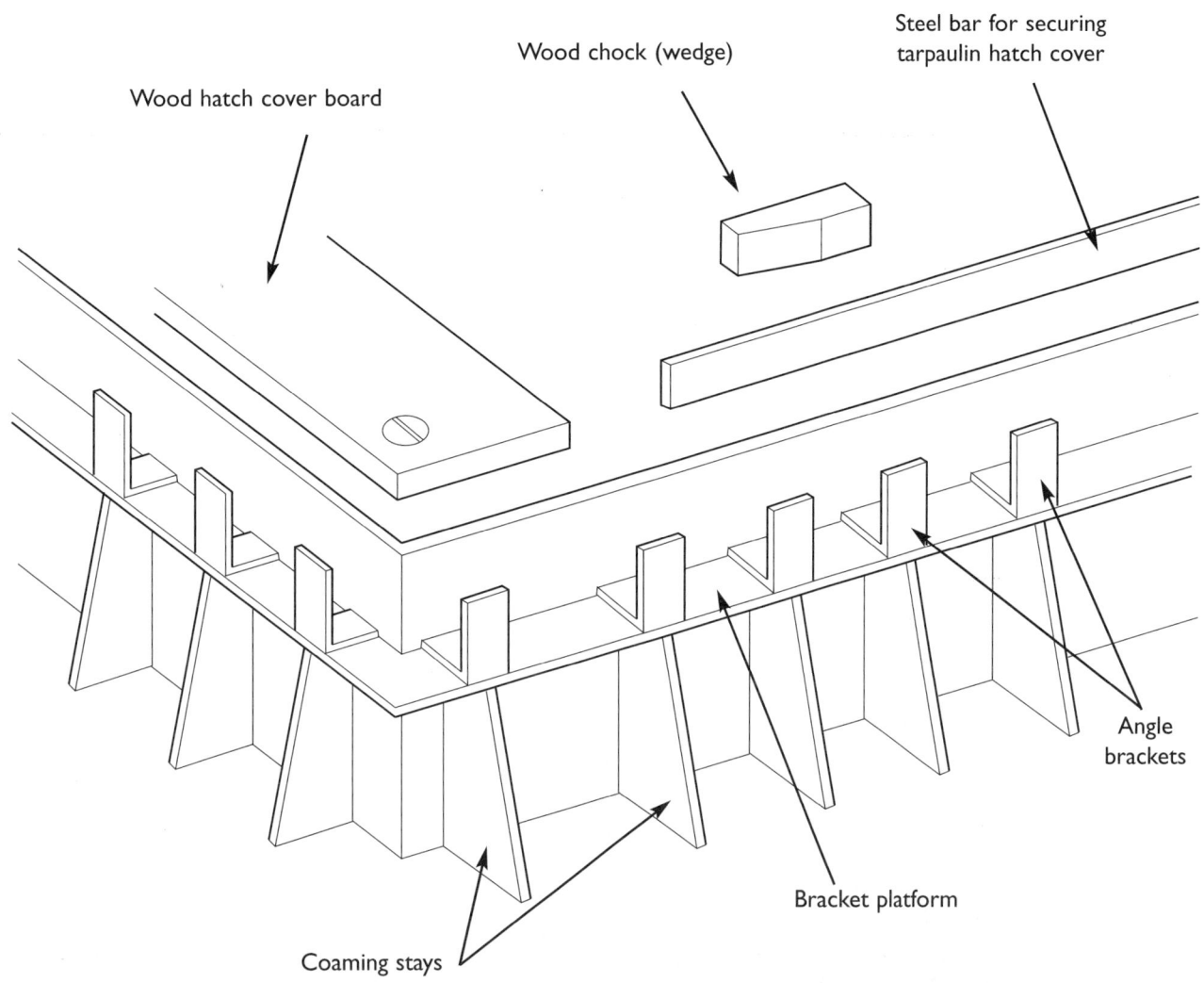

55

Fig. 98 A small circular hatch on the forecastle of a coastal motor ship.

Fig. 99 Detail of the main hatch with tarpaulin cover and flat steel securing bars on the model of ARRAN MAIL.

Fig. 100 A cargo of timber stowed on the steel hatch covers of the motor ship LIZRIX.

The more modern cargo ship is generally fitted with steel hatch covers which run on rails and which are arranged to open by being drawn along the rails and folded on top or beside each section to leave a clear opening. Such sliding hatch covers of MacGregor or similar manufacture, are often strengthened to allow cargo such as containers, timber etc. to be loaded on top. This type of hatch is shown in the accompanying photographs.

Coamings and hatch covers are subject to the rules of the Classification Societies and such rules are strictly enforced. Not all of the rulings are published, as many applications require individual assessment and approval of the surveyors in place. For example, coamings for hatches on weather decks are required by Lloyds to have a minimum height of 24in (600mm) although they are often made much higher and the stiffening and bracing of such coamings must comply with the rulings.

The methods of securing tarpaulins over hatch boards and the number of tarpaulins required are also a matter of set ruling; frequently the tarpaulins must be secured at intervals by steel straps clamped in place and tensioned using rigging screws (bottle screws). The arrangement of bars and wedges used round the hatch of a small coaster is shown in model form in the photograph of Arran Mail built by the author. Such loose hatch covers and tarpaulins are rarely seen today but pictures can be found in most good reference books that cover cargo ships of yesteryear.

Fig. 101 Details of hatch coamings, stays and covers with chains and pulleys on the LIZRIX

Fig. 105 After end of hatch on a motor ship showing covers, guide rails and fire pipes. The hatch covers are stowed in this space when the hatch is opened.

Fig. 102 Hatches of the MacGregor pattern being drawn open by winch on the LIZRIX.

Fig. 104 Alternative to the winch mounting of Fig.103 is this arrangement where the winch is below deck and the towing hawser is guided by pulley and guide pipe mounted on the front of the superstructure

Fig. 103 Winch used for drawing hatch covers open, mounted on a platform on the main superstructure of a coaster.

HAWSEPIPES

Hawsepipes are the pipes that extend from the forecastle deck to the sides of the ship near the bows and through which the anchor cable passes. Usually they are made from cast iron or steel and carry heavy flanges of oval or similar shape on and to protect the shell plating. With the stockless anchors commonly in use today the pipe is large enough to permit the stock of the anchor to be drawn up into the pipe so that the flukes and arms of the anchor can be drawn snugly against the ship's plating. Many ships have recesses (anchor boxes) formed in the shell plating to accommodate the anchor within the line of the hull. Such boxes are heavily strengthened against wear caused by movement of the anchor. The small ships that are the subject of this volume rarely carried stern anchors and they have thus been ignored.

When building a working model ship it is necessary for the modeller to ensure that the hawse pipes are sealed to the hull and deck to prevent water leaking into the hull. If a working model anchor system is installed it is necessary to ensure that the anchor stock can be easily accommodated within the bore of the pipe used to make the hawse pipe. The termination points of the hawse pipes at the deck must also be of correct form and shape for the model to be authentic in appearance and such detail should be noted carefully. The line of the anchor cable from hawse pipe to windlass through the cable stopper needs careful attention to ensure that all lines up correctly.

Fig. 107 Hawse box with 'Hall' anchor stowed on a stern trawler. Note reinforced edges of the hawse box.

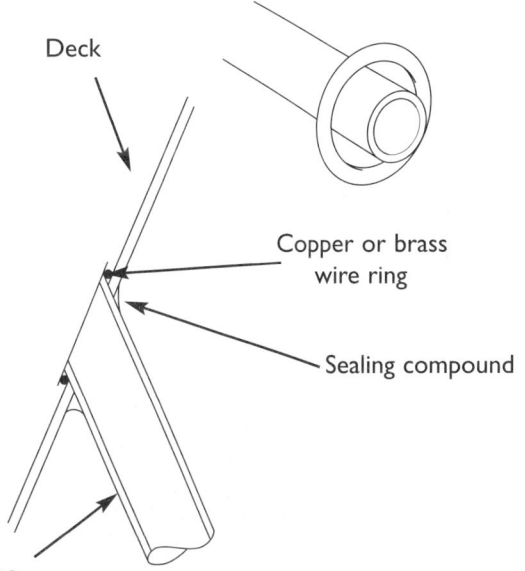

Fig. 108

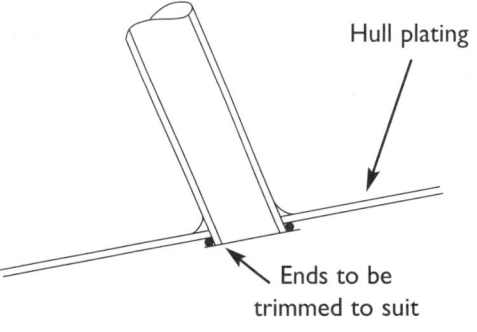

One Method of Making a Hawse Pipe

HULL CONSTRUCTION

The building of the hull of the small ship is of interest, so far as the ship model builder is concerned, only to ensure that the hull of the model looks right and in proportion. The timber-built ship of earlier times is generally considered to be the best study when constructing a model, as the form and designs are similar. Once a hull has been built in timber it is comparatively easy to either smooth the surface to represent a welded hull or to plate it with card or similar material to simulate a plated hull. It is possible to build a ship model in other materials such as tinplate and brass but this type of construction is not considered herein. There is, too, a kit available from which one can build a type SD14 cargo ship entirely from card and in the same way as was the original ship built. This can be waterproofed and made to be seaworthy but it is a complex subject and outside the scope of this work.

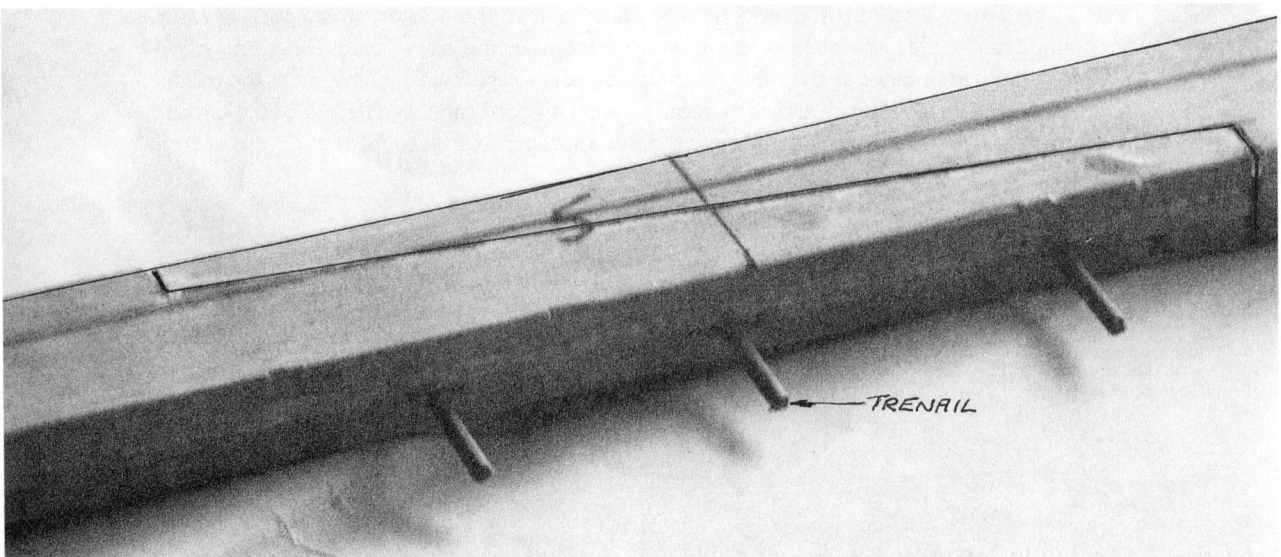

Fig. 109 Joining two sections of keel together using a scarf joint and trenails.

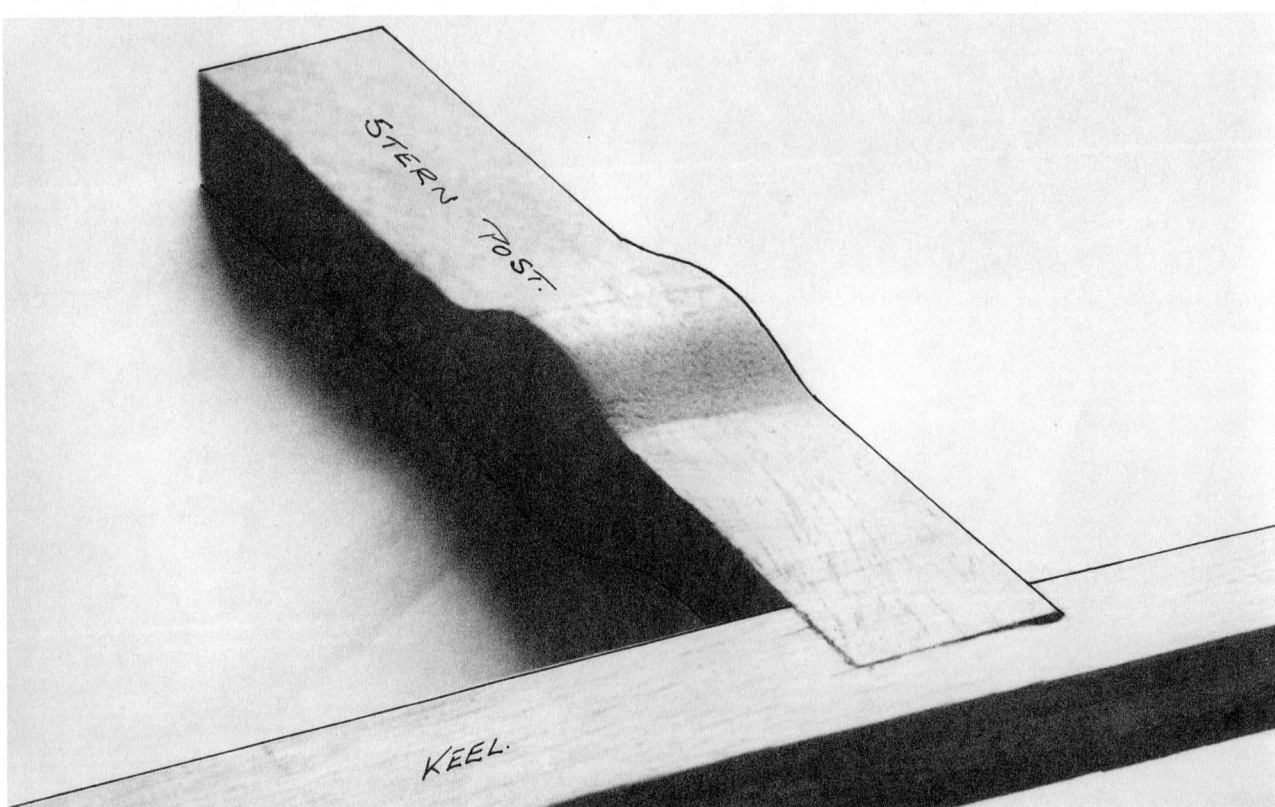

Fig. 110 Fitting stern post to keel.

The frames of a ship of steel construction are generally spaced along the keel at intervals of 24in, which today means a spacing of 650 millimetres. Towards the bow and stern these intervals are often decreased slightly to around 600mm. Much has been written regarding the building of model ship hulls and there is little point in going into detail here of such methods. Model hulls can be made by a number of methods; they can be carved from a solid block of timber although this is wasteful of material and usually restricted to making only very small hulls. The more usual methods are 'bread and butter' where the hull is built up from a series of planks of timber glued together, the 'bread' being the timber and the 'butter' being the glue. The bottom plank is usually roughly pre-shaped and the 'lifts' (planks) are usually shaped both inside and out before assembly, the whole being clamped together until the glue has cured before the final outer shape is planed and sanded to the required finish. For some static models the inside is left solid but for the working model it is cut away to give adequate room for the machinery. Sensibly the modeller using this method will prepare a number of templates from the lines drawings to ensure accuracy as the work proceeds. One method of bread-and-butter hull construction that shows a serious saving in material is the Kirby method, which has been described in a number of publications. This method uses a single plank of timber and gives excellent results.

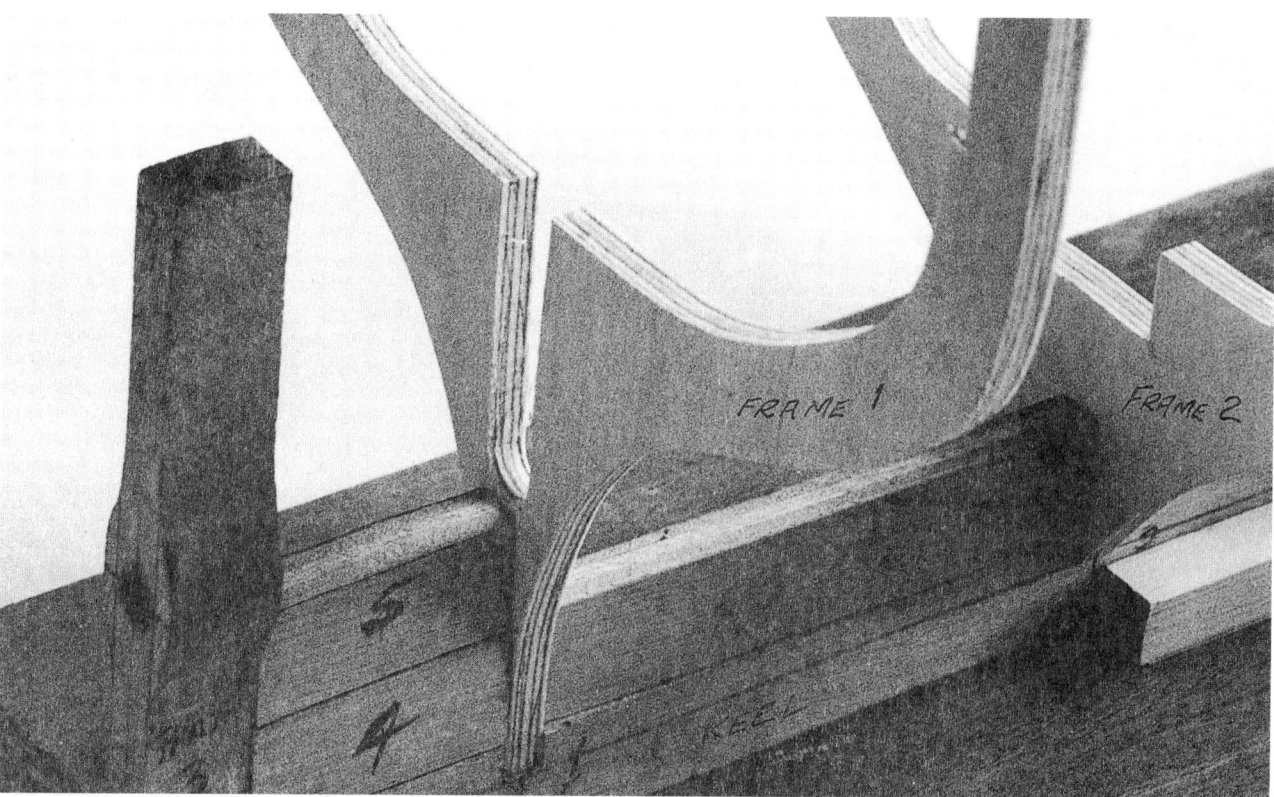

Fig. 111 Stern of the model showing frames and deadwood (4 & 5)

Fig. 112 Completed keel and frame assembly - model is a wooden herring drifter.

By far the most common method of building a model hull in timber is that of the 'plank-on-frame' method. This requires that a keel be cut over which a number of bulkheads or frames can be fitted to which are glued (and pinned) thin planks in the same way as a timber ship or small boat would be built. Some builders carry the shell planking through to the bow and stern while others use blocks of balsa or jelutong timber to permit the finer curves of the bow and stern to be carved and sanded. Some of the photographs illustrate the open framework of a model under construction using this method. Depending upon whether the model is to be a working one or a static one will determine whether open frames or solid bulkheads are used. **Figs. 109 to 114** refer.

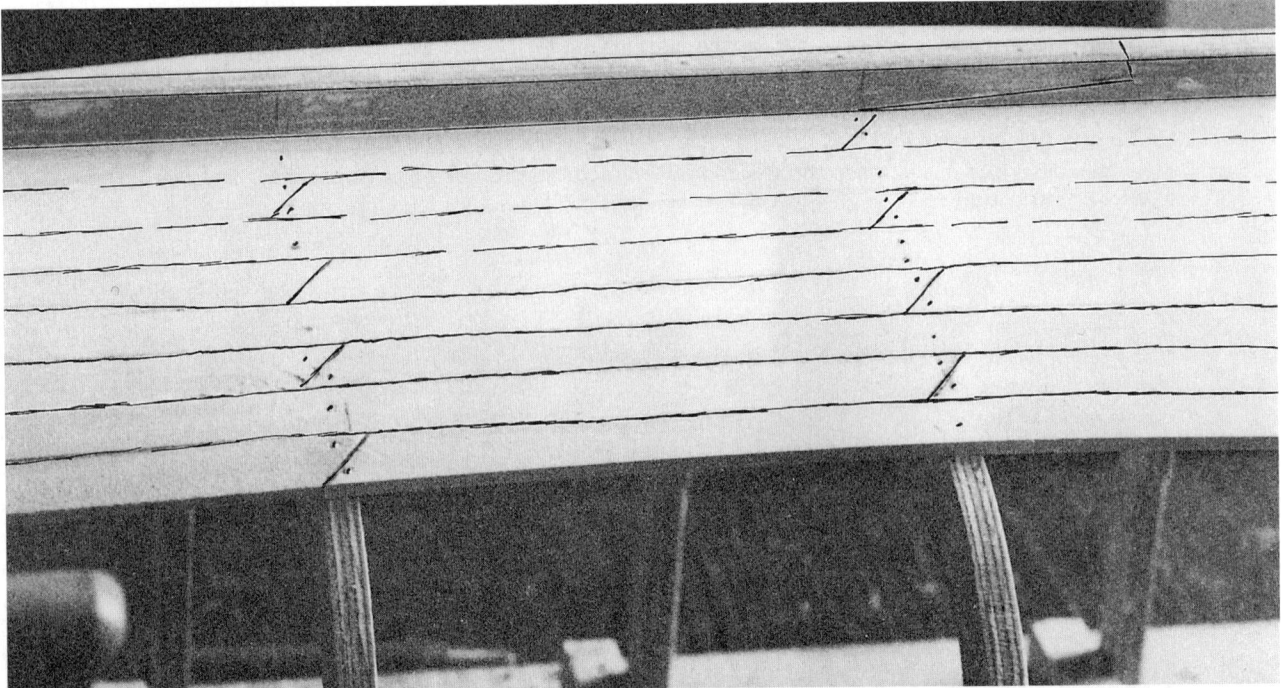

Fig. 113 Method of planking over frames.

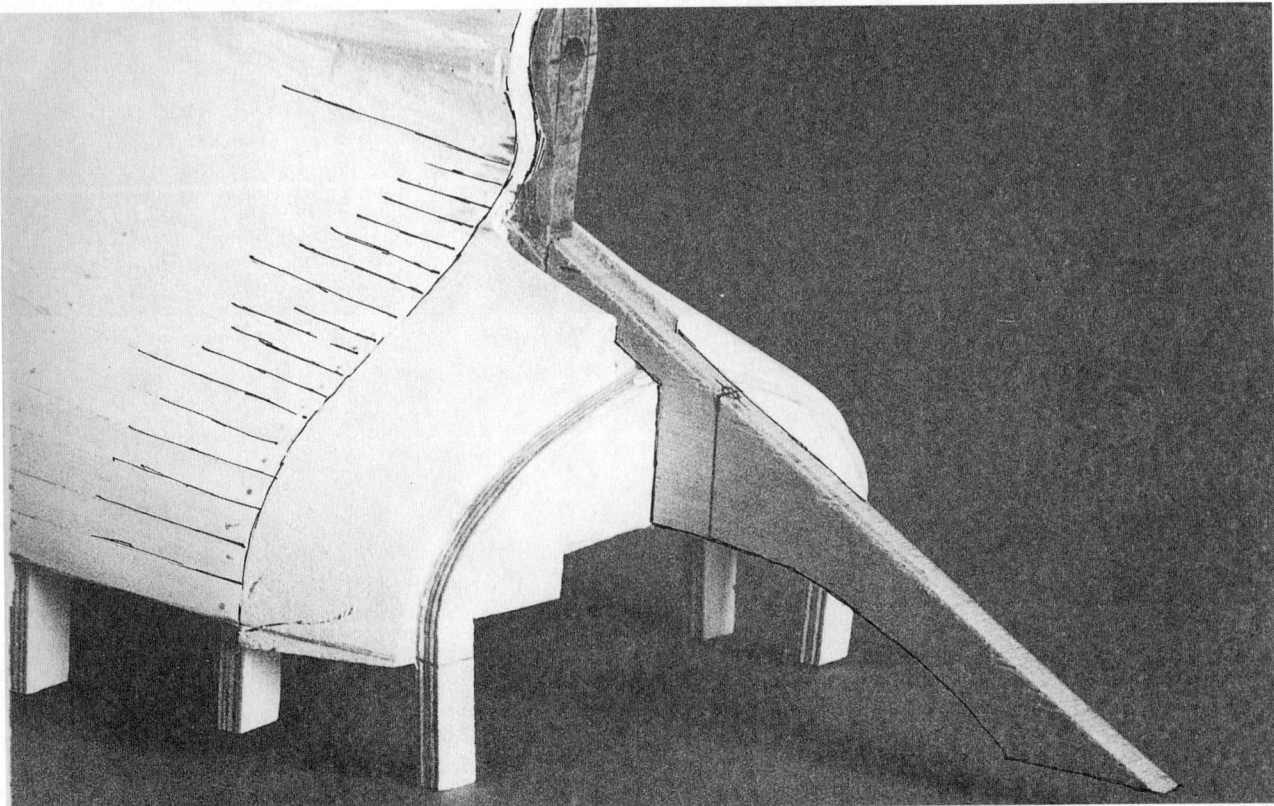

Fig. 114 Stern of model almost completed and showing fitting of balsa blocks.

Fig. 115 Keel and frames of model tug SEGUIN set up and prepared for planking.

Fig. 118 Bow of a short sea trader showing welding of plates.

Fig. 119 The side of a motor ship showing effects of plate welding.

Drawings

Mention must be made of the drawings needed by the ship modeller. The person working from scratch will need a copy of the ships 'lines' together with a 'general arrangement' and any other drawings that can be obtained and that are relevant. The modeller working from a kit containing a pre-formed hull or who purchases a ready-formed hull will not need the lines plans. The lines plans are the key to the shape of the ship's hull **Fig. 116**. They comprise three sections. At the top is usually a side elevation depicting the starboard side - the bow being to the right of the drawing. This is known as the sheer plan and shows the outline of the stem, keel and stern with a line indicating the main deck. On this are three sets of lines, the first comprising vertical lines drawn up from the base and known as stations. The second comprises a series of horizontal lines parallel to the base line and known as waterlines. Finally, and running from stern to bow, a number of curved lines known as bowlines and buttock lines.

Below the sheer plan is usually a plan of the hull showing the port side of the ship from the fore-and-aft centreline and from above. Once again there are vertical lines showing the stations at the correct intervals. There are next a series of curved lines showing the waterlines as if they could be seen from above with one showing the outline of the main deck. Finally the third plan is the body plan comprising the base line with the vertical centreline drawn up from the base. On the right side of the vertical centreline are a number of curved lines which show the shape of the stations from amidships to the bow while on the left side are the outlines of the stations from amidships to the stern. The waterlines are shown parallel to the baseline once more. The body plan is sometimes superimposed on the sheer plan with the vertical centreline at the centre of the ship.

Conventionally all ship's plans are drawn to show the starboard side, i.e., with the bow to the right of the drawing. In addition almost all lines plans are drawn to the extreme outside of the ship i.e., to the outside of the hull planking or plating. Thus if the drawings are used to cut stations for use as frames when building a plank-on-frame model, the outsides of such frames need to be reduced by the thickness of the material to be used for planking or plating.

General arrangement drawings show the layout of the ship in some detail but builders' drawings can vary greatly in the detail they provide. Some will show the interior of cabins at each level of the superstructures and others will show only outlines. Some will give full outlines of engines and auxiliaries and others will not. Very few show the front and rear elevations of accommodation, bridge and other superstructures. Most builders' drawings are quite complex and provide information that is of no special value to the ship modeller. Most drawings provided by the plans services (see appendices) for use by model builders have been drawn by modellers from the builders' drawings and have been simplified to suit the building of a scale model **Fig. 117**. Many will give details of superstructures from all needful aspects and many will also give large-scale details of some of the deck fittings.

The most important aspect of ship's drawings as far as the ship model builder is concerned is the scale. The great majority of builders' drawings are to a scale of 1:48 or today 1:50 and this is not always the scale the modeller requires. Carefully-drawn plans can readily be enlarged or reduced by drawing-office supply companies or specialist copy services for nominal fees. Such enlargements or reductions can be very accurate and very useful to the modeller and the fees are generally reasonable. Some of the more specialist services will reproduce drawings on transparent film permitting copies to be easily made. Care must be taken to read scales correctly; for example, a drawing is logged as 1/4in to 1ft equates to a scale of 1:48. Either of these two definitions is correct, it is not correct to state that this scale is a 1/4 scale drawing, as it is not. A drawing to 1/4 scale is in effect drawn at 3in to 1ft. The effect is similar when detailing drawings produced in the metric scales. A good rule marked with both imperial and metric scales will be of value and most good drawing-office supply or artists' shops can supply rules providing scale measurements.

Fig. 116 Typical line drawing for Fishing Vessel

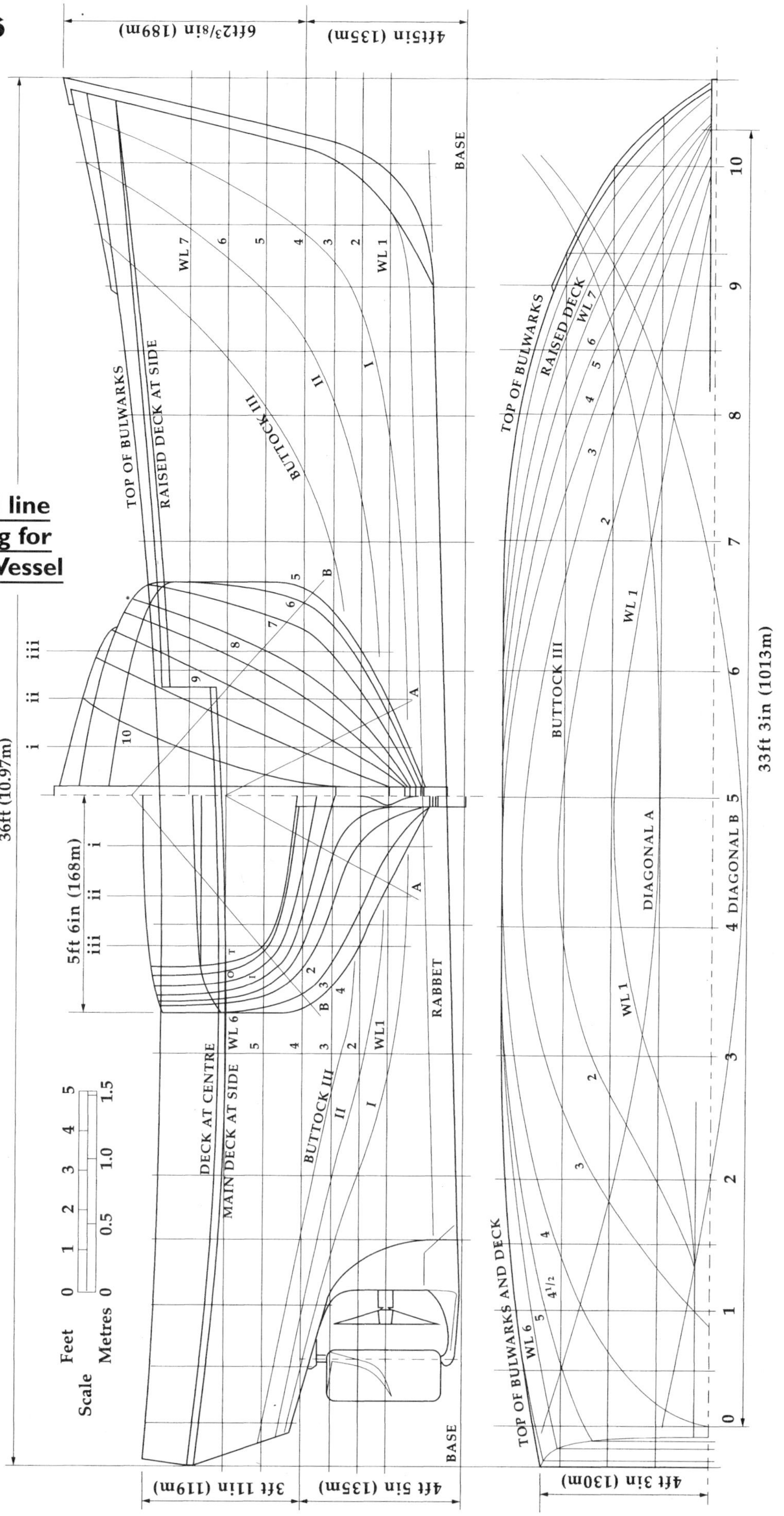

Typical Lines drawing

Fig. 117

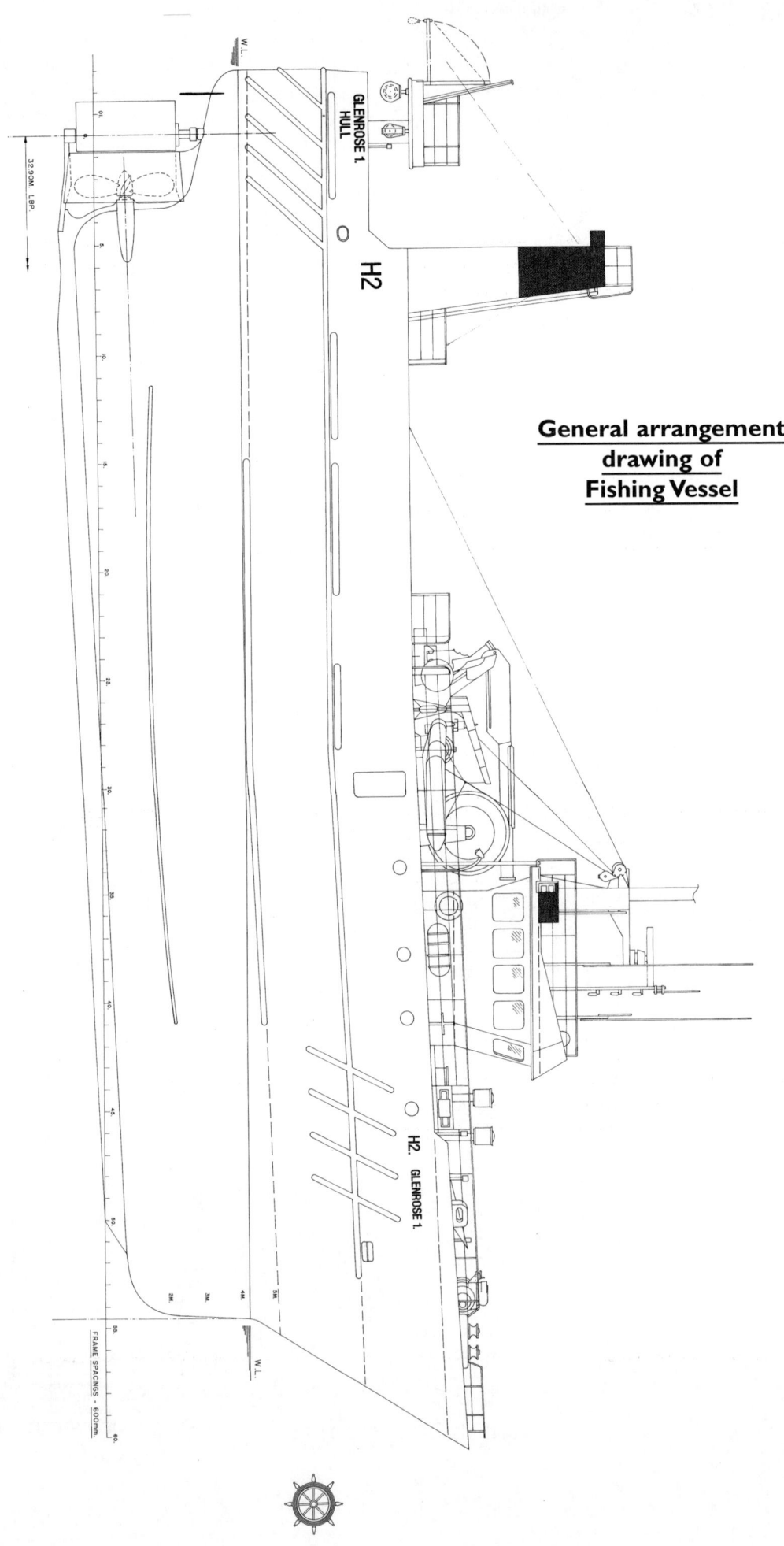

General arrangement drawing of Fishing Vessel

Hull Plating and Details

Many modellers plate their hulls with card, litho plate or similar thin material to simulate the plating on the ship. Whichever method is used it is very necessary to ensure that the work is carried out accurately. Sometimes the modeller will have access to the ship's plate expansion drawing that lays out the shapes of each of the plates used in construction but such a drawing will often be difficult to read. In the days of the riveted ship, hull plates overlapped each other from bow to stern; in other words the first plate fitted would be at the stern. The next plate would overlap the first sufficiently to allow the two to be drilled and riveted and this carried on to the bow. Plates were usually joined at the frames, too, with the rivets securing the plates to the frames. Sometimes the steel plates were butted at the ends and riveted using a piece of plate behind to give a more flush appearance to the hull lines.

Ships that were of welded construction had the plating welded at the edges to give a flush finish although the finished hull was generally quite wavy due to unequal expansion of the plates during the welding process. The modeller desiring accuracy will need to consult as many photographs of the selected ship as possible to determine the method used to plate the hull. For further details of riveting plating see the appropriate section later.

Care must be taken when producing shell-plate riveting for the model hull. The rivets used when constructing the shell of a ship were of the countersunk round-head or raised countersunk pattern where part of the rivet head was sunk into a counterbored hole in the plate. This resulted in the head of the rivet having very little projection above the plate surface. Once the ship had received a number of coats of paint the rivet heads became almost invisible from a short distance away. To reproduce such detail on the plating of a ship's hull is one that needs serious consideration. If the model is of large scale, say of 1:24 or more, then such rivet detail may well be visible and should be added. For models of smaller scales then riveting would certainly be unnecessary. Furthermore the shell-plate riveting was carried out according to classification society rules which detail the number of rows of rivets, the size of the rivets and the spacing of them relative to their location and the thickness of the plates. Thus while it is good to see such detail on a large-scale ship it would seriously impair the quality of the model if the correct number of rows, spacing etc. of the rivets were not shown. Another instance of research being needed by the ship model builder.

Decks and their plating or planking have been detailed in the appropriate section.

LADDERS & COMPANIONS

All ships with almost no exceptions have ladders and companions to permit personnel to move from deck to deck. In effect a ladder on board ship is essentially similar to that used ashore, comprising two long, flat sides and with rod-type rungs. A companion or companionway is a staircase with treads of chequerplate, flat plate, round rods or even timber.

The ladder generally conforms to a set of dimensions that are of long standing; the rungs are usually spaced at intervals of 9in (230mm) and the sides or risers are usually a minimum of 12in (250mm) apart and normally 15in (380mm). In some cases the fixed ladder will have a handrail but sometimes it does not depending upon its location and duty on the ship.

Fig. 120 Portable companion for boarding on a model paddle steamer.

Fig. 121 Companion leading from well deck to forecastle on model coaster, treads and risers from Plastruct range (see appendices) with wire handrails continuing down from top guard rails.

Fig. 122 Vertical ladder to wheelhouse roof on model coaster, ladder of cast white metal with handrails from guard-rails above.

Fig. 123 Companion on stern of model coaster ARRAN MAIL built by the author. Risers were made from thin plywood and the treads are of twin lengths of brass rod all assembled in a purpose made jig.

Fig. 124 Companion ladders on the stern of the motor vessel JONRIX.

Companions generally have treads spaced some 7in (180mm) apart with the sides or risers varying from 24in (600mm) apart or more. Companionways almost always have handrails and these are quite frequently on both sides of the risers. Where a companion leads to an upper deck and is not led close to a deckhouse or other superstructure, the opening in the deck will be provided with an encircling guardrail. The very small ship will rarely have companions visible as they occupy valuable deck space that cannot be spared. Note that handrails for both ladders and companions are frequently extensions of the top rails of the upper guardrails. Details of guardrails can be found later.

Fig. 125 A very substantial welded steel companionway leading down to the cargo deck of a motor ship.

Fig. 126 Welded rungs on a post to give access to the post top.

Fig. 127 A substantial companion with hand rails on an oilrig support ship.

Pre-made and very accurate model ladders and companions from a number of makers can be bought through the specialist ship model shop or mail order supplier. According to scale, some are formed in fine, hard plastic, some are cast in white metal and some are etched in brass or nickel silver. It is also possible to find both ladders and companions as kits of parts neatly packed in small bags for home assembly.

Access to masts and similar structures is often formed of rungs welded in a ladder formation to the unit and as shown in one or two of the photographs. Such rungs can be simply made for the model from thin hard wire bent up and glued into a series of suitably-drilled holes. Wire staples for the office stapling machine can be a good and inexpensive source of ladder rungs. The photographs here provide some views of a varied selection of ladders and companions and, for the model builder, the watchword is, be certain of the scale and sizes you need before investing. Such items can, of course, be made from scratch using a variety of materials as indicated in some of the pictures. Not all the differing types of ladders and companionways can be found within the ranges of the commercial model makers.

LIFEBOATS

Lifeboats are a feature of model ships that require care and attention on the part of the ship model builder. It is all too easy to purchase a lifeboat shell and fit it to a model without realising that it is not the correct model needed. It is necessary to research into the type of lifeboat(s) that would have been or is fitted to the ship of which the model is a replica. Most model makers' general arrangement drawings and plans will show details of the lifeboats fitted and the modeller must then produce the correct shape and type of lifeboat in miniature. As with many of a ship's details, it is quite possible that the lifeboats were changed during the period the ship was or is in service and this must be verified before the lifeboats are made.

Ship lifeboats have undergone a number of changes over the years. The clinker-built lifeboat was common on almost all vessels for many years **Fig. 133**. Although in the period before the Titanic disaster the number of boats carried was inadequate, today there are strictly enforced rules that govern the safety of life at sea. In the U.K. the Board of Trade (Department of Trade and Industry) governs size and construction of lifeboats and the outfitting of such boats also come within their remit. The early wooden and clinker-built boats have been superseded by boats built in aluminium, steel and glass fibre; boats of glass fibre being by far the most common today.

Fig. 128 A GRP lifeboat on the port side of the JONRIX. Note the cantilever type cranes for placing the boat in the water.

Propulsion of lifeboats was initially by oars (sweeps) but a number were constructed with levers located at each seat and connected by a system of rods to a central shaft that led to a propeller. Each person in the boat could thus assist to propel it through the water. The advent of the internal combustion engine led to a number of lifeboats being outfitted with small engines. Not all lifeboats on a ship would be thus fitted but some would remain fitted with oars.

Research into safety led to other improvements over the years. All lifeboats are now fitted with buoyancy tanks so that they can remain afloat even when swamped. The most significant improvement is, of course, the introduction of lifeboats that are virtually totally enclosed and that give protection to the occupants from the ravages of the wind and sun as well as the sea. These latest lifeboats are slowly replacing the older units and there are but few modern small ships that carry such boats as yet. The ship model builder needing further information on the construction and regulations governing lifeboats should seek such data from the libraries and maritime museum services. The accompanying photographs will help. Quaycraft today produces some of the best model lifeboats seen by the author, details of whom can be found in the appendices.

Fig. 129 Close-up detail of the GRP lifeboat on the JONRIX.

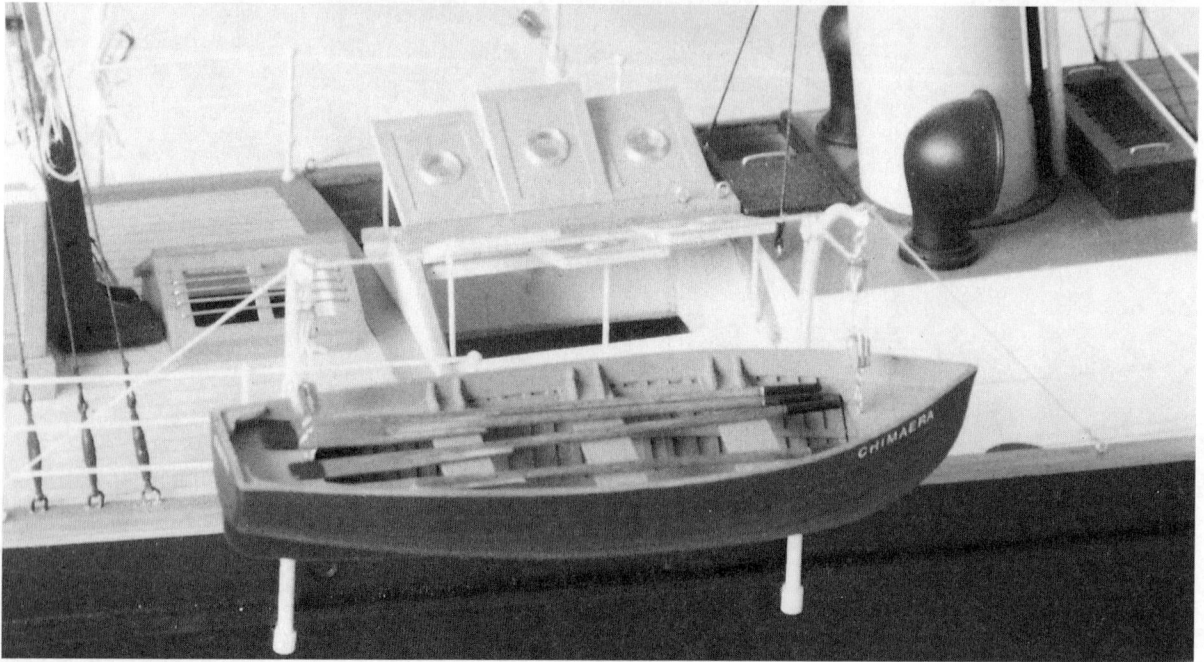

Fig. 131 A model lifeboat suspended from radial davits on the port side of a model pilot cutter.

Building model lifeboats from scratch is a satisfying task; they can be made from all manner of materials: thin timber, card, tinplate and papier-maché. Mine are made by first carving and sanding a plug former to the size of the required model but allowing for the thickness of the material to be used. To this is fixed a keel generally made of thin 0.8mm plywood and then the sides and transom or ends are formed of card. If the model is to be of clinker build then the sides are made of strips that overlap. If it is required to simulate steel or GRP construction then the sides will be made of papier-maché or in thin card. The timber plug needs to be well treated with wax before construction is commenced but generally the shell will part from the plug with a little gentle persuasion. With a suitable plug it is possible to make a master mould using latex with a filler powder incorporated and in which, once the rubber has cured, repeat models can be moulded in GRP or papier-maché. Latex and filler powders can be bought from a number of outlets reference the appendices. The book 'The Construction of Model Open Boats' by Ewart Freeston is worth reading in this connection, regretfully it is currently out of print but the library services may be able to assist here.

The sketch **Fig. 135** shows the general arrangement of a modern enclosed motor lifeboat of the type that is mounted on the stern of a ship upon a sloping ramp from which the boat can be slid into the water or, where the water depth is shallow, from a davit system as shown. This type of lifeboat, or ones that are similar, can also be found beneath davits of the gravity pattern on the modern passenger-carrying vessels and larger ships. In time they will have more general use on the smaller ship.

Fig. 130 Detail of one of the winches fitted to the JONRIX for raising and lowering the lifeboats.

Typical Arrangement of Lifeboat Falls

Fig. 133

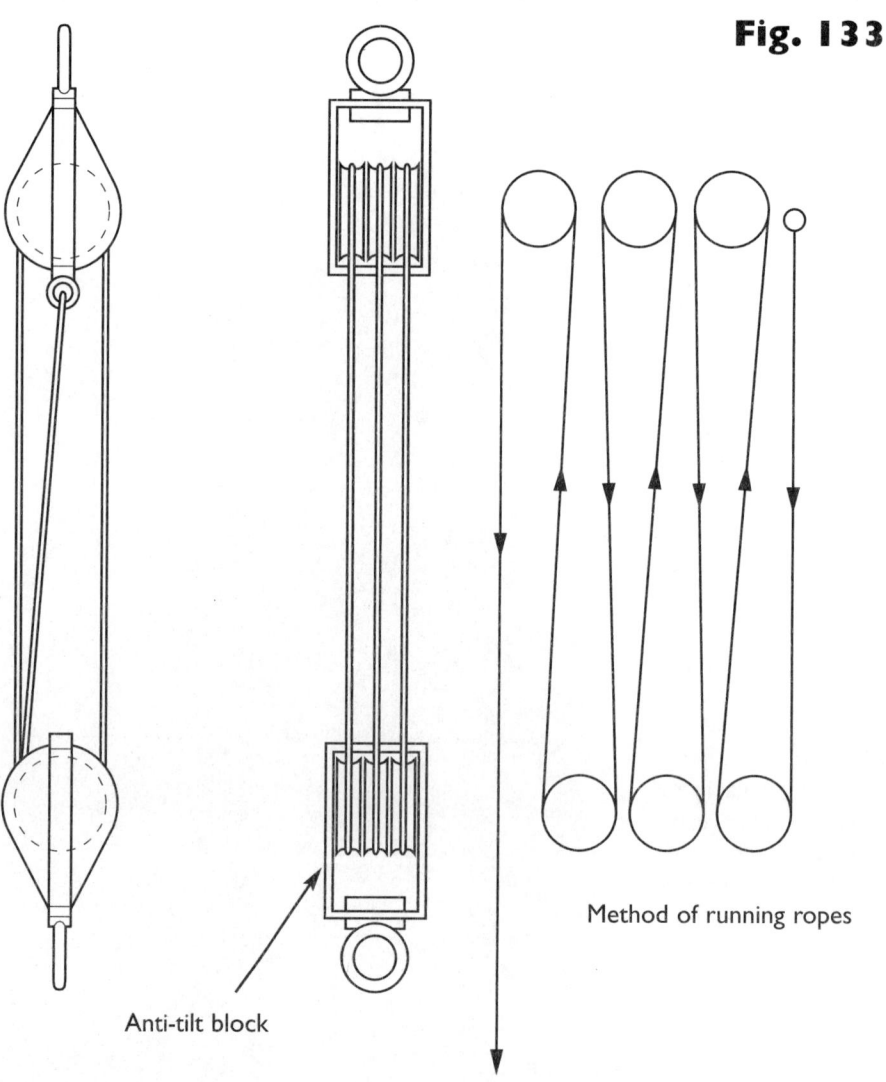

Anti-tilt block

Method of running ropes

Fig. 132 Model herring drifter showing dinghy used as a lifeboat on such vessels, it was lowered and raised by the sail gaff.

Fig. 134 Model lifeboat cast in resin and supplied by Quaycraft (see appendices) for the model of the side-fishing trawler KINGSTON PERIDOT.

Sketch of Totally Enclosed Lifeboat

Fig. 135

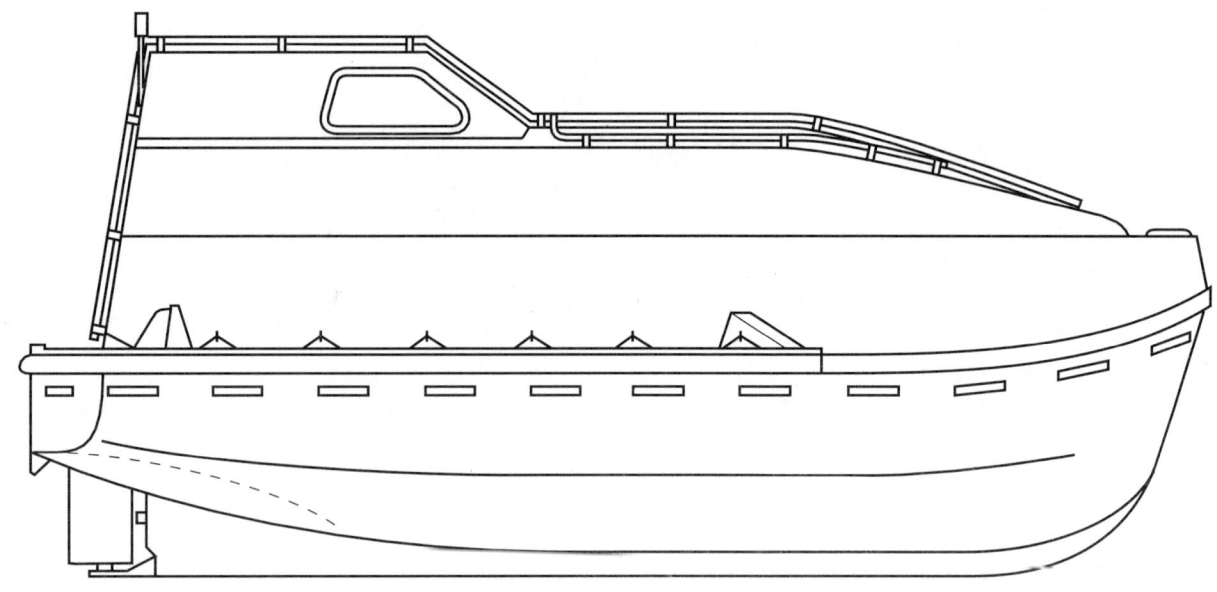

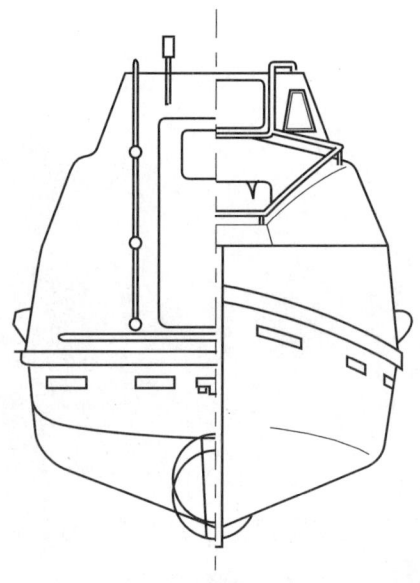

This example has a length of 6770mm, a beam of 2500mm and a height overall of 3000mm for a capacity of 20 persons. Laden, the boat has a weight of 5000kgs.

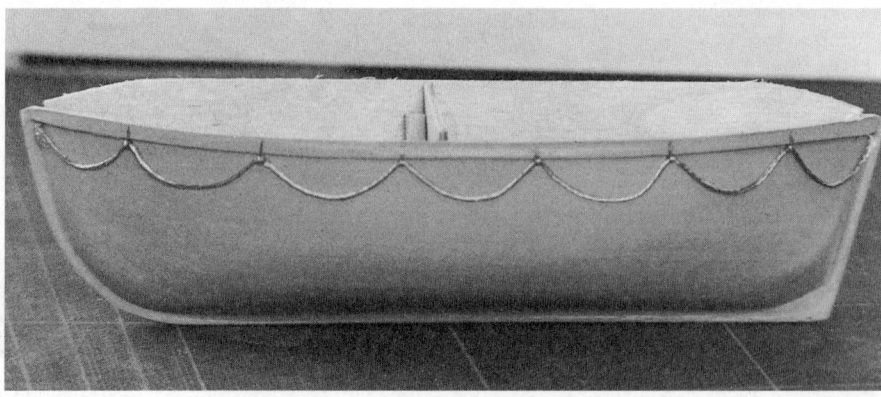

Fig. 136 Model lifeboat under construction.

LIFEBUOYS

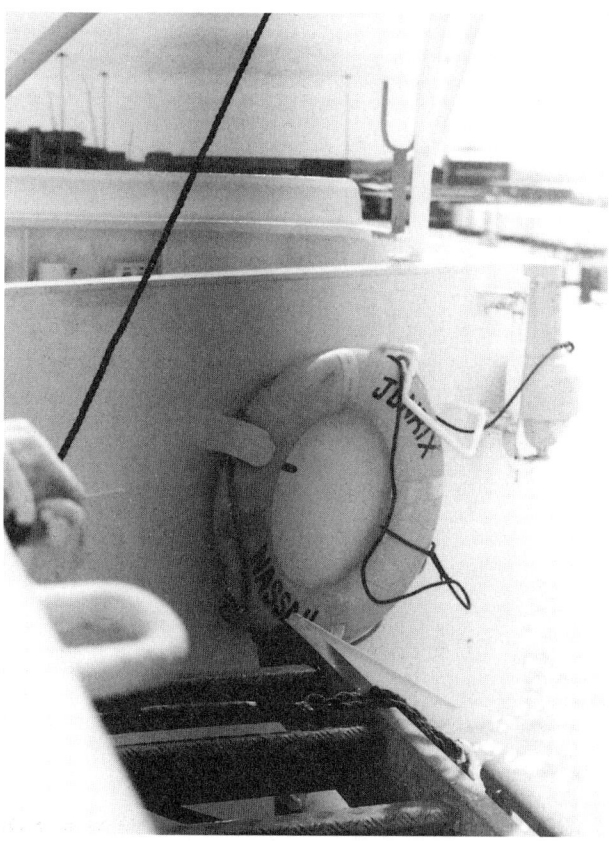

All ships carry lifebuoys located in strategic places and on brackets that allow them to be readily available in an emergency. They are of standard size 30in (750mm) outside diameter x 18in (460mm) inside diameter and of oval cross section, 6in x 4in (150 x 100mm). Originally they were made of cork and canvas covered with grab lines secured to the buoy by 4in wide bands of canvas stitched in place. Modern lifebuoys are usually of moulded PVC with an inner of expanded polyurethane. The grab lines of synthetic rope are secured through the core and knotted. Lifebuoys are usually painted red and white in quarters but more recently they have been painted in 'dayglow' orange for better visibility.

Stowage of the lifebuoy is a matter of where it is located and usually they are hung on a three-point bracket system. Those mounted on the bridge wings of ships are usually in chutes with a quick-release mechanism and generally, too, fitted with a self-igniting light or flare. It is important for the modeller to locate and secure lifebuoys correctly if authenticity is to be maintained.

Fig. 137 A chute mounted, 'dayglow' orange lifebuoy with self igniting light on the starboard bridge wing of JONRIX.

Fig. 138 Red and white painted lifebuoys on a model tug.

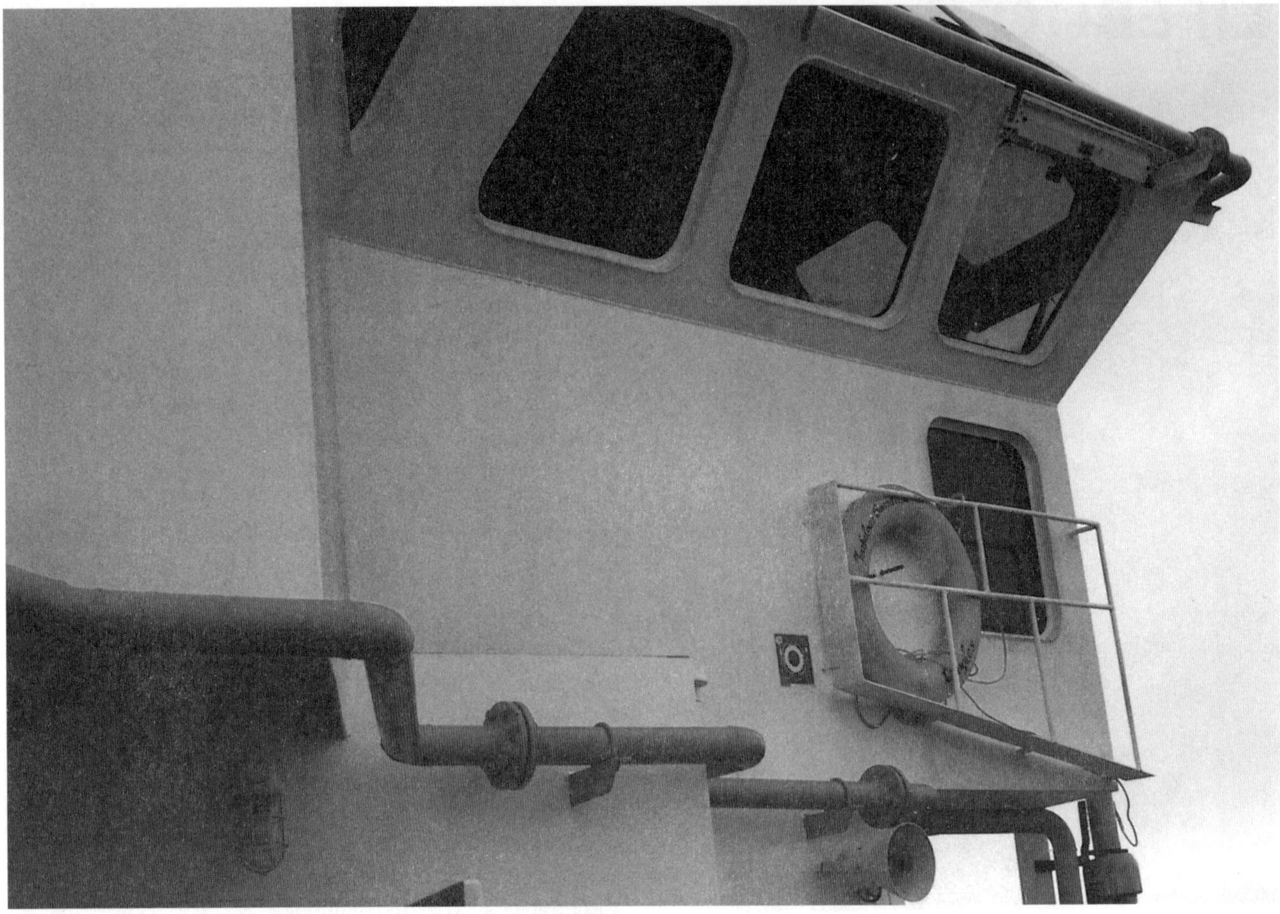

Fig. 139 A llifebuoy in a chute on the bridge wing of an oilrig support ship.

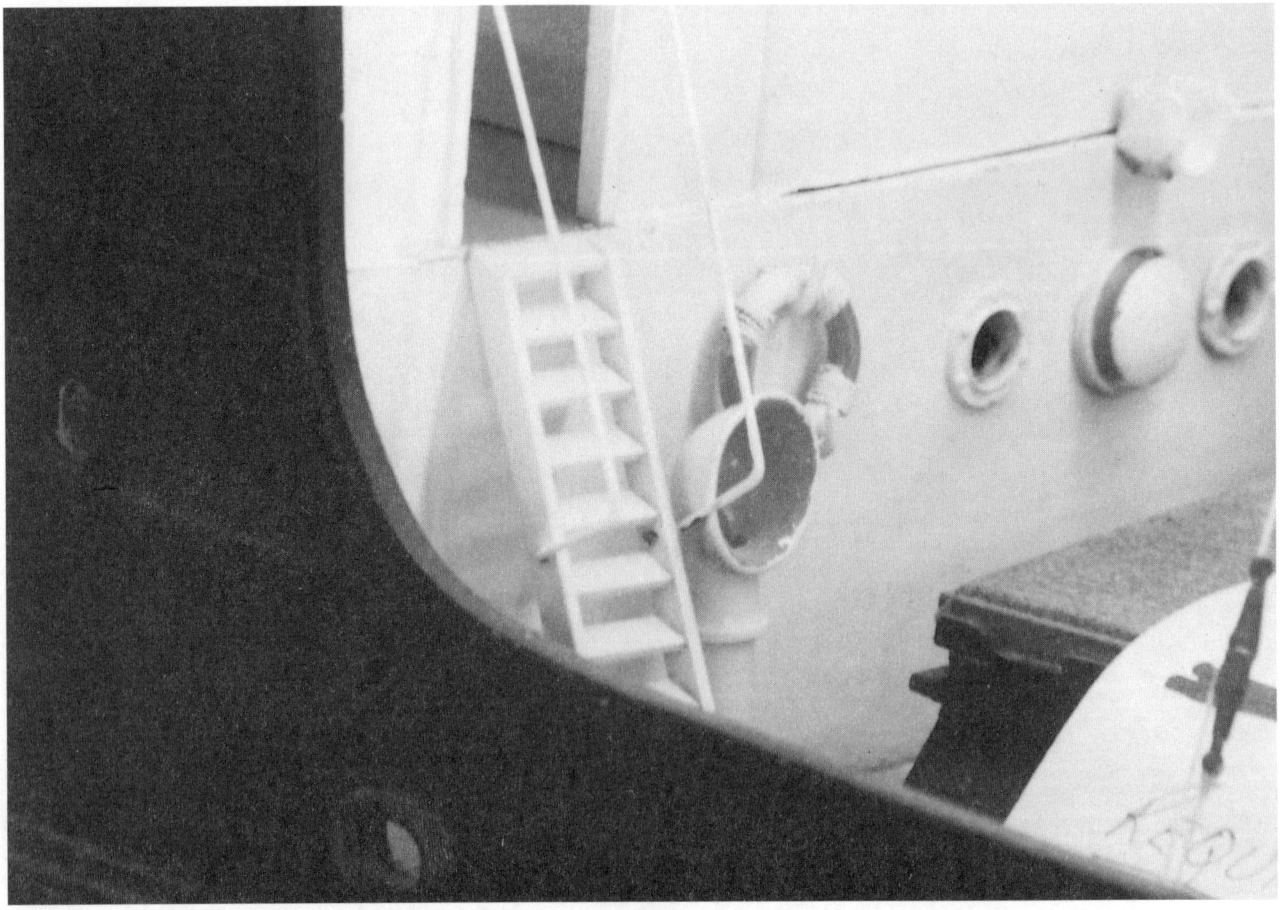

Fig. 140 Clear stowage of a lifebuoy on a model motor coaster.

LIFERAFTS

The inflatable liferaft is, today, a standard feature of almost all ships. Some ships carry such liferafts in place of a standard lifeboat. They come in canisters which, when placed in the water, open to release and inflate the liferaft. The liferaft is generally circular, has a protective canopy and contains emergency rations, flares etc. The canisters are usually stowed singly on deck in a cradle but they sometimes are fitted on a track where two or more can be released quickly. This latter arrangement is generally confined to the larger vessels. The illustrations show a number of canisters. Such liferafts have to comply with the rules of the Department of Trade and Industry and must be tested and inspected at regular intervals. Present day regulation by SOLAS (Safety of Life at Sea) apply to the outfit of ships' liferafts, and associated equipment for life saving, particularly with reference to those ships that carry passengers.

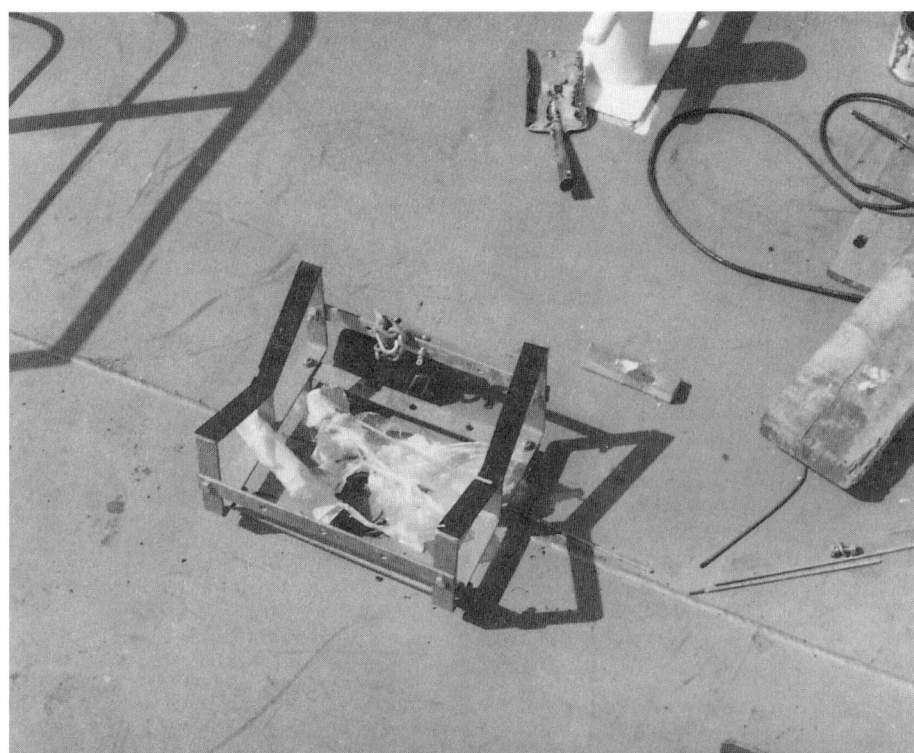

Fig. 141 A liferaft canister cradle prepared and awaiting the canister to be fitted.

Fig. 142 Liferaft canister mounted on the starboard side of a bunkering tanker.

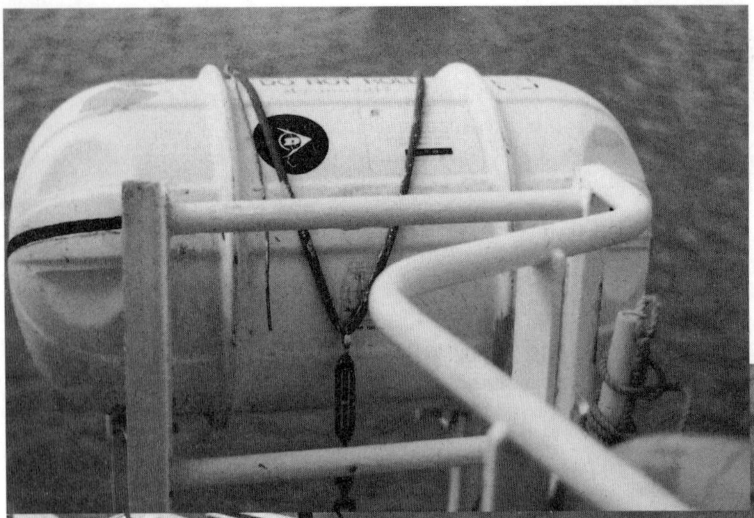

Fig. 143 Liferaft canister on a fishing vessel.

Fig. 144 Liferaft of timber on the superstructure of the model of the Customs launch BADGER.

Fig. 145 A fine view of the motor ship TIMRIX clearly showing lifebuoys, liferafts and lifeboats on the superstructure.

LIGHTS

Here again is a situation where ship model builders often fail: the type and disposition of a ship's navigation lights is important. Failure to fit the correct pattern lamp is one reason why an otherwise well-built model will be decried. In the days of the sailing vessel and the early steam ships, the port and starboard and mast lamps were illuminated by oil (paraffin). Some of the early herring drifters and trawlers had deck lights that used acetylene made within the base of the lamp by dripping water on to carbide, but the navigation lights were oil lit.

Fig. 146 Lights on a motor ship, the upper to indicate towing and the lower is the stern navigation light.

When the steam-engine-driven dynamos came into service ships lights were illuminated by electricity but they were required to carry oil lamps for use in the event of a power failure. Today, ships' lights still use electricity but the standby lights are illuminated by power from batteries kept charged from the vessel's auxiliary plant. One will, therefore, always see two lamps at each position, whether on masts or bridge wings. The upper lamps are generally lit from the main power supply on the ship and the lower lights from the emergency system.

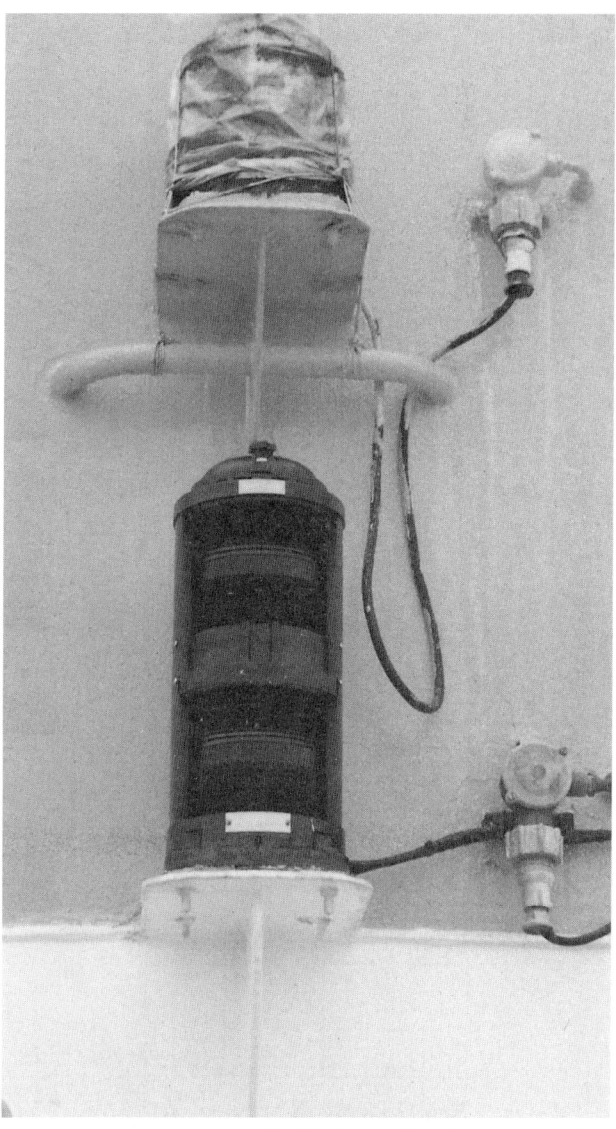

Fig. 146 Stern light unit on a motor ship.

As with all other parts of the ship the lights come under the rules of the classification society or other ruling body. Each light has to be visible over a given arc and each has a specific colour. The lenses of the lights are of dioptric type and each light has a built-in baffle to ensure that the light spreads over the designed arc. Under way or being towed a vessel must show a red port light and a green starboard light, each arranged to show a light from ahead to two points abaft the beam or over an arc of ten points of the compass. Each must be fitted with a board to prevent light being seen from the other side

Fig. 149

Sketch of mast of fishing vessel Glenrose 1 showing lights

Continuous Loop Signal Halyards P & S

Safety Hoops

Square bar dogsteps 300 mm apart

Double Electric All Round White Fishing/Anchor Light

Safety Hoops

Double Electric All Round Red NUC/Aground Light

TV Antenna

300mm Wide Single Rung Ladder

Deck Floodlights

900 P & S

25 Tonne Roller Sheave

Section 'X X'

84

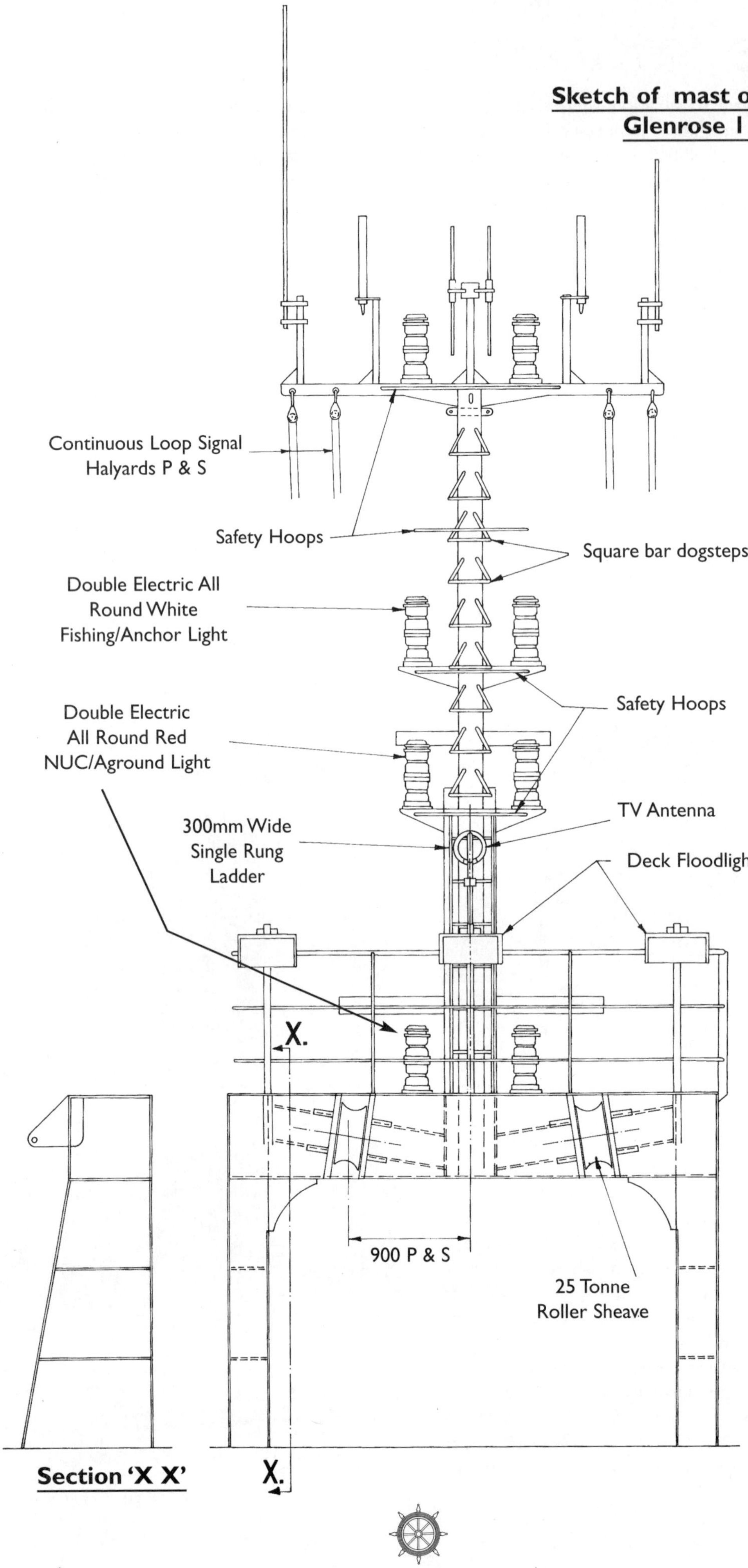

of the ship and with boards to prevent the light from being seen from astern or from beyond the centreline of the ship. The vessel will also show a bright white light on the foremast that will show an unbroken light over ten points of the compass on either side of the centreline. A second, forward-facing white light with the same range and visibility is also usually carried a little further aft and at 15ft higher than the former. A fixed stern light is also usually carried which must be white and show over six points of the compass astern on either side of the centreline. The photographs show various arrangements of lamps ranging from oil pattern in model form to two-high units on a modern ship. Until the early 1970s the side screens for the port and starboard lights were painted red and green respectively but today the sidelight screens are painted black.

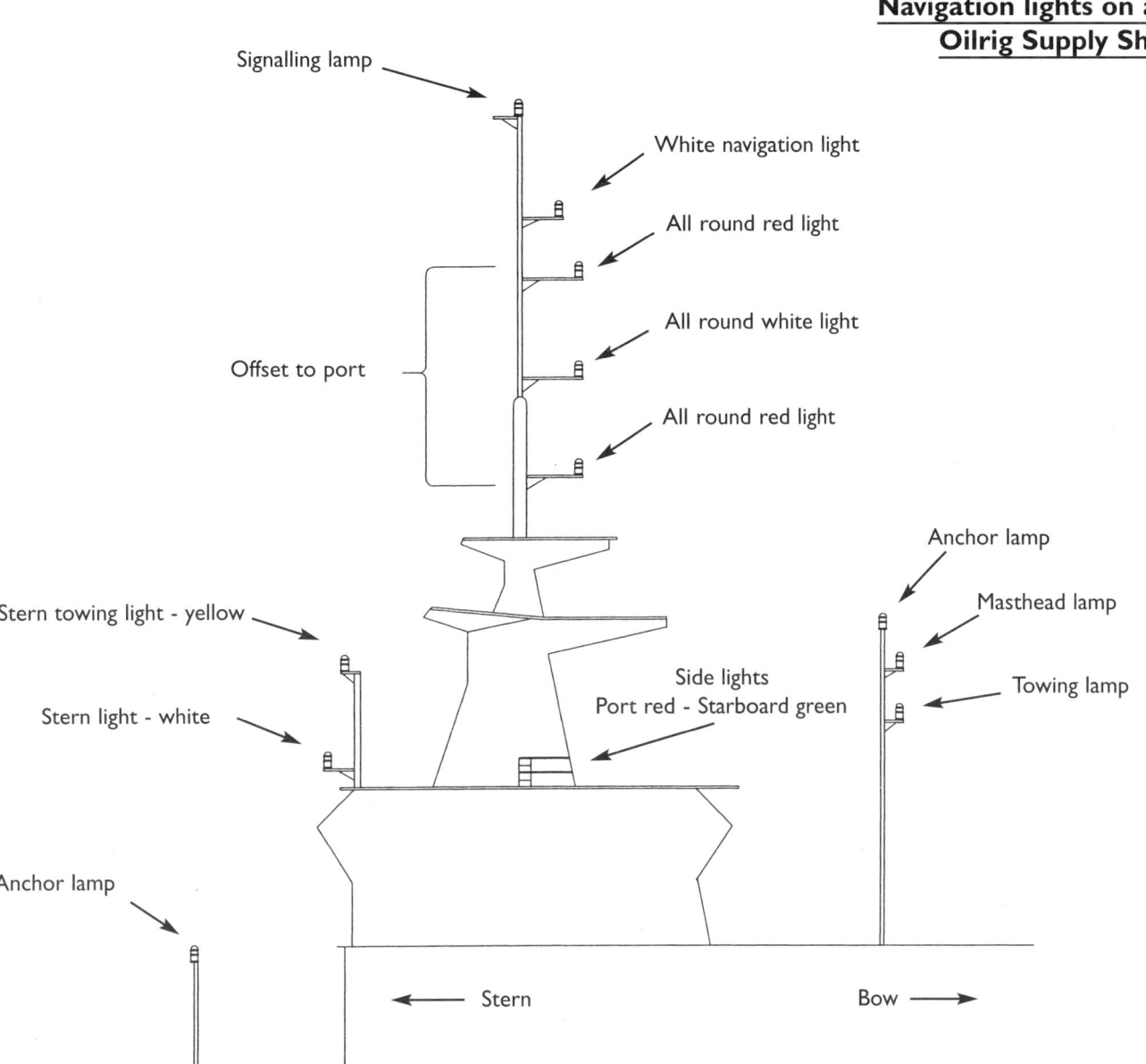

Fig. 150

Navigation lights on an Oilrig Supply Ship

In addition to the foregoing arrangement of lights, which are mandatory, all ships carry additional lights that indicate conditions such as the ship is not under control or other conditions. These are detailed and described in the sketches and can be seen in some of the photographs. Fishing vessels, too, carry lights to indicate that they are fishing as indicated in **Fig. 149** applicable to a stern trawler. The tug and the oilrig support ship have a Christmas tree of lights as illustrated in **Fig. 150**.

The ship model builder should make every effort to ensure that the lights fitted to the model are correct both for period and in location. Many models are spoiled by inaccuracies that can be avoided with a reasonable effort at research.

Fig. 148 Main mast on a fishing vessel with lights as described in the text.

Fig. 153 Lights on main mast and gantry of stern trawler ONWARD CHALLENGER.

Fig. 151 Starboard light box on model coaster showing both electric and oil pattern lamps.

MASTS & DERRICKS

The masts of the tall ships with their yards and rigging were soon replaced when ships turned to steam and, subsequently, diesel power. Most ships retained two masts, one forward and one astern of amidships and aft of the funnel(s). Tall, tapering masts of the pole type were usual on the early steamers and the masts served a useful purpose. They carried the derricks needed for cargo handling and the aerials for the new radio equipment in addition to the crow's-nest on the foremast needed for the lookout. The navigation lights were also raised on the foremast before the days of the fixed electric units that became a feature when generators were the norm on all ships.

As the cargo-handling equipment developed the masts were modified; the crow's-nest disappeared with the coming of radar and whip-type units replaced the long aerial wires. Thus the more modern ship quite often has but one mast forward and has Samson or derrick posts to handle the blocks and rigging needed for cargo handling. Many modern coastal cargo ships today have dispensed with derricks, cranes and other cargo-handling equipment and rely totally on the facilities provided by the ports or harbours.

Fig. 154   Typical Derrick Swivel and Mountings

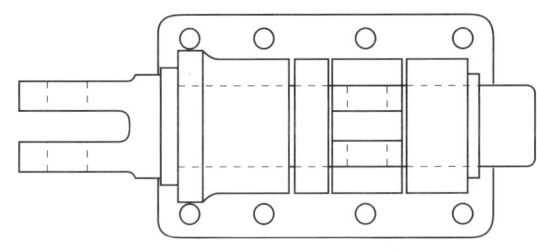

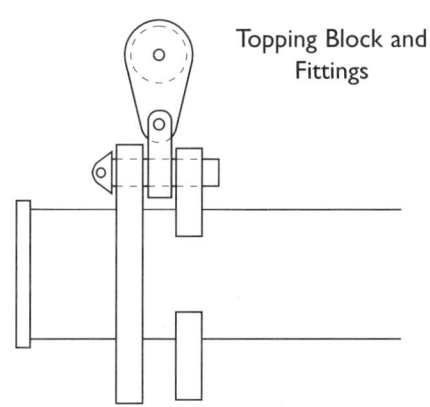

Topping Block and Fittings

Derrick Fittings

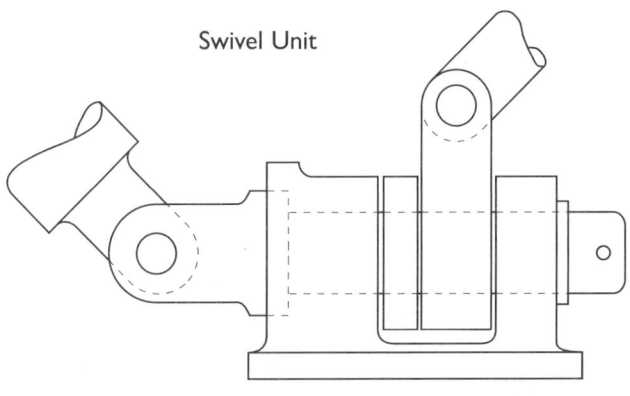

Swivel Unit

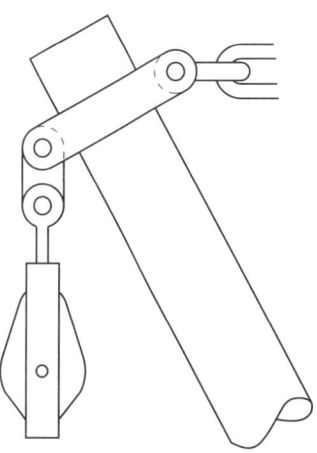

The early wooden and rope-bound blocks have progressively been superseded by the more modern all-metal block for all manner of work when cargo handling and the drawings and photographs should provide some data. The ships round which this volume is written rarely have or had more than two cargo hatches although some of the early coastal steamers did have a small hold aft of the accommodation and machinery block. It was common on many small cargo ships to have Samson posts to serve the after hatch while the derricks for the forward hatch were mounted from the foremast. Sometimes, of course, the foremast was sited between the two hatches as can be seen in the photographs.

Today on some modern vessels the foremast has become a feature and is streamlined and fitted with platforms for radar equipment etc. although this is much more a feature of the passenger ship than the cargo vessel. Some of the more specialised ships such as large tugs and oilrig service and support ships have very distinctive masts forming a feature that is part of the funnel and main superstructure. These masts carry radar equipment, aerials and a veritable Christmas tree of lights as can be seen in the illustrations. The ship model builder needs to be certain of such features in order to reproduce them correctly.

Fig. 155 **Samson Post with Derrick and Blocks**

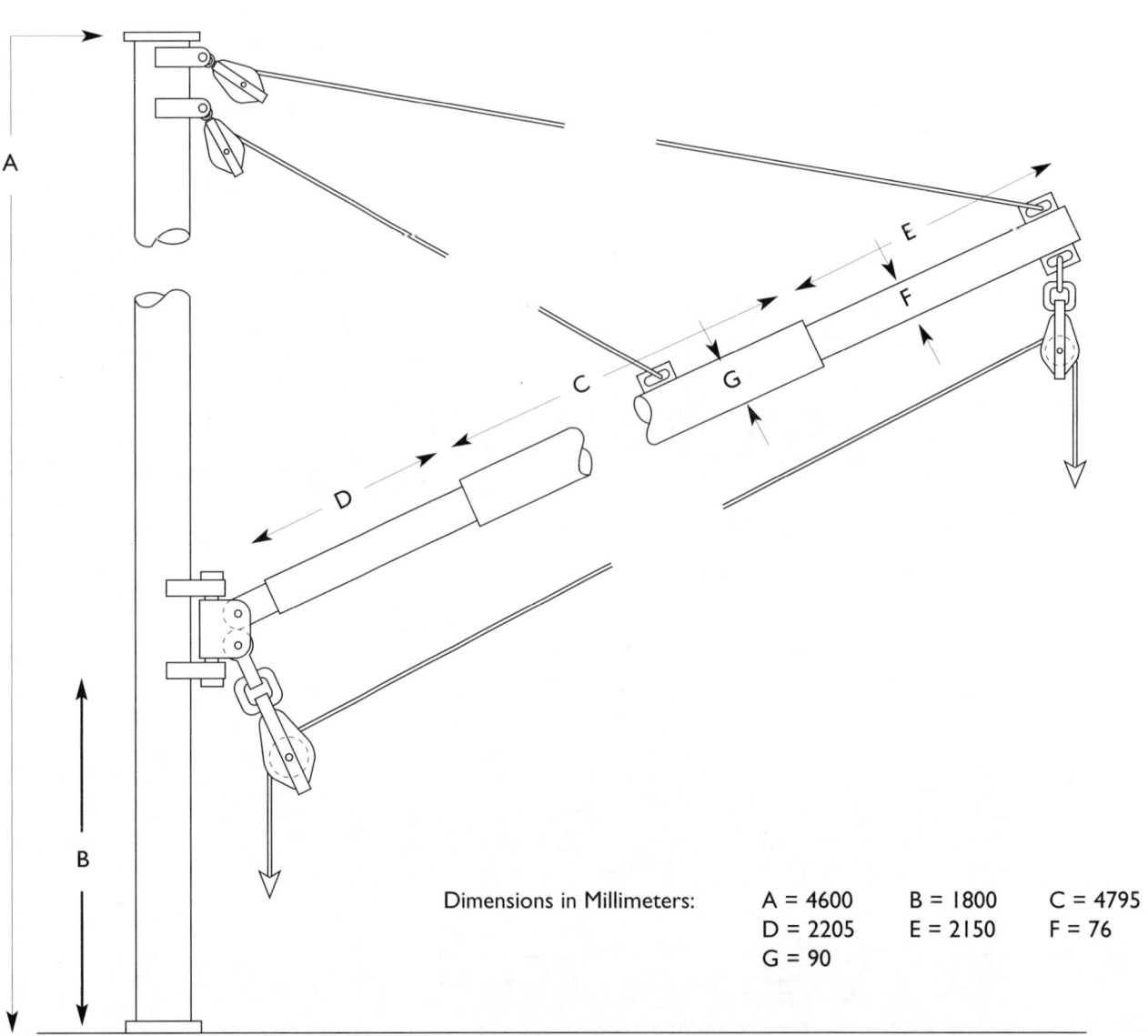

Dimensions in Millimeters: A = 4600   B = 1800   C = 4795
D = 2205   E = 2150   F = 76
G = 90

Fig. 156 Mast, spars and deckhouse for a model pilot cutter.

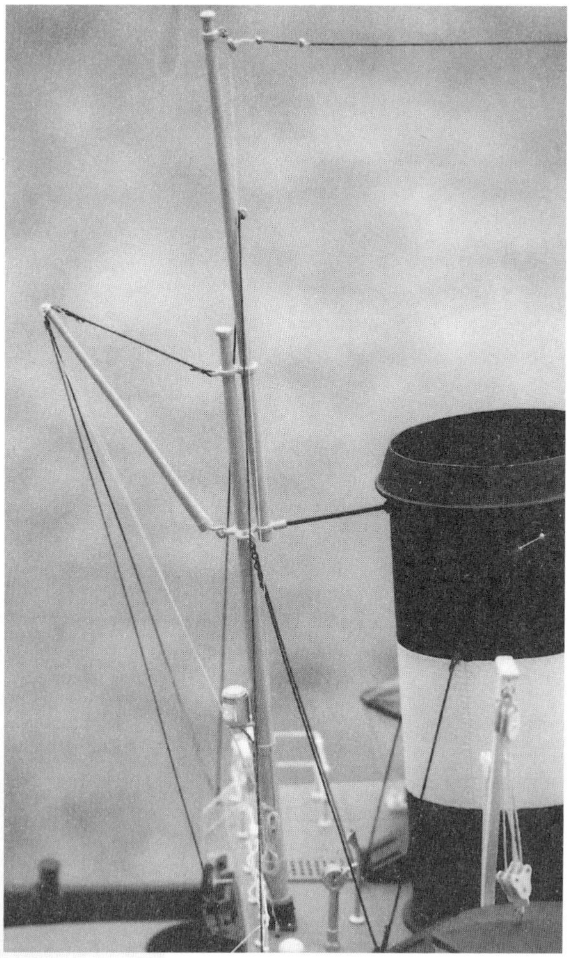

Fig. 157 Main mast and loading derrick for a model steam tug.

Fig. 158 Lower section of foremast on a modern motor ship.

Derricks for cargo handling, as do the masts and their mountings, come under the ruling of the Classification Societies and some of the various methods of mounting derricks are shown in the accompanying sketches and pictures. Whether mounted close to the base of the mast or on a derrick table at the base of the mast, the derricks had sufficient length to reach across the hatches that they served. The topping blocks were sometimes mounted on a bracket on the mast and sometimes at either end of a crosstree fixed to the mast. Where there were Samson posts the topping blocks were mounted as shown. Most derricks are today of tubular steel but in earlier days they were of timber and tapered at both ends. The herring drifters and steam trawlers mounted derricks from the foremast and frequently had booms and sails mounted from the main or mizzenmast. The herring drifters particularly carried a sail used when the vessel drifted to the nets and this was a prominent feature of such ships.

Fig. 159 Middle section of the mast shown in Figure 158.

Fig. 161 Samson post with two derricks on the stern trawler DOROTHY GRAY.

The blocks used over the years were progressively modified, more by the material used in manufacture, than in actual design as will be seen in the sketches provided. Certain patterns were used for specific applications while others have a more general use. The blocks used in lifeboat falls are special as the lower blocks are of the anti-tilt pattern to prevent fouling of the ropes. A number of kit manufacturers produce model blocks for ship models but most are of the early timber pattern. Modern steel blocks in model form are much more rare and it will frequently be necessary for the modeller to make such items in house. The photographs and sketches will help in this.

Typical Rope Blocks for Marine Duty   **Fig. 162**

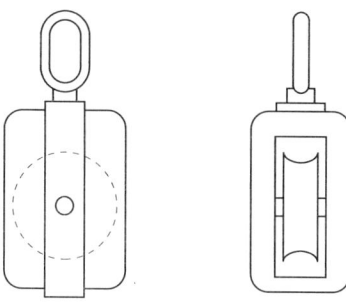

Single Sheave Wood Block with Strops and Swivel

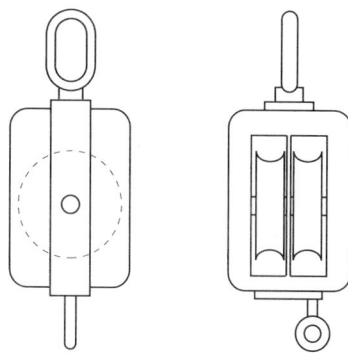

Double Sheave Wood Block with Strops, Swivel and Becket

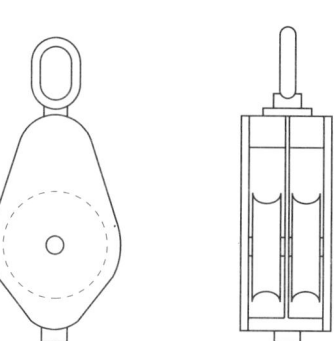

Double Sheave Steel Block with Swivel

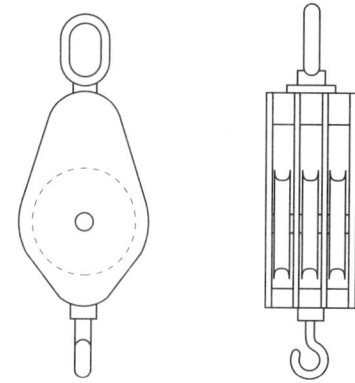

Triple Sheave Steel Block with Swivel and Becket

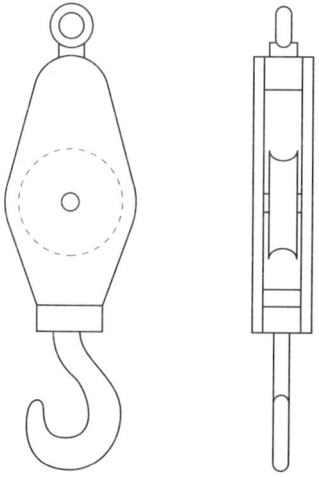

Single Sheave Block with Hook

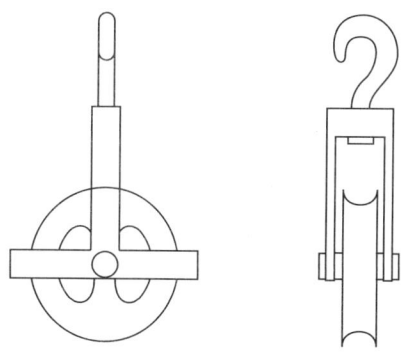

'Gin' Block for Lightweight Duty

Fig. 160 Tripod foremast with derrick and swivel on a fishing vessel under construction.

MOORING PIPES

These are heavy castings, oval or circular in shape and fitted into the plating of the bulwarks on many ships. Small versions can be found in most tugs and coasters. The sketch **Fig. 163** gives some indication of sizes and if the diameter of the opening is known, then it is possible to calculate the remainder reasonably accurately. The purpose of such mooring pipes is obvious, providing a smooth surface through which ropes can be guided.

Fig. 164 Mooring pipe in the bulwarks of a large coaster.

Fig. 165 Plimsoll line and markings on the side of a small coastal vessel.

Standard Oval Type Mooring Pipe

Fig. 163

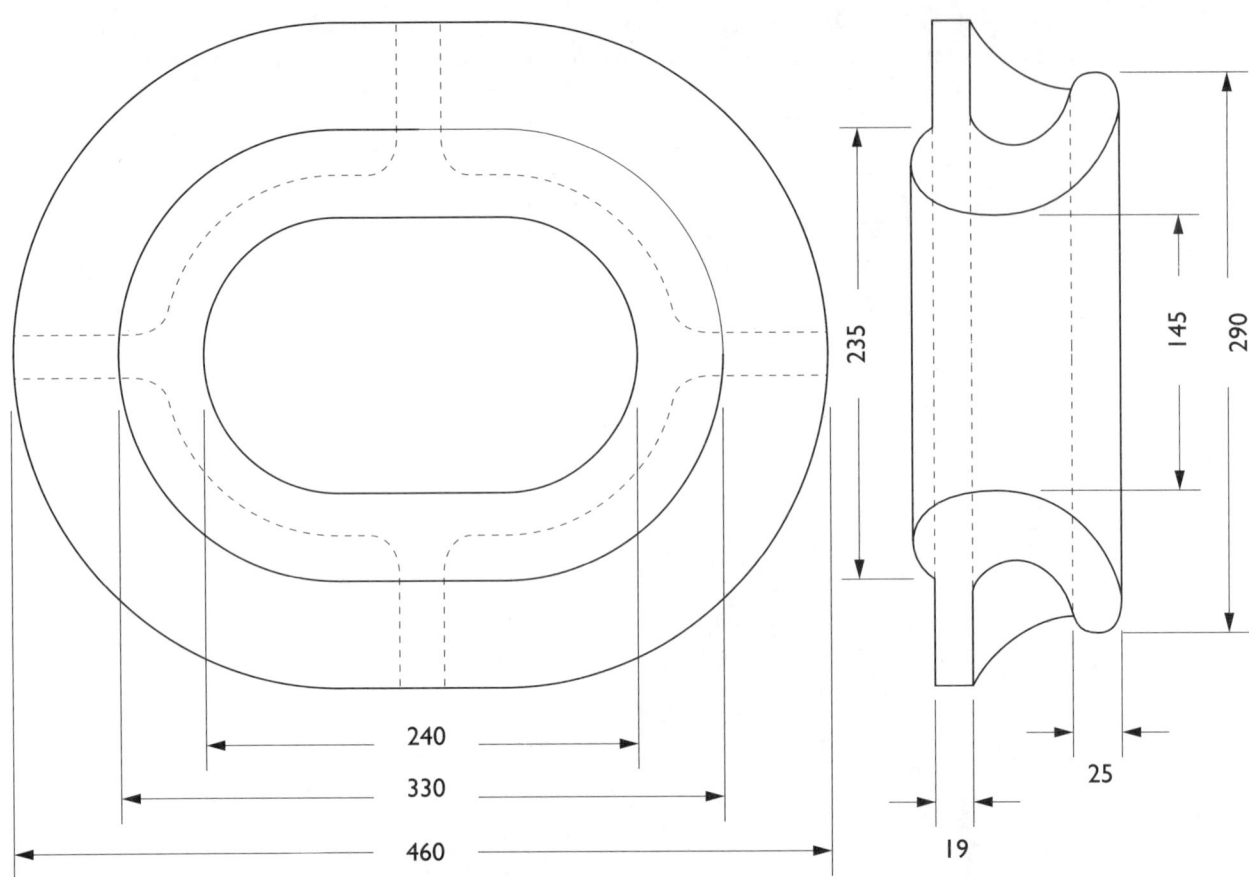

Dimensions in Millimetres

Fig. 166 Stern deck of the motor ship TIMRIX showing capstan, bollards and mooring pipe at extreme right.

PORTHOLES

These are often also called port-lights and a number can be seen in the photographs. While they are often only visible as a ring set into the plating of the hull or a deckhouse, they can be seen in more detail when fitted to a skylight or similar construction where the hinges and latches can be clearly seen. Portholes are generally sized by the diameter of the glass and model port-lights can be bought at the model shops in a variety of sizes and materials. The best are made of brass and glazed but they are often available without glazing. Many very accurately modelled portholes can be bought formed in white metal with good detail although rarely glazed. The modeller must be careful to ensure that any portholes used in the building of a model are of accurate size and adequately sealed against water ingress when fitted low in the hull. Those fitted high up and in superstructures may be left unglazed, particularly when a steam plant is fitted, to assist in provided a free air flow to the burner system, but again the possibility of water entering through an unglazed port must be considered.

On some of the early iron and steel steamships portholes in the shell of the hull sometimes had eyebrows or rigoles fitted over them to prevent water washing down and obscuring the view from them and to assist in rendering the opening watertight.

PROPULSION

The ships considered here are powered vessels as the sailing ship is a particularly specialised subject and dealt with comprehensively in many other publications. Propulsion, therefore, covers the methods used to drive the ship and the machinery needed for the purpose. Steam was the prime mover for many years and really only slowly disappeared in the late 1950s to be replaced by the compression ignition engine which rules supreme today. The model ship in the same way was first driven by steam and the small steam plant was superseded by the electric motor that is now the most common form of drive. The small steam engine is, however, making a significant comeback mainly due to the efforts of a number of small companies and the use of readily available bottled liquefied petroleum gas (LPG) for firing the boiler.

Compound engines, where the steam was fed first to the smaller of two cylinders and then fed to the second, larger cylinder drove the early small ship. The compound engine, in fact, lasted for a considerable period especially in ships such as the herring drifter and trawler. Of course the fuel first used to fire the crude, early boilers was coal and steam pressures were low. As boilers improved, pressures increased and the triple expansion engine became the norm. In the triple expansion engine the steam is fed in turn from the high-pressure cylinder to the intermediate cylinder and lastly to the low-pressure cylinder before being discharged to the condenser system. Such engines were economical of steam and quite compact. Fed with steam at pressures up to 250psig, they were very responsive and reliable. Many steam-driven coasters and small cargo ships lasted into the late 1960s but there are few to be found today.

The majority of small ships, tugs, fishing vessels and others are today driven by compression ignition engines using gas oil that is very similar to the diesel fuel used in road vehicles. Larger cargo ships, cruise vessels, tankers and ferries use heavy fuel oil that needs to be heated before it is used and which is much cheaper than the lighter fuels. Such heavy oil is rarely used in the smaller ship due to the complexity of handling the fuel and the fact that heavy-oil engines are usually of the two-stroke pattern and uneconomic unless of large size and power.

Fig. 167 Paddle wheel of a large model showing operating linkage to feathering paddles.

Model steam engines and boilers are today readily available from two or three specialist manufacturers and there are many small ships that lend themselves to be modelled and steam driven. The modern model steam plant is designed to be easily controlled by radio equipment and the current prices are almost compatible with the more sophisticated electric-drive systems. Before dealing in more detail with the methods of powering the model ship we must look at the drive systems.

The earliest of powered ships were driven by paddle wheels, in some cases by a paddle wheel at the stern but more frequently by side wheels. Most early tugs were side-wheel driven with the wheels being under independent control. Passenger ships using side wheels were and are required by law to have their wheels locked together. It is fairly easy to overturn a side-wheeler if one wheel is run full ahead and the other full astern as there is a tendency for one wheel to try to climb out of the water while the other submerges. This condition applies equally to a model particularly if the model has high superstructures. In the U.S.A. the majority of paddle-driven vessels (mostly riverboats) are driven by a single stern wheel and while they have very high superstructures and shallow draught, they are beamy and thus quite stable. The paddle steamer, particularly the pleasure steamer, lasted well into the 1960s on the rivers Clyde and Thames and there is a paddle steamer still running under the control of the Paddle Steamer Preservation Society. Paddle tugs, too, lasted many years and a number still exist although they are now mainly static exhibits. On the mainland of Continental Europe paddle steamers may be found working on a number of large lakes and on some rivers. It is possible to buy a kit from which to build a model of a paddle-driven tug Glasgow produced by Graupner and this kit includes paddles of the fully-feathering type.

Fig. 168 A selection of brass propellers (courtesy of the 'Prop Shop').

Fig. 169 A four-blade propeller fitted to the hull of a model tug.

However, research and development of engines, boilers and methods of firing for steam raising led to development of alternative methods of propulsion and to the screw propeller. The screw propeller is more efficient than the paddle wheel and capable of providing considerable thrust even from the low-powered engines of the early days and, of course, this is how the vast majority of ships are driven today. Model propellers can be made in-house using suitable jigs and with care but the huge range of such units available to the ship model builder obviates the need for home building by all but the most avid enthusiast. Model propellers can be bought made from hard plastics, nylon, cast white metal and brass or bronze. All are carefully made under controlled conditions and those of brass or bronze are particularly well made and balanced. They all come in a variety of sizes with blade configuration varying from two to seven blades. By far the most common type of propeller found on the small ship, tug or tanker etc. is of four blades. The scale of the model will dictate the size of the propeller(s) that needs to be fitted. Most coasters and short sea traders carry a spare propeller, one such being illustrated.

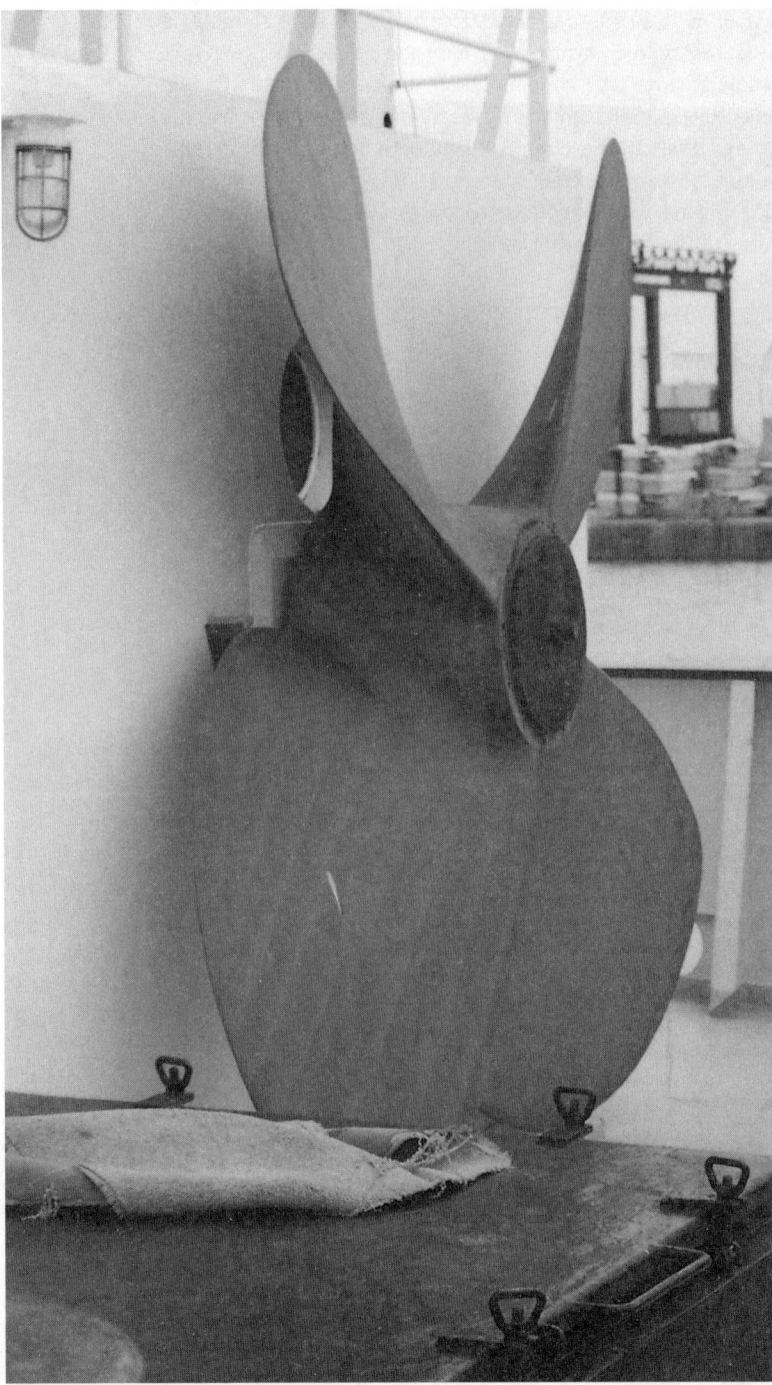

Fig. 171 Spare propeller fastened to the superstructure of the motor vessel LIZRIX.

Some ships, mainly tugs and fishing vessels and also some oilrig service ships, have propellers running in Kort nozzles. The Kort nozzle is a short tube with walls of aerofoil shape that acts as a venturi and increases the power of the propeller. Some Kort nozzles are fitted with a rudder blade behind the propeller and are arranged to turn to guide the ship (steerable nozzles). Such nozzles have a benefit, particularly on the small working ship and some are illustrated. By far the most useful propeller in service today is the variable-pitch propeller. This unit has the blades mounted in a swivel arrangement at the boss and the blades can be turned to alter the pitch. In effect, with the main engine running at constant speed, the propeller can be set to allow the ship to stand still, move ahead or move astern by altering the blades. This alteration is carried out through the drive shaft and by levers and equipment in the engine room of the vessel. The main advantages of this arrangement are as follows. First the saving of fuel; manoeuvring a ship in harbour or in berthing requires frequent changes in direction and speed of the engine resulting in increased fuel consumption. Constant running at economical speed thus saves fuel. Second, the capital cost of the gearbox system is offset by the deletion of the reversing gear and clutch system. Third; complete control of the speed and direction of the ship can be done from the bridge with additional controls on the bridge wings. Thus the officer of the watch has the ability to move the ship precisely without the delays needed by first stopping the engine before reversing or sending telegraph signals to engine room staff. Such variable-pitch propellers are now available in model form but only, to date, in a limited range of sizes.

There are alternative forms of propulsion found today particularly for driving tugs and similar small ships that need to be highly manoeuvrable. These include the Azimuth thruster, which is a unit that carries the propeller system on a stalk below the ship and allows the propeller to be turned through 360 degrees to move the ship in any direction, the Schottel drive, which is similar to the Azimuth unit but capable of being turned through a maximum of about 260 degrees and the Voith Schneider drive unit that is a complex system. Fitted beneath a vessel it permits complete speed and direction control. Several model ship kit makers produce Schottel drive units in small scale but there is none making Azimuth thrusters or Voith Schneider drives at the time of writing.

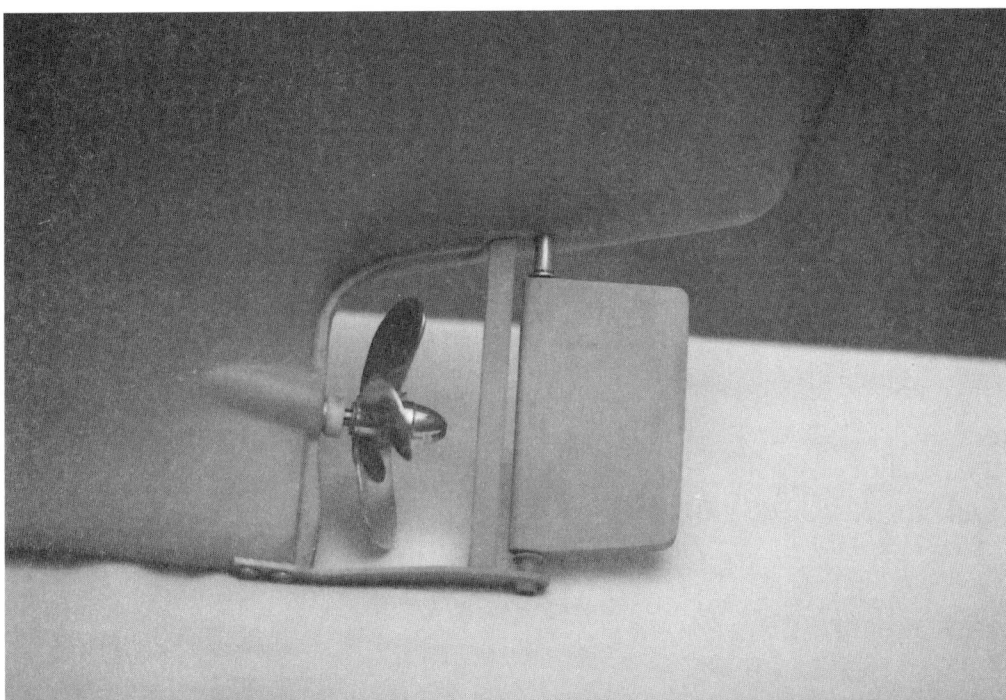

Fig. 170 Four-blade propeller fitted to a model fishing vessel.

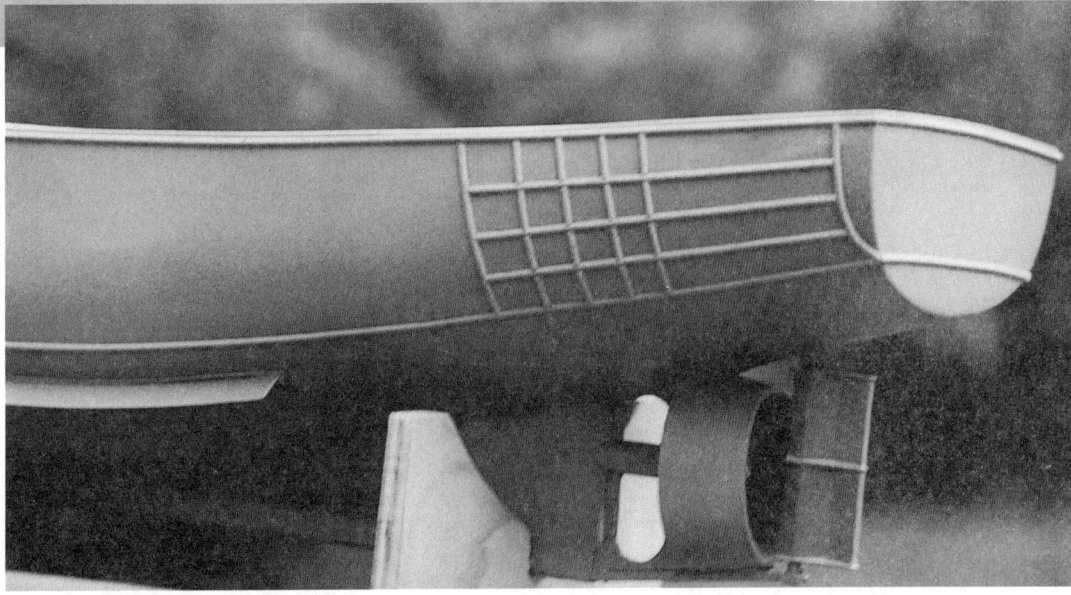

Fig. 172 Stern of model fishing vessel showing Kort nozzle and propeller.

The most recent development in ship propulsion is the water-jet unit wherein water is drawn from under the ship and expelled at high pressure through a venturi-type exit near or at the stern. These can be bought in model form complete with electric motor drive for fitting to suitable models and there are illustrations here although the author has not been able to obtain a great deal of data relative to the full size unit.

The full size ship and, of course, the model requires a shaft or shafts to drive the propeller from the chosen prime mover. For the model one can find a range of propeller shafts of good and acceptable quality from a number of specialist makers and from most model ship shops. The shaft needs to be connected to the drive motor or engine using a flexible coupling or Cardan coupling also available from the model ship shop. Note that the drive motor or engine shaft, coupling and propeller shaft should be carefully aligned. Single couplings will not take care of more than the very slightest misalignment. If the prime mover needs to be out of line with the propeller shaft then it will be necessary to use a double coupling or even a second shaft and two couplings. Under no circumstances should the drive train place a load on the motor or engine over the minimum resistance of an in-line drive. Out-of-true drive systems will cause motors to overheat and burn or model steam engines to seize which, in either case, will result in costly replacements.

Fig. 173 View of GLENROSE I in dry-dock illustrating Kort nozzle, rudder etc.

Electric motors

The most common form of driving a working model ship is by electric motor. Small DC electric motors can be purchased from almost all model shops and many are suitable for driving a model ship. They can be fed with current from a sealed lead acid pattern battery or by rechargeable NiCad or similar batteries. Most motors are either 6 or 12 volts and rated according to the amperage required. For the working model ship covered herein virtually all motors will need to be fitted with a reduction gearbox as the usual speed of the motor will be too high for the marine propeller of the model **Fig. 178**. Control of the motor(s) can be by simple on/off switch, wire-wound resistance with wiper arm driven from a servomotor, resistance board and wiper (Bobs board) or by electronic speed controller. All such controls have their merits but the most sensible for the scale model builder will be the Bobs board or the electronic speed controller and the latter is the more superior although more costly. Obviously the question of what to fit is a matter of personal choice in many cases and often of the size of the pocket in others. The best advice is to consult the shop staff or an informed club member, buy the very best that can be afforded and install the equipment as carefully and accurately as possible.

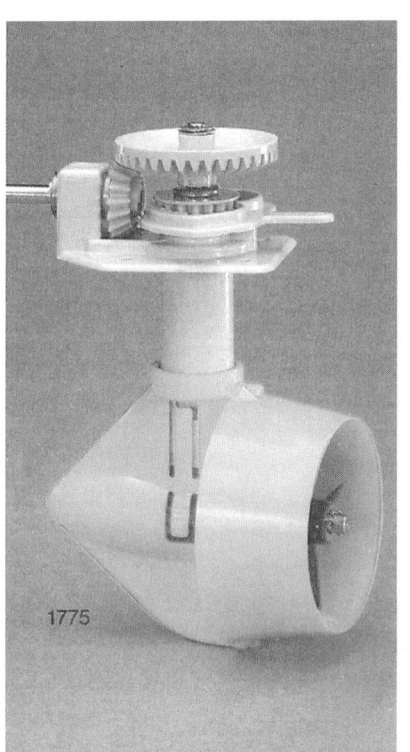
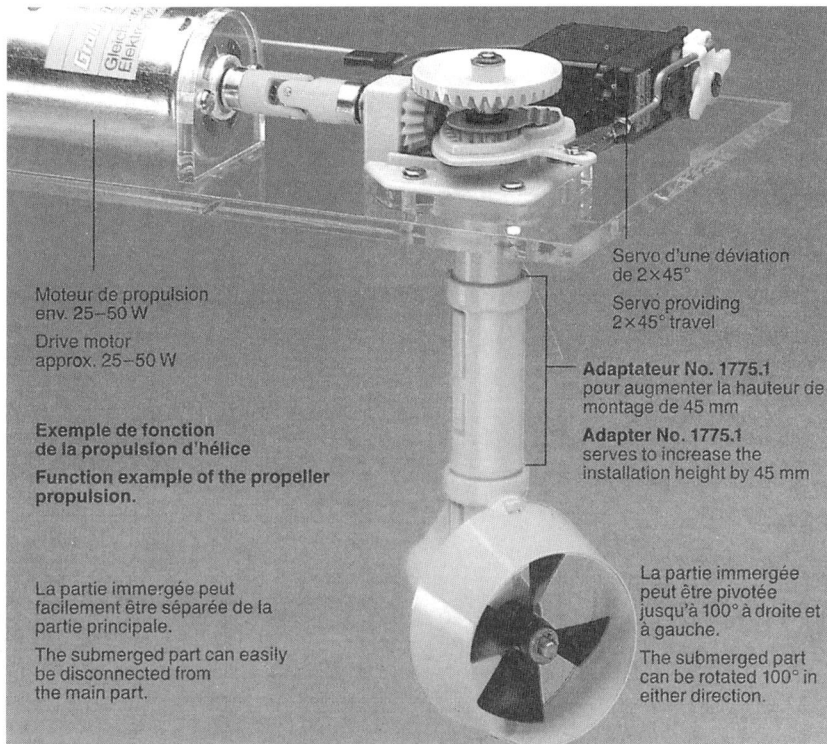

Fig. 174 Schottel drive unit in model form (photo courtesy of Graupner).

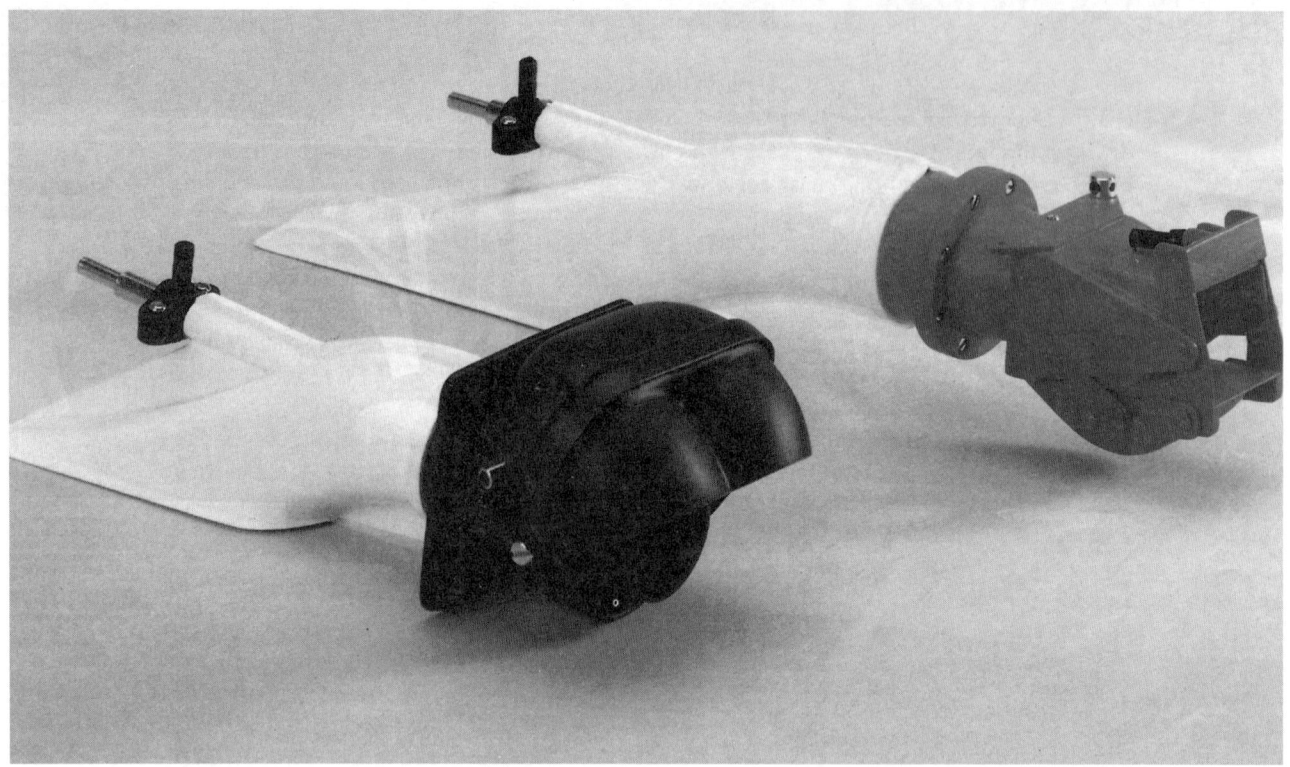

Fig. 175 Two types of water jet units in model form available from Graupner (photo courtesy of Graupner).

Fig. 176 Model hull with two propeller shafts & couplings installed to allow model steam plant to be fitted forward of a saloon on an open steam

Fig. 177 Some types of electric motor available to the model ship builder.

Suggested Arrangement for
Electric Motor with Reduction Gear

Fig. 178

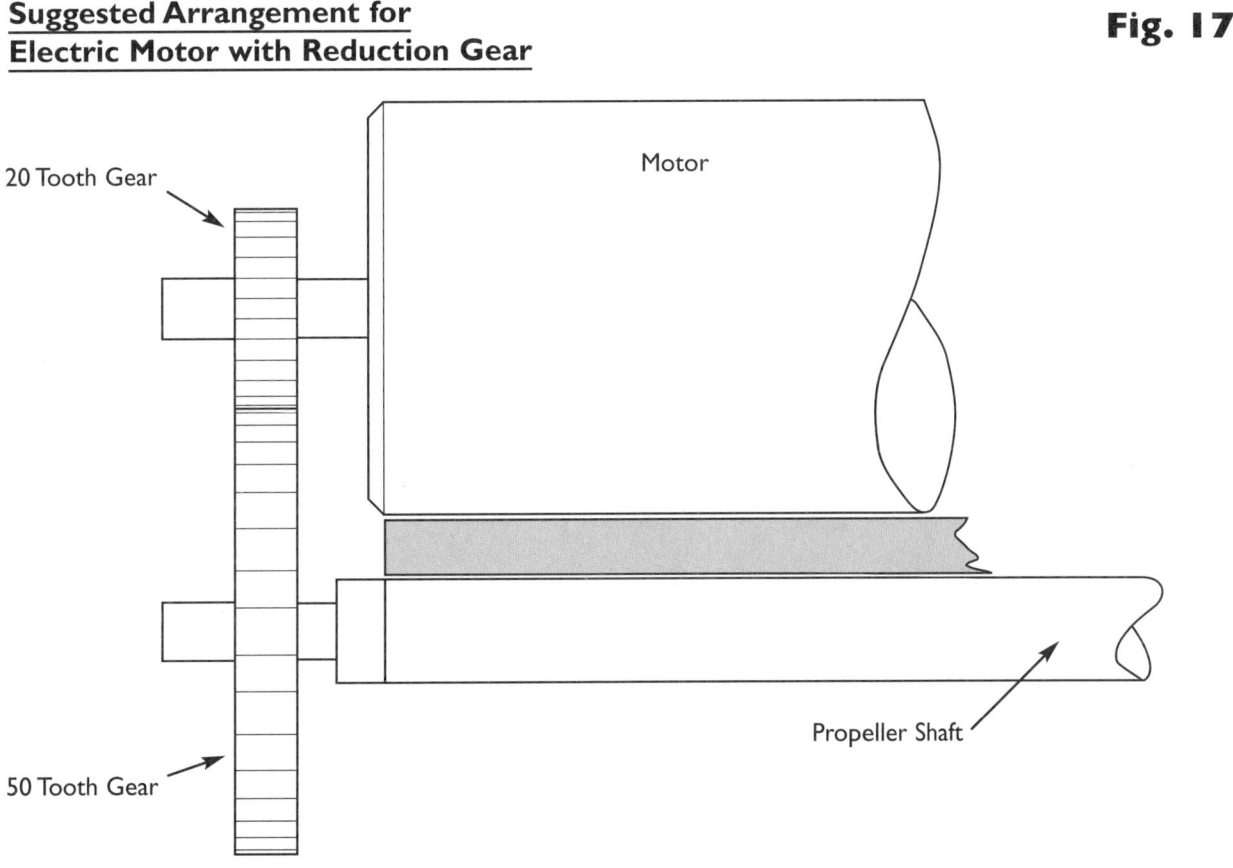

Steam plants

Many of the small ships round which this book is written were steam driven in earlier times. Such steam ships, tugs and fishing vessels had and have a special aura and fascination. Today it is possible to buy a small steam plant comprising engine and boiler with all the necessary connecting pipes and instruments and fitted with a burner or burners for firing by gas or by methylated (killed) spirit. Most come fully assembled and tested but it is possible to buy some of them in a stripped-down form for home assembly using simple tools and, of course, at a small saving in cost. The very smallest cost very little more than the equivalent electric motor, battery and speed controls and they are simple to set up and run. However, steam boilers are pressure vessels and, as such, require to be handled with care and in accordance with the manufacturers' instructions. Model boat clubs will not permit steam-driven models to be fired up or sail on their water unless the modeller can produce valid test certificates for the boiler and its associated rechargeable gas tank. Such test certificates are supplied with the boiler and other pressure vessels on purchase and the boilers and tanks need to be tested and the certificates renewed at two-yearly intervals. This is not to imply that the steam plant is in any way at fault but simply to warn those who have had no experience, to treat such equipment with care and respect the instructions provided by the makers.

The keen modeller who has access to and the ability to use a metalworking lathe can, of course, make small steam engines. Model boilers, too, can be built in the home workshop by the modeller capable of brazing or silver soldering. Good model steam boilers should always be made from copper although there are some, very low-pressure boilers produced by some makers constructed of brass. The home boilermaker should not consider brass under any circumstances as it generally has very uneven expansion rates and will not readily stand up to easy working. Brass boilers are not acceptable at testing stations except for very low-pressure applications.

Fig. 179 Twin cylinder slide valve steam engine and gas fired boiler installed in the framework of a model pilot cutter. Mounting thus, prior to planking the hull, allows easy alignment of engine shaft, coupling and propeller shaft. Once the mountings have been made the steam plant can be removed to allow the hull to be completed.

The firing of the modern small boiler by gas or by methylated spirit is now almost entirely foolproof. Burners for gas operate either by the pressure of the gas producing a flame from a ladder in a similar manner to the domestic oven or central heating boiler or by the heating of a ceramic element. Both types of burner are fitted to the appropriate boiler and use LPG that can be butane alone or, for preference, a mixture of butane and propane (30% propane to 70% butane). Such liquefied petroleum gases are available from camping stores and similar outlets in canisters that can be used in the model, if small enough, or used to charge a gas tank for installation in the model. It should be remembered that these gases are heavier than air and that unburned gas can collect in the bottom of a model ship and cause a fire if not exhausted. The model hull should be inverted to exhaust unburned gases or a small fan can be used to scavenge the hull.

Fig. 180 Steam plant of Maxwell Hemmens manufacture installed in a slender model steam yacht.

Fig. 181 Vertical boiler and twin cylinder steam engine in a model open steam launch. Note steering wheel and 'Windermere'

Spirit burners of the type illustrated are pressure burners of the self-pressurising pattern; they are efficient and give a very hot flame. Care is necessary with this fuel, as the flames are invisible in even slight sunlight. Some very small boilers use a spirit burner that has a series of small tubes with wicks that draw up the spirit and can be lit. This type of burner is also quite efficient but needs to be handled with care, as it is usual to light it before placing it under the boiler. Finally the small simple boiler can be fired with solid fuel tablets (Meta tablets) placed in a tray and lit before being inserted under the boiler. These have a very short duration of burning and are only suitable for the smallest of boilers.

Most small steam engines fall into two categories: oscillating engines and slide valve engines. The oscillating engine is that where the cylinders oscillate over a plate that permits steam to enter and drive the pistons and also has ports that allows the exhaust to escape after use. They are the simplest pattern steam engines and are easily reversed when there are two cylinders either in-line or mounted in a V format. One or two enterprising makers have built such engines with four cylinders comprising two V-form pairs. The more efficient engine is the single, or twin, cylinder slide-valve engine and this is the type most generally used for the larger units. Although the most common steam engine built for marine duty in full size ships was the triple expansion engine, this is not available commercially in model size. The savings of steam using progressive expansion is important in large engines but in miniature engines such savings are negligible and, in any case, could only be effected if complex vacuum and condense systems were to be installed to make the savings. Some keen engineering modellers have built multiple-expansion model engines but they are not, to date, of serious commercial consideration.

Fig. 182 A Cheddar Models 'Proteus' steam outfit in the hull of the model side fishing trawler KINGSTON PERIDOT.

Fig. 183 A Stour Valley Steam outfit suitable for installing in a model ship. (photo courtesy of Stour Valley).

Steam boilers

The simplest boilers mentioned here are those where the water/steam cylinder is set into a casing and where the burner is placed in the bottom of the casing and heats the whole cylinder. A more efficient and refined make of this type of boiler has water tubes in the fire space; these increase the heating surface and thus the speed of steam generation. In general model steam boilers are of the firetube pattern very similar to full size cylindrical boilers and these are shown in the accompanying sketches. Steam boilers for such models as Clyde Puffers and steam launches almost invariably use a vertical boiler similar to those illustrated. Details of steam boilers and engines can be found in many publications.

Fig. 184 Maxwell Hemmens 'V' four cylinder steam outfit fitted into the hull of a model steam launch.

Fig. 185 An azimuth thruster on an oilrig support vessel.

PUMPS

We are concerned with the machinery, fittings and structures visible on the small ship in this volume. While all ships have a substantial outfit of pumps for a variety of duties, these are generally installed in the machinery spaces below decks and they are, therefore, invisible as far as modelling is concerned. The small hand pump used mainly for transferring water from deep tanks to a header tank are generally located above deck and therefore easily seen. The illustrations show these; they are small units that could be ignored on models of very small scale but must be considered for the large-scale model.

Pumps for providing effects on the model ship, such as feeding water to model fire monitors or simulating engine-cooling discharges, are different. Small electric pumps for this type of duty can be bought from the specialist ship model shop; they are made by such manufacturers as Graupner and Robbe specifically for this purpose. The pipework connecting these pumps to the hull and to the fitting concerned needs to be carried out with care to ensure that there are no leaks. Even the smallest pump can rapidly fill a hull with water. An alternative to the specially made pump is the screen washer pump normally fitted to the family car, such pumps can be bought from second-hand car dealers or breakers for a few pounds and are adequate to feed water to the fire monitor etc.

Fig. 186 A hand pump with capped outlet on the side of the superstructure of a small fishing boat.

Fig. 187 A model water pump for 6 volt DC supply (photo courtesy Robbe Schluter UK Ltd)

RADAR EQUIPMENT

Radar equipment was developed during the early part of the Second World War and is, today, fitted to virtually all ships. The early steam-driven coasters, short sea traders, tugs, fishing vessels, etc., did not have the benefit of such equipment and the masts and upperworks of such ships are noticeable by its absence. It is the means of projecting an outline picture of the objects at sea and of the surrounding area of a ship upon a screen located in a position on a ship where it can be used to aid navigation and to avoid other ships in close proximity. Usually the radar screen is fitted on the bridge of the ship and sometimes also in a chartroom beneath or near the steering position.

The most obvious items relative to the radar system are the transmitter/receiver units that are positioned on platforms or towers on top of the bridge or on masts. These units revolve at steady speed and are readily visible. On some smaller ships, yachts and the like, the radar transmitter/receiver units are totally enclosed in cylindrical covers. Both types are illustrated here. Many ships carry two revolving units that, in the main, detail data at different ranges. The automatic pilot of most ships has an audible warning connected to the radar system that warns the watch-keeping officer of approaching danger, ship or obstruction usually when the ship is about one mile from such danger. The watch-keeping officer need not necessarily be on the bridge at all times when the automatic pilot (often called George) is in operation.

Fig. 188 Radar units on the main mast of an oilrig ship.

Fig. 189 Radar unit in a casing on a small oil tanker.

RAILS & STANCHIONS

The rails and stanchions are significant parts of a ship's outfit. The rails, correctly called guardrails, form a highly visible part of the model ship. If the rails and their supporting stanchions are incorrectly fitted, are of the wrong size or fail to be truly in line then the whole look of the model will be wrong. Many models lose valuable points in competitive events because of ill-fitting or poorly aligned railings. The modeller should be aware that those stanchions that have a ball through which the bar of the rail fits generally taper from the base upwards. This taper is quite slight but is quite obvious. Furthermore the size of the ball of the stanchion is proportional to the diameter of the rail, the ball at the top of the stanchion being much bigger than the others to accommodate the larger diameter top rail **Fig. 190**. Multi-ball stanchions are rarely seen on the modern ship where the stanchions tend to be made of flat bar, drilled to suit the size of the rails and with the top rail welded to the top of the stanchion **Fig. 191**.

Some ships and especially those designed to carry passengers frequently have the top rail made in timber, usually teak or mahogany **Fig. 192**. The early steam ships often had the tops of the iron or steel bulwarks finished with a timber rail. Many herring drifters had a timber top rail to the timber bulwarks surmounted by single-ball stanchions threaded with a rope as an additional safeguard along the sides of the superstructure. The model ship builder should take care to ensure that these small touches are added with accuracy.

On the steel ship the stanchions could be mounted using cast bases bolted down, or sometimes, with a flat palm for welding to the curtain plate of the deck edge. The photographs give some indication of these fittings. With the flat-bar-pattern stanchion these were invariably welded to the deck. In certain places, where the surveyor required additional supports; some stanchions had angled braces fitted.

Fig. 193 Flat bar stanchions and welded hand rails on a fishing vessel.

Fig. 194 Flat bar stanchions and rails on the forecastle of a fishing vessel.

Fig. 195 Rails and stanchions modelled in styrene strip and rod for a small static model fishing boat.

Fig. 196 View of large diameter top rail and smaller diameter lower rails on a fishing vessel.

As a general rule of thumb the height of the top rail above the deck was set at 3ft 6in. (1070mm) but on passenger-carrying vessels this was often increased to as much as 4ft 6in. (1370mm). The teak or mahogany top rail, where fitted, was and is usually 6in wide x 2.5in thick (150 x 64mm). Many manufacturers make stanchions of the single and multi-ball pattern in a variety of sizes mostly of brass but some of white metal or Britannia metal. Similarly flat bar stanchions with a number of holes in a variety of configurations can be purchased from selected outlets. The range of scales in both cases seems to run from 1:96 to 1:24 (1:100 to 1:25) which cover most working model sizes. For those modellers working in smaller scales some specialist manufacturers produce lengths of rail etched in brass or nickel-silver in a number of sizes. The discerning ship modeller can even make flat bar stanchions from strips of styrene and use styrene rod from which to fabricate the rails. Such rails could well be very accurate to scale but may prove to be too fragile for a working model being handled frequently. The photographs depict rails on both full size ships and on models and the sketches give some details too.

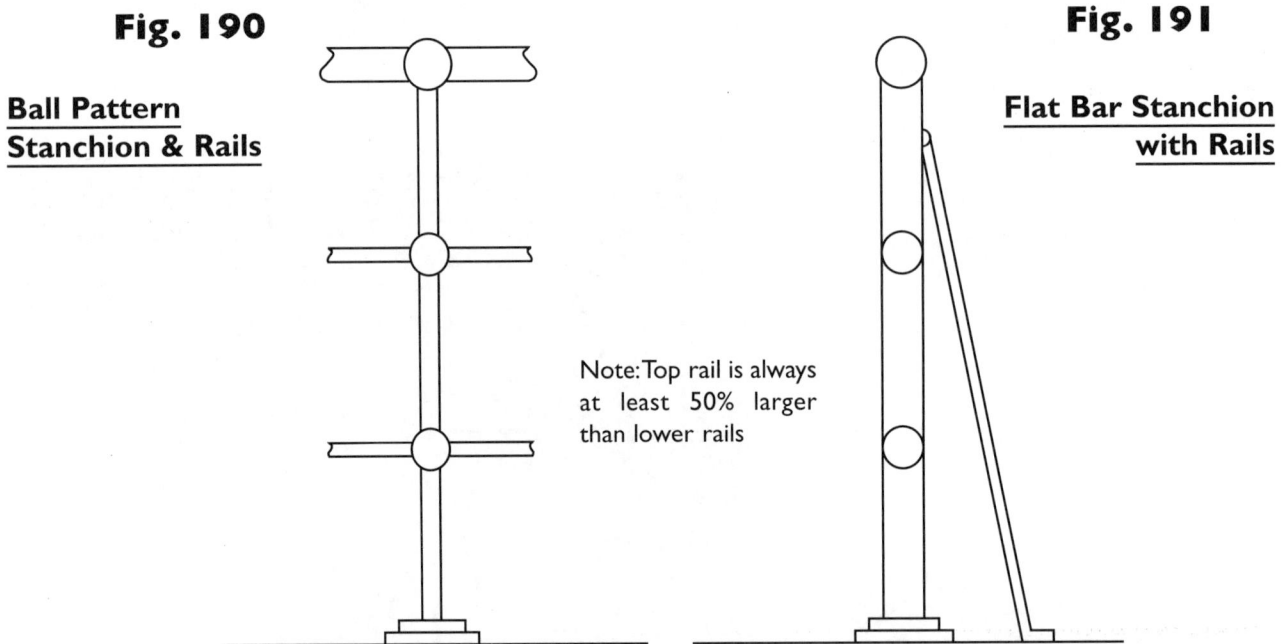

Fig. 190

Ball Pattern Stanchion & Rails

Fig. 191

Flat Bar Stanchion with Rails

Note: Top rail is always at least 50% larger than lower rails

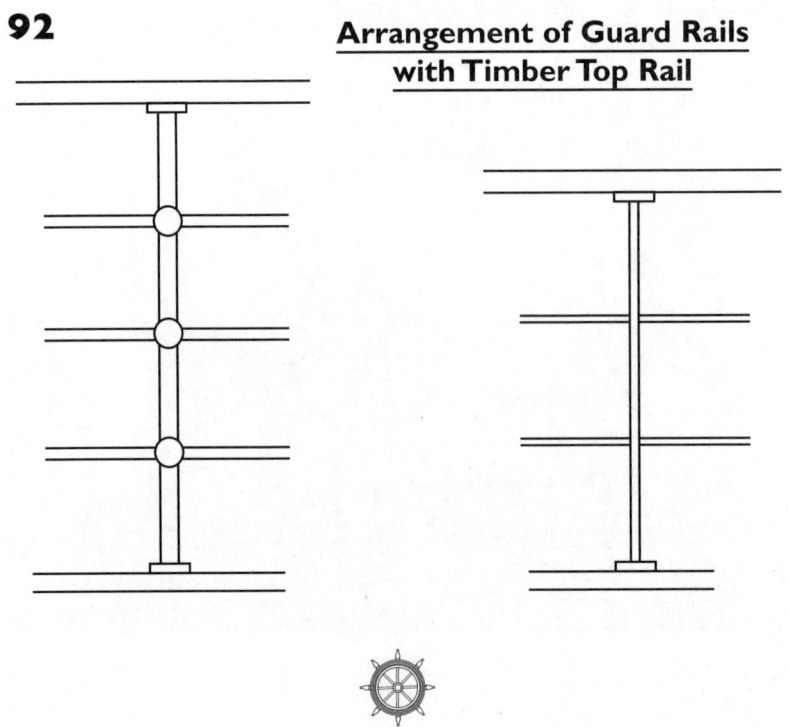

Fig. 192

Arrangement of Guard Rails with Timber Top Rail

Fig. 197 Flat bar stanchions, some with braces, on the fishing vessel DENEBULA.

Fig. 198 Rails, stanchions, platforms and companions on an oilrig support ship.

RIGGING

The rigging of a ship is, in effect, the ropework. This is divided into two distinct parts: standing and running rigging. Standing rigging is the ropework that supports items such as masts, funnels etc. and is fixed in place. Running rigging is the ropework that runs through blocks and similar tackle and is used for lifting, pulling, lowering, etc.

Standing rigging is, in the main, used on masts and, on the early ships, was of hemp rope which was treated with Stockholm tar to render it waterproof. In general such standing rigging was secured to the bulwarks or edges of the decks using deadeyes and tensioned with lanyards **Fig. 199**. This is illustrated in the sketches and photographs. This method of securing standing rigging was common on most early ships including the herring drifters and steam trawlers almost until the end of the side-fishing trawlers in the 1950s. The more modern standing rigging is usually of wire rope tensioned using rigging screws (bottle screws) at the bulwark or deck edge for the masts **Fig. 200**. In the earliest ships the standing rigging for the masts, known as shrouds, was also rigged with finer rope to form ladders, known as ratlines, up to the crosstrees and crow's-nest or platforms. Fine data, drawings and photographs of the rigging of the early ship can be found in publications such as 'Sails Last Century' and 'The Masting & Rigging of English Ships of War' both published by Conway Maritime Press.

Fig. 199   **Arrangement of Deadeyes for Standing Rigging**

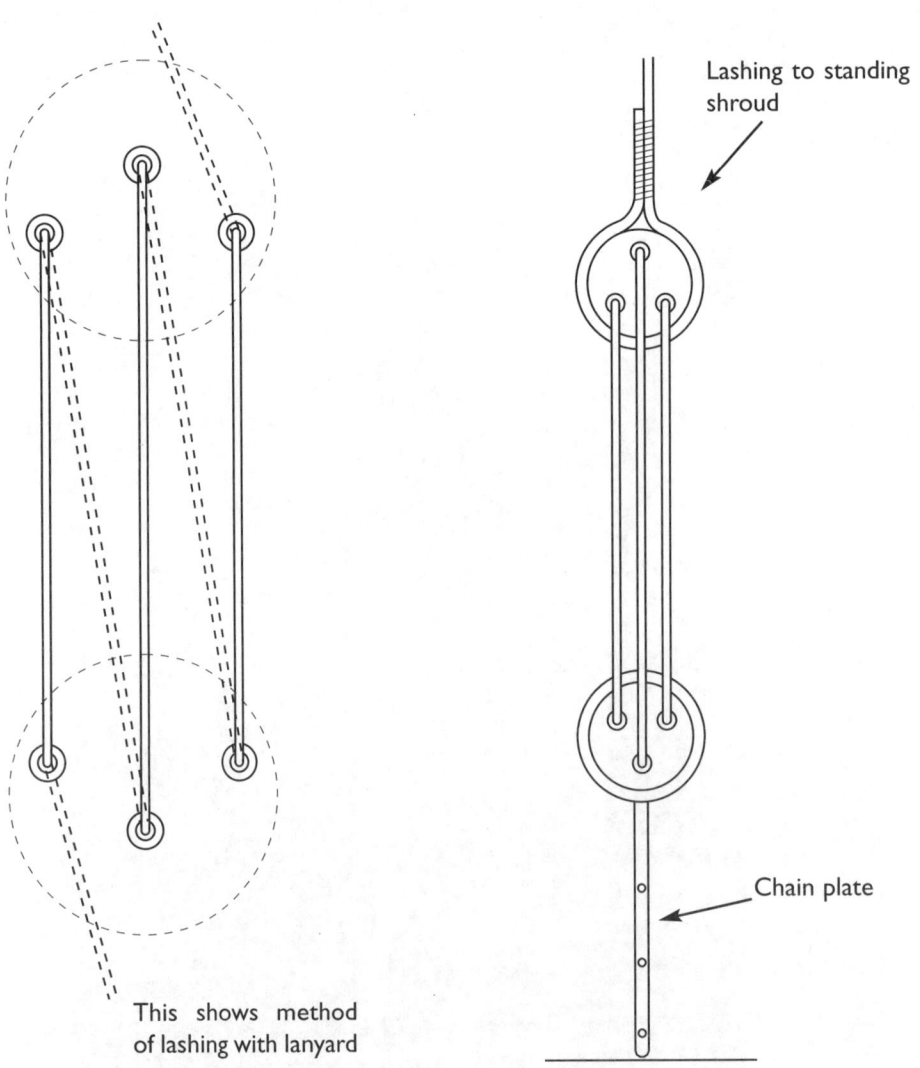

This shows method of lashing with lanyard

Lashing to standing shroud

Chain plate

There would be a series of drawings provided when a ship was under construction showing the rigging and known as the rigging plan and such are invaluable to the modeller. These drawings sometimes form part of the plan sets from the Plans Services for given ships. If a rigging plan is not available then the modeller will have to rely upon photographs or upon data provided for a similar typical vessel.

The running rigging is totally dependent upon the type of deck machinery fitted, derricks, davits etc. Each ship will carry the necessary blocks and ropes to allow the duty, for which the ship was designed, to be carried out efficiently as possible at the date of the building. It should also be noted that, when a cargo ship was under way between ports, the running rigging and blocks for the derricks and cargo handling would be dismantled and stowed. Such rigging would only be installed when the ship approached its berth preparatory to loading or unloading cargo. In the case of lifeboat falls and similar running rigging it was usual to leave this in place to be ready for immediate use.

The rigging of even a small fishing vessel or coastal steamer could and can be quite complex and it is wise for the prospective ship modeller to obtain as much information as possible when preparing to rig his/her model. The photographs here are included to provide data of rigging on a number of models.

Fig. 200 **Rigging Screw (Bottle Screw) for Tensioning Standing Rigging**

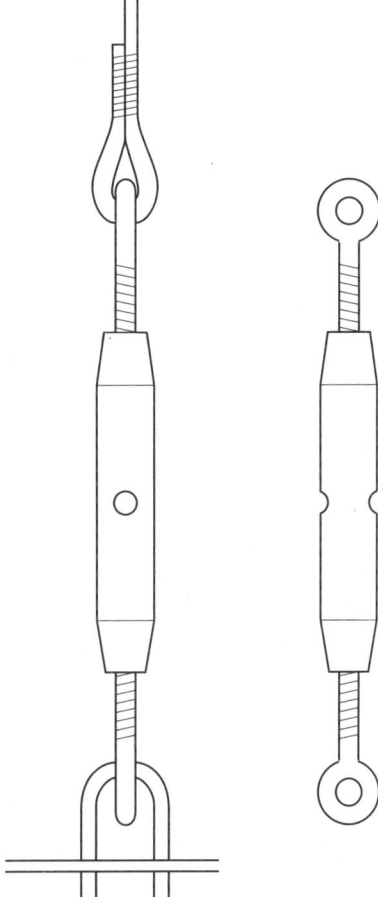

Fig. 201 Foremast of model side fishing trawler showing standing rigging with ratlines.

Fig. 202 Main mast of model yacht SKEANDHU showing shelf, deadeyes and chainplates.

Fig. 203 Bowsprit of model yacht SKEANDHU illustrating standing rigging & decoration.

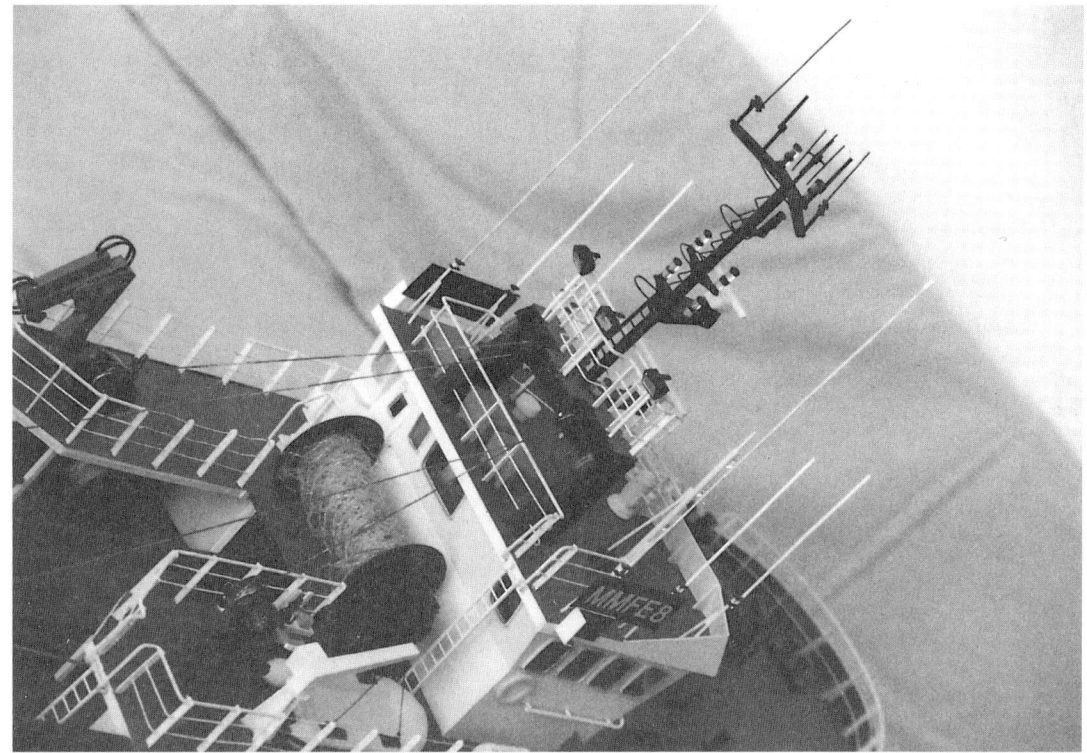

Fig. 204 Foremast of a model stern trawler GLENROSE I showing lack of standing rigging on a free standing structure.

Fig. 205 Standing rigging clearly visible on the model of SKEANDHU.

RIVETS

As previously mentioned rivets and associated riveting work can cause problems for the modeller. The simulating of rivets on the scale model ship is a 'bone of contention' and one that has caused some judgmental arguments on many occasions. The majority of rivets used on the hull and superstructures of the iron and steel ships were of three types illustrated in **Fig.206**. The shell plates were almost invariably fixed with rivets of the countersunk/roundhead pattern where the hole in the upper plate was countersunk to accept the rivet. The resultant degree of head showing once the rivet was fitted was quite small compared to the other types of rivet. Thus such rivets tend to disappear below the coats of

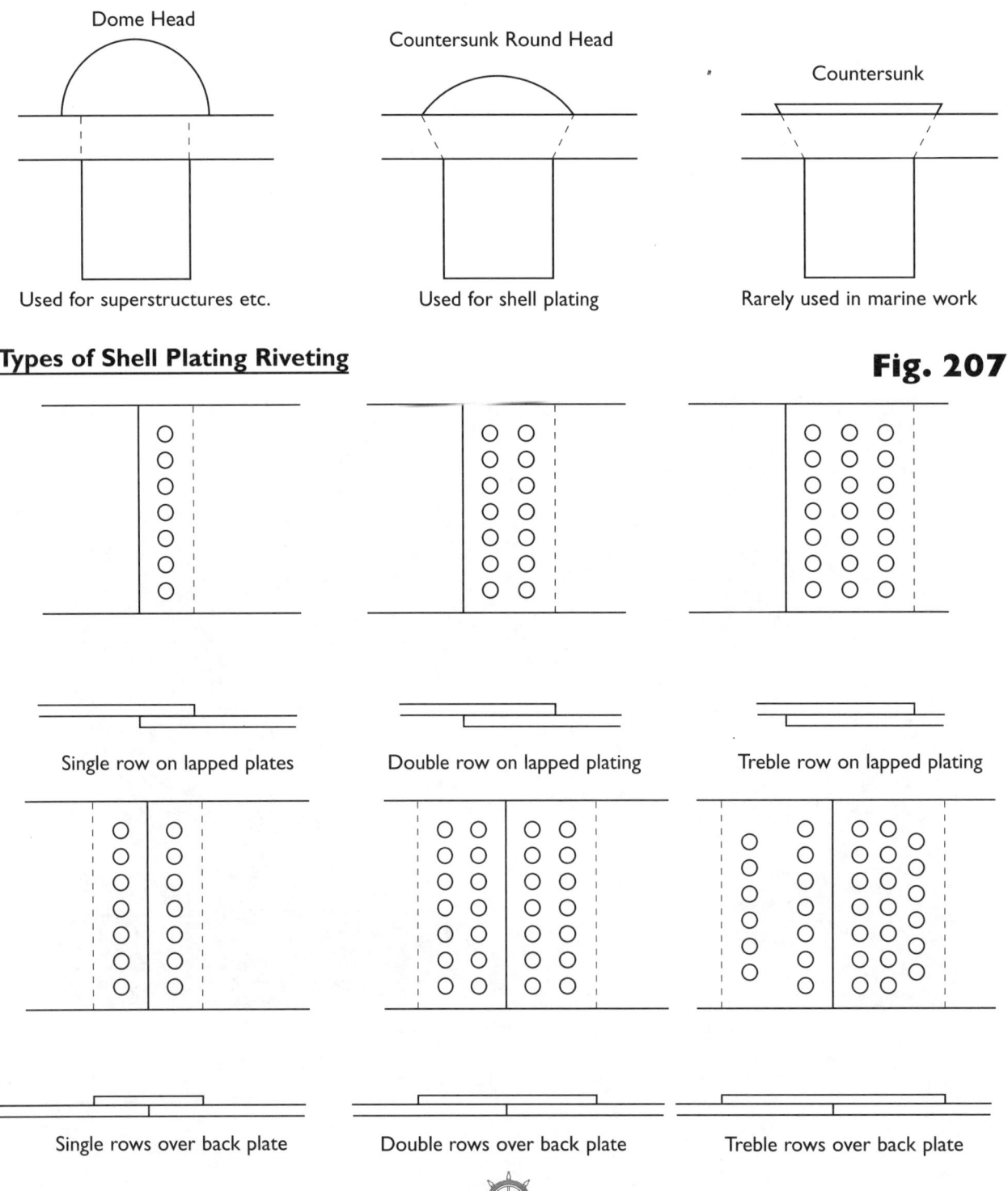

paint applied to the ship over a period of time. Unless the model being built is of a fairly large scale it is unwise to attempt to show rivets in the hull plating. Furthermore the classification society rules governing the spacing and number of rows of rivets in specific places on the shell plating call for a great degree of accuracy on the part of the model builder. It is not sufficient to suggest plate riveting by positioning a few blobs of glue or a pinhead or two; such a course is best forgotten and omitted. If the model is being built to the scale of 1:24 or larger then it would be possible to simulate correctly the plate rivet work but less than this scale it would be difficult and, viewing from a short distance away, unnecessary **Fig. 207**.

Rivets on the superstructure of ships and to deck machinery bases etc. were much more prominent as standard round-head rivets were almost always used. They remain visible despite many coats of paint and the number of rows and spacing was quite different allowing easy and accurate simulation. Were I, for example, required to express a judge's opinion on a model scaled at 1:48 with visible superstructure riveting and only plate lines showing on the hull, I would award high marks if the work was carried out sensibly and accurately to my eye. If, however, the riveting were haphazard and the rows out of line then I would mark the model down. It is very necessary to be careful of fine detail when building a scale model, as it is so easy to make slight mistakes that eventually show up clearly. It is also possible to make errors and fail to see them when concentrating hard on a particular task. I find that a friend having a look at the work in progress quite often sees an error that I have inadvertently overlooked.

Rivets are most prominent on such items as mountings for deck machinery or hatch seatings and here the modeller can so easily enhance a model. Seek out photographs and sketches of such items in encyclopaedias and other tomes of ships and their fittings in the local library. Many books of shipbuilding and ships do have some illustration that will be of value. The modern welded steel ship has machinery seats and mountings of prefabricated welded steel often bolted down to the deck using very large bolts which can be suitably simulated using very small real brass bolts. Take care with all such items. The rivets illustrated in the photograph **Fig. 253** show clearly superstructure work but in this case, on an Admiralty tug. The rivets here would soon become indistinct under a number of coats of paint.

ROPE REELS

There are few ships that do not carry reels for the storage of wire and synthetic or coir rope. Such reels vary in size dependent upon the quantity and type of rope that needs to be reeled in. Most rope reels today are made in standard sizes and the sketch **Fig. 208** is typical of such a reel. Note the ratchet used to prevent the drum from running off when the handle is released. Produced by a number of makers there are many variants and some are even fitted with electric motor drive. The photographs show some rope reels in both full size and model form.

Fig. 209 Rope reel on an oil rig support ship.

Fig. 208 **Typical Drawing of Manually Operated Rope Reel**

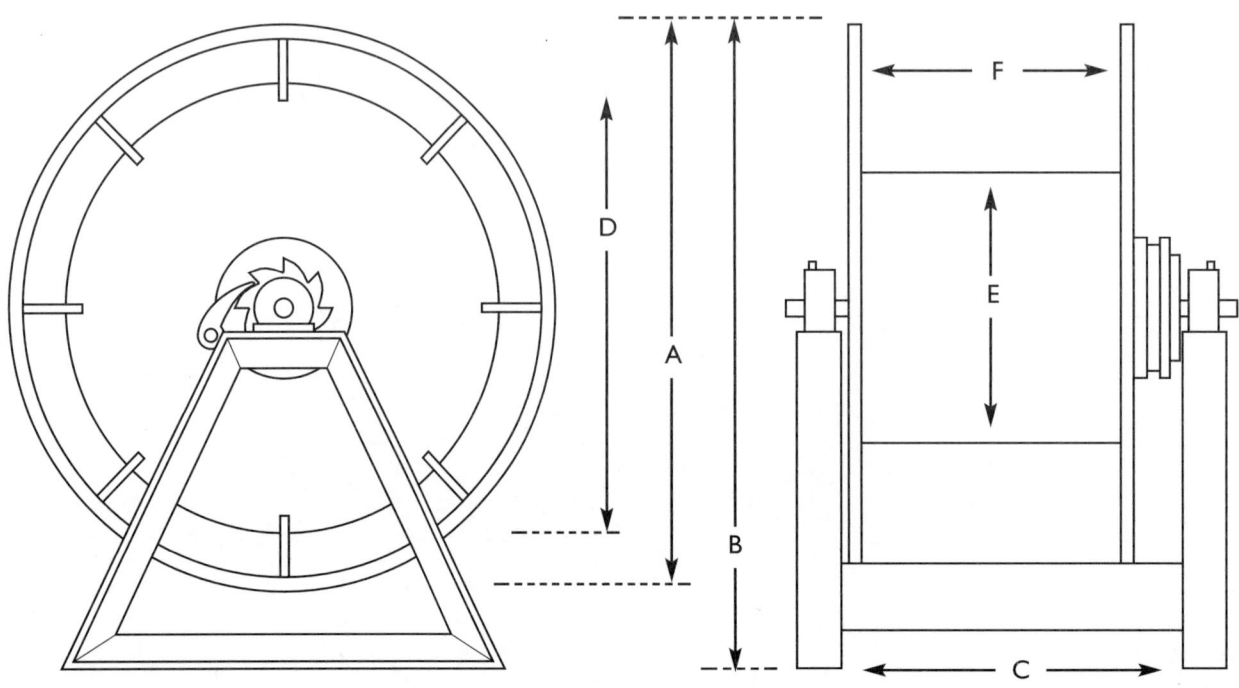

All Dimensions in Millimetres

A	B	C	D	E	F	Weight - Kilos
950	1100	685	750	320	500	60
950	1100	685	750	400	500	60
950	1100	935	750	320	750	75
950	1100	935	750	400	750	75
950	1100	1185	750	320	1000	90
950	1100	1185	750	400	1000	90

Fig. 210 Two rope reels on the motor ship LIZRIX.

Fig. 211 Rope reel on the model of oilrig rescue ship SCOTT GUARDIAN.

RUDDERS & THRUSTERS

With few exceptions the early powered ships were fitted with a single, plate rudder, the blade being a single plate secured to the stock (shaft) by arms. The thickness of the plate varied between 3/4in and 1in and sometimes less depending upon the size of the ship. The arms were similar to those of large hinges found on big wooden gates and connected the rudder to pintles secured to the plates of the ship's stern. Single-plate rudders are now found only on the very smallest of ships.

The rudder of built-up construction using two or more plates followed where the section of the rudder was found to be tapered or streamlined as shown in Fig. 212. Further development led to the semi-balanced and balanced pattern rudders much more common today as illustrated in Fig. 213.

Some Types of Ships Rudders

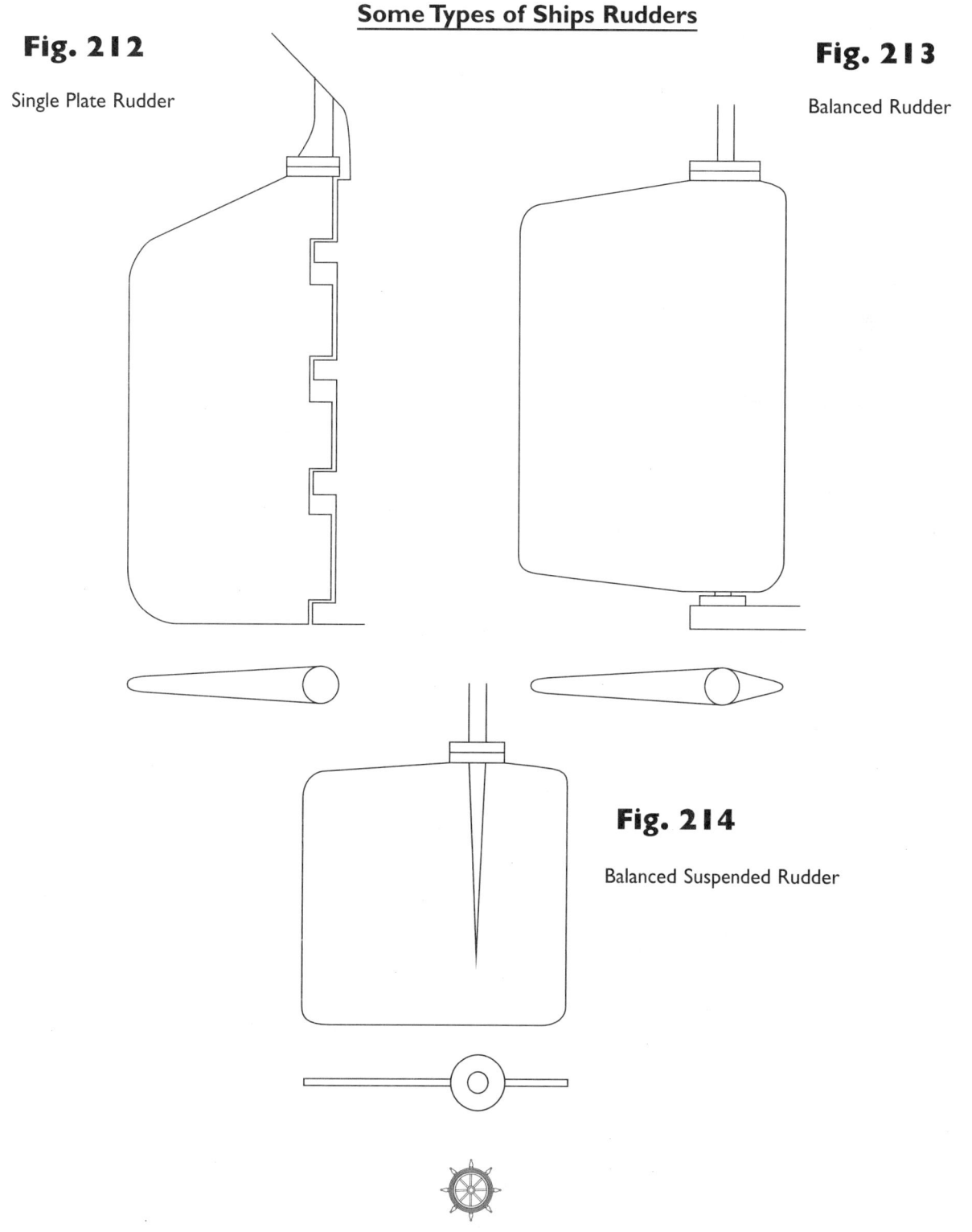

Fig. 212

Single Plate Rudder

Fig. 213

Balanced Rudder

Fig. 214

Balanced Suspended Rudder

The diameter of the stock is dependent upon the area of the blade of the rudder and is subject to the ruling of the classification society concerned. The centre of gravity of the unit and the designed speed of the ship also contributes to the size of the stock. In the case of the twin-screw ship it is usual for two interlinked rudders to be fitted sited behind each screw. Such rudders are usually of the balanced type without lower bearings as are generally fitted to the rudder of the single-screw vessel Fig. 214. As has been observed in the notes on propulsion the steerable Kort nozzle often has a rudder blade incorporated.

One small point that should be noted by the modeller is that the rudders of most ships rarely move more than 35 degrees either side of the centreline of the ship. Where there is a steerable Kort nozzle this movement is generally restricted to a maximum of 25 degrees each side of the centre.

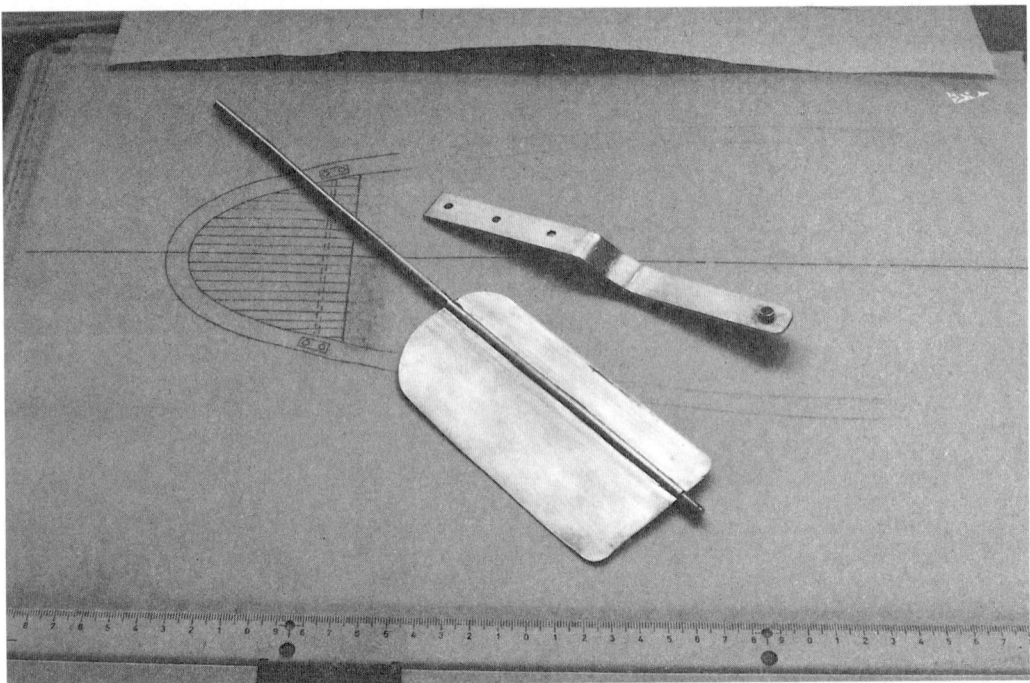

Fig. 215 Component parts of a single blade balanced rudder for a model steam launch.

Fig. 216 Model rudder assembled on steam launch.

Some vessels that have to manoeuvre in restricted places have been fitted with a rudder at the bow to aid rapid turning but this practice has largely been superseded by the installation of the athwartships thruster. Thrusters are fitted today on many ships both large and small. Initially the thruster was fitted close to the bow of the vessel and called a bow thruster. It consists of a tube, within the hull, open at both ends to the water in which is fitted a propeller system driven usually by an electric motor under control from the bridge of the ship. Such a thruster is ineffective except when the vessel is moving slowly but is of great benefit in turning the ship in either direction. Modern ships are often fitted with thrusters at both bow and stern to give a fine degree of manoeuvrability in confined waters and it is not unknown for some large ships to have a multiplicity of thrusters at both bow and stern. So successful has the thruster become that the number of tugs once needed at most ports has been seriously reduced. For example ships such as roll on/roll off ferries of large size can be moved through locks, turned and berthed successfully without the need of any assistance.

Model bow thrusters can be bought at most good model ship shops, most having the tube arranged so that it can be fitted to the model hull securely and allowing the motor and propeller system to be fitted separately and yet remain watertight. One pattern produced by Graupner has a small diameter tube and the drive made through a paddle system which is particularly effective. In every case it is always wise to fit a small grille over the openings in the hull to prevent the ingress of weed and other detritus that can cause the small works to seize. The ship model builder wishing to enter steering regattas will find the installation of a working thruster of great value particularly to the single-screw ship where steering can be difficult running ahead and almost impossible running astern.

Fig. 217 Model bow thruster with electric motor (photo courtesy of Graupner).

SAILS

The early powered ships carried sails to reduce the heavy coal consumption by using sails under favourable sea conditions. The herring drifter and some trawlers carried sails to allow them to drift to the nets and from this method of fishing the drifter got its name. In more recent times some ships have had sophisticated metal 'sails' installed operating under computer control to assist the engines and create some economies although such experiments do not seem to have been successful.

In general the modeller building the model herring drifter or an early pattern trawler or similar fishing vessel will have the option of fitting a sail. Whether this sail should be displayed hoisted or stowed is, of course, a matter of choice. If the model is to be built for static display then a correctly made and hoisted sail will greatly enhance the model. If the model is to be a working one and sailed upon the local lake then it is a different matter. A hoisted sail creates the problem of windage where turning the model one way will be very difficult because the wind on the sail tries to prevent the turn, whereas turning the other way will be rapid as the wind on the sail aids the turn. In reasonable breezes it is very difficult to sail a model carrying a sail at the stern as on a herring drifter as has been the case many times in the author's personal experience and it is wise to have the sail furled when sailing the ship. It is quite possible to make a sail or have one made that can be hoisted when the model is on display but stowed when the model is on the water.

Sails are made from panels of cloth as anyone who has seen sails on a ship of reasonable size or on a yacht such as a sailing dinghy or cruiser knows. In the early ships sail material was of very heavy cloth similar to that of the tarpaulin. The herring drifter sail was treated with a type of tar solution to prevent it from rotting and this gave a colour close to that of strong, milky

Fig. 218 Model herring drifter with mizzen sail hoisted.

coffee although the soot from the funnel very soon blackened the sail. Model sails for a herring drifter or similar model can best be made from fine cotton such as handkerchief material. My drifter sails have always been made from handkerchiefs when the lady of the house was otherwise occupied although she sometimes did do the sewing. With such a small sail it is not necessary to sew panels of material together but simply to make a turned seam all round the sail and simulate the panels with rows of fine close stitches. A sewing machine is of great value here but it is not impossible to do all the work on the sail by hand **Fig. 218**.

The general arrangement drawings for the ship will usually give details of the sail on the same sheet as the rigging is detailed. Some ships of early times also carried a triangular pattern sail from the foremast and such will also be detailed on the rigging or GA plans. Note that all sails on ships except those of the small yachts are never snowy white but usually a darker creamier colour and on the working ship very dark indeed.

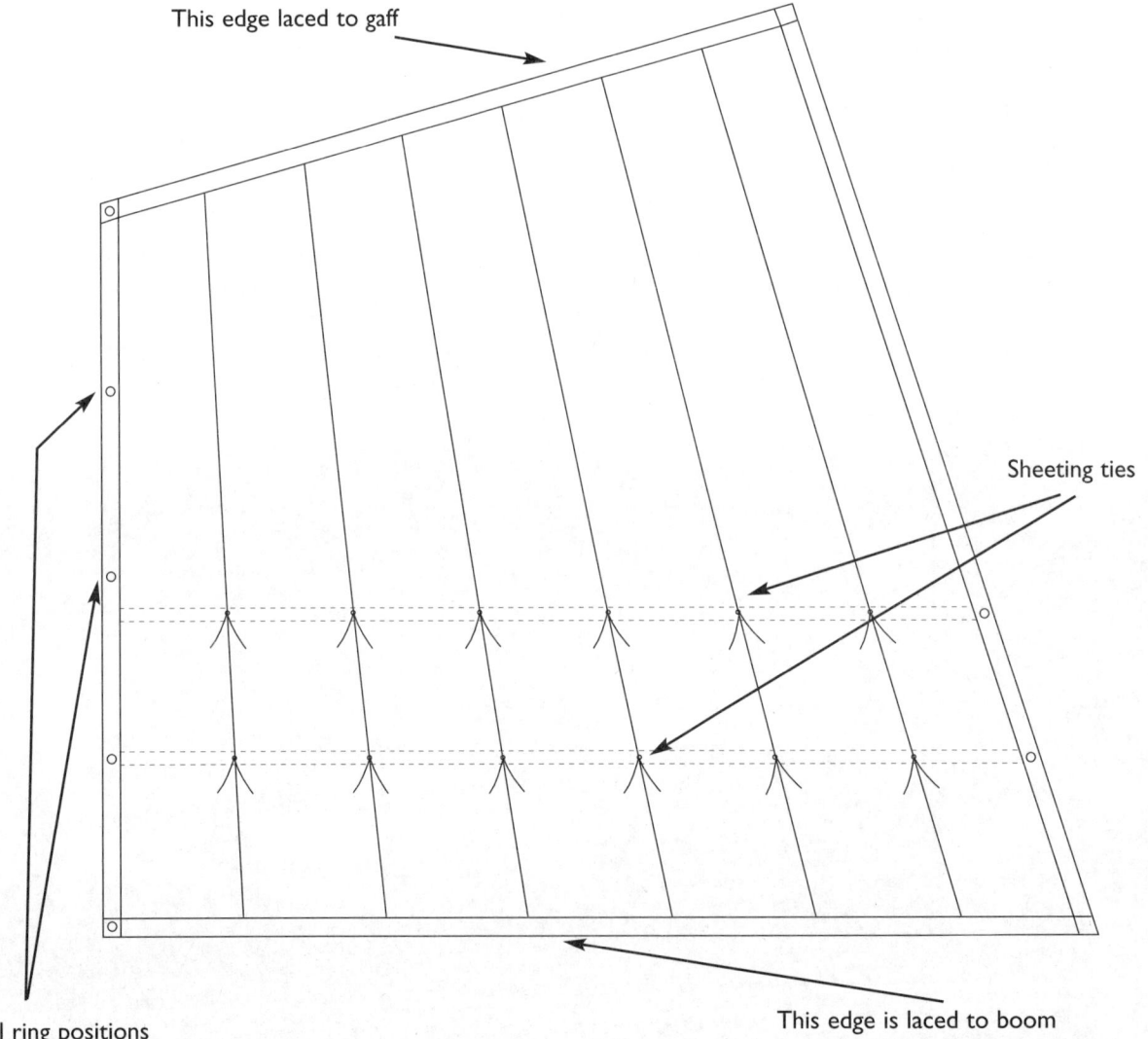

Sail for Model Herring Drifter

Fig. 219

SHAFTS

Not necessarily a visible part of the ship but a vital one never the less, the propeller shaft is as necessary to the working model as to the full size ship. On full size vessels the propeller shaft has a complex sealing system at the point where it exits from the hull. Up to recent years the tail shaft bearing was composed of a number of shaped pieces of lignum vitae timber lubricated by the water and with a system of seals to prevent the water from entering the ship and a pumping system to control the water. Further up the shaft and often very close to the engine flywheel or outermost bearing there is fitted a thrust bearing that directs the thrust produced by the propeller away from the engine and into the structure of the ship's hull. In the case of twin-screw vessels there would, of course, be a thrust bearing attached to each shaft.

The model propulsion engine, whether it be a steam engine or an electric motor, is not designed to accept end thrust on its shaft or bearings and thus it is necessary to include a thrust bearing of some sort between the propeller and the engine. This, in the case of the model shaft, is usually a washer inserted between the propeller and the end of the shaft. Such a washer will transmit the thrust to the outer casing of the propeller shaft and in turn to the hull of the model. Motor or engine failure can occur if such arrangements are not fitted and where the propeller shaft is allowed to float even slightly in a fore-and-aft direction. The majority of scale model ships are fitted with shafts that are similar to that illustrated in **Fig. 220**. The best of such propeller shafts are composed of stainless steel inner shafts with the outer made of brass tube and the bearings formed of either bronze or brass bushes. Finer still are the shafts where the inner shaft is carried in ball bearings but it is necessary to ensure that there are O-ring type seals fitted to prevent water from passing the bearings and flooding the hull.

Plain shafts as described in **Fig. 220** need to be packed with fine waterproof grease such as that used in water pumps of cars or, alternatively, fitted with an oiling tube through which the shaft can be filled with heavy oil. Oil will tend to leak from the shaft over a period of time and it is less likely to prevent water from running up the shaft. Fine adjustment of the end float will assist in preventing water from leaking up the shaft. Such leakage generally occurs when the model is running astern when there is end float that lifts the thrust washer from the end of the shaft casing. A small amount of water entering from the propeller shaft(s) is not usually serious provided that the modeller does not allow it to build up enough to cause damage to motors or delicate radio equipment.

There is a wide variety of propeller shafts available from a number of makers, some of which are quite slender. Most makers produce their shafts in a number of lengths and normally the shafts are sold by length of the outer casing. So that a 10in shaft will have an outer casing 10in long and the inner shaft will usually be 1in longer. Some inner shafts will have plain ends; some will have a thread for the propeller on one end and a plain end on the other while the majority will be threaded at both ends. Most shafts for models today use metric threads although it is still possible to have shafts made with BA pattern threads if the propeller is so screwed.

Typical Model Propeller Shaft **Fig. 220**

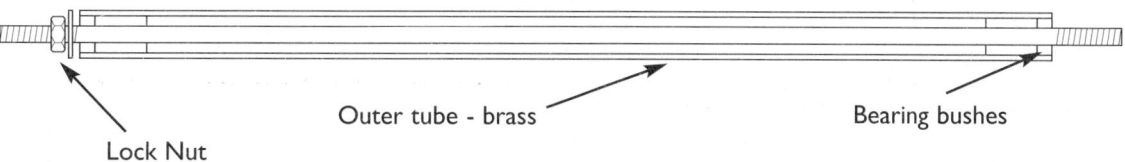

Lock Nut Outer tube - brass Bearing bushes

As has previously been mentioned it is always wise to use a suitable coupling between the engine or motor and the shaft to take up any misalignment that may be present and to ensure a smooth drive train. In the author's experience the very best couplings to use are the Cardan pattern produced by Marx Luder or Graupner all of which come complete with a selection of bushes to suit shaft sizes but only to suit plain shafts. These particular couplings can accept a reasonable degree of out of true in the aligning of the drive train but, of course, the smaller the degree of misalignment the better.

At the end of the sailing season it is wise to remove the propeller, the inner shaft, the coupling and the drive equipment and to store them safely. The outer casing of the shaft should be repacked with grease and the inner shaft replaced after ensuring that it is not damaged. The propeller, if of brass or bronze, can be cleaned and polished and also replaced. The coupling should also be examined and replaced on the model but the drive motor or steam plant and batteries should be carefully stored after cleaning and suitable attention.

Fig. 216 Range of couplings for connecting drive unit to propeller shaft - courtesy of Graupner.

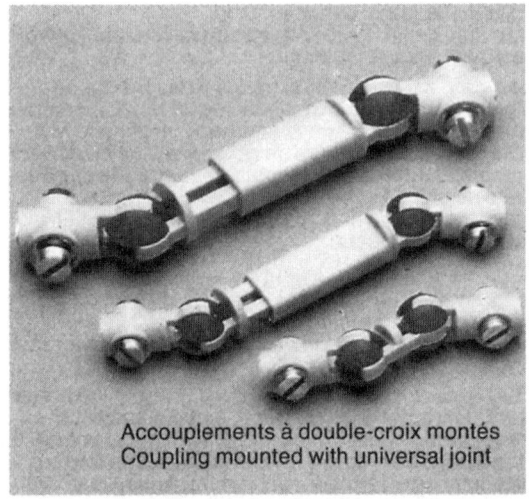

Accouplements à double-croix montés
Coupling mounted with universal joint

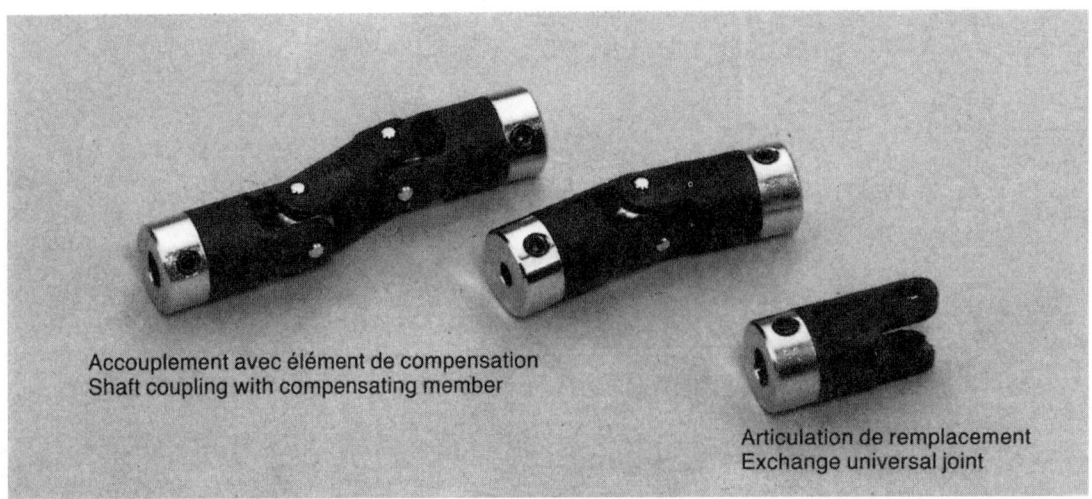

Accouplement avec élément de compensation
Shaft coupling with compensating member

Articulation de remplacement
Exchange universal joint

Fig. 222 Stern of motor ship TIMRIX in dry-dock illustrating projecting tail shaft and rudder.

SKYLIGHTS

There are skylights on very nearly every ship that can be thought of; they serve to allow light to enter enclosed spaces in the hull where portlights or windows can not be used. The most often seen and highly visible is the engine room skylight which gives, not only needed daylight in the engine space, but ventilation, too, by releasing the hot air that collects at high levels. In the days of the steam-engine-driven ship it was rare to see an engine room skylight closed even when the weather was bad and rain was falling heavily. The need for release of heat was much more necessary than the entry of some rainwater. Some small ships would need to close the engine room skylight if the sea was breaking over the decks and could enter the engine room in reasonable quantities but even here it was rare to see them closed. The photographs illustrate some engine room skylights.

In other places the accommodation would be illuminated through a skylight where cabins or a saloon located below deck needed the allowance of daylight. Most of such accommodation would have the glazing protected by steel or iron bars and sometimes the skylight tops would be fixed closed. On some small vessels the provision of a skylight was a raised box-like construction fitted with an opening lid in which there would be two or more circular portlights. This type of skylight is also illustrated among the photographs.

Some of the side-fishing vessels and ships of that period had heavy glass 'lights' set into the decks to let light into the cabins below. These 'deck lights' were set into steel frames let into the timber deck and fitted with very thick glass to withstand the work that could be carried out over them. In a sense they were not really skylights but a form of portlight except that they were fitted into the flat deck.

The ship model builder needs to seek out the location of such small items as deck lights as well as the more obvious skylight and the scale model will be enhanced by such attention to detail.

Fig. 223 A very basic skylight over the saloon of the bunkering tanker RIX HARRIER.

Fig. 224 Skylight of timber under construction for a model pilot cutter.

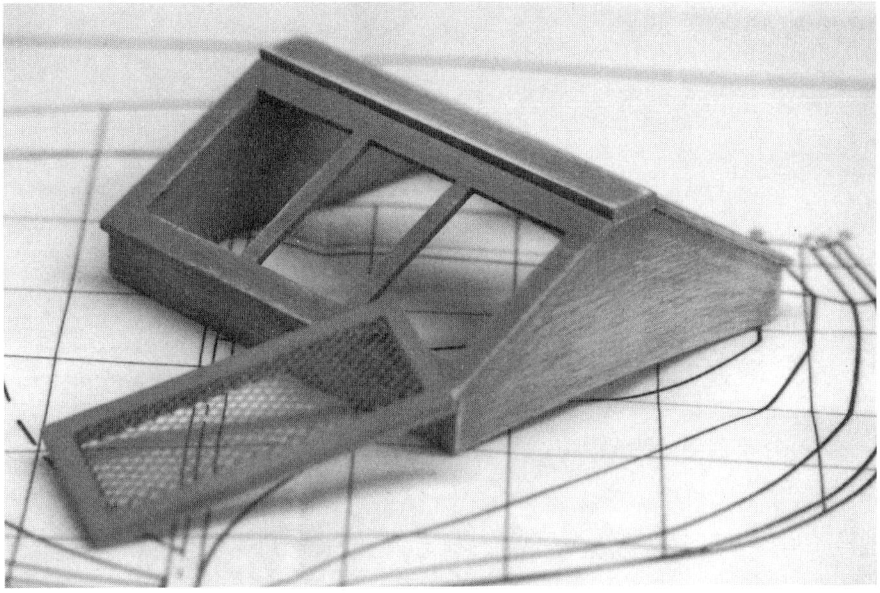

Fig. 225 Engine room skylight for the model tug CRUISER.

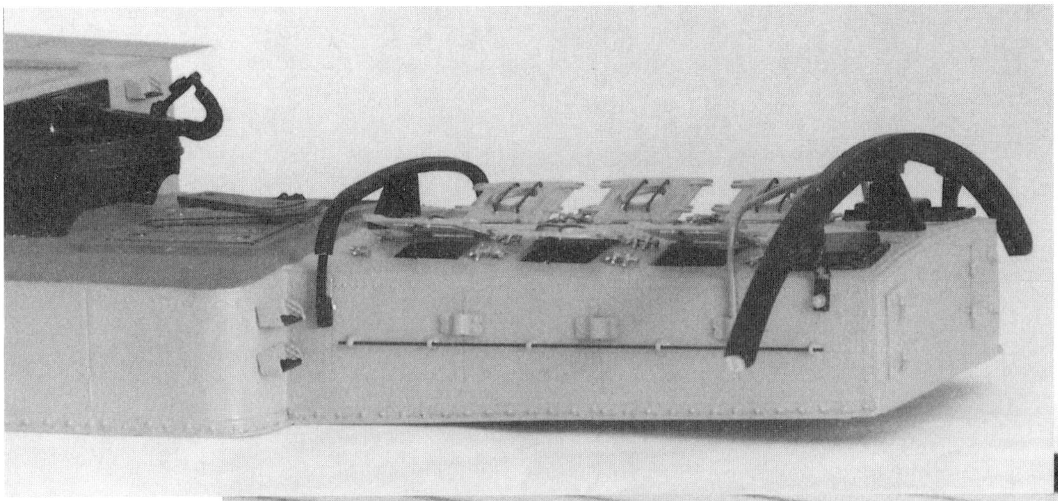

Fig. 226 Skylight under construction for model of the Tyne pilot cutter BRITANNIA.

135

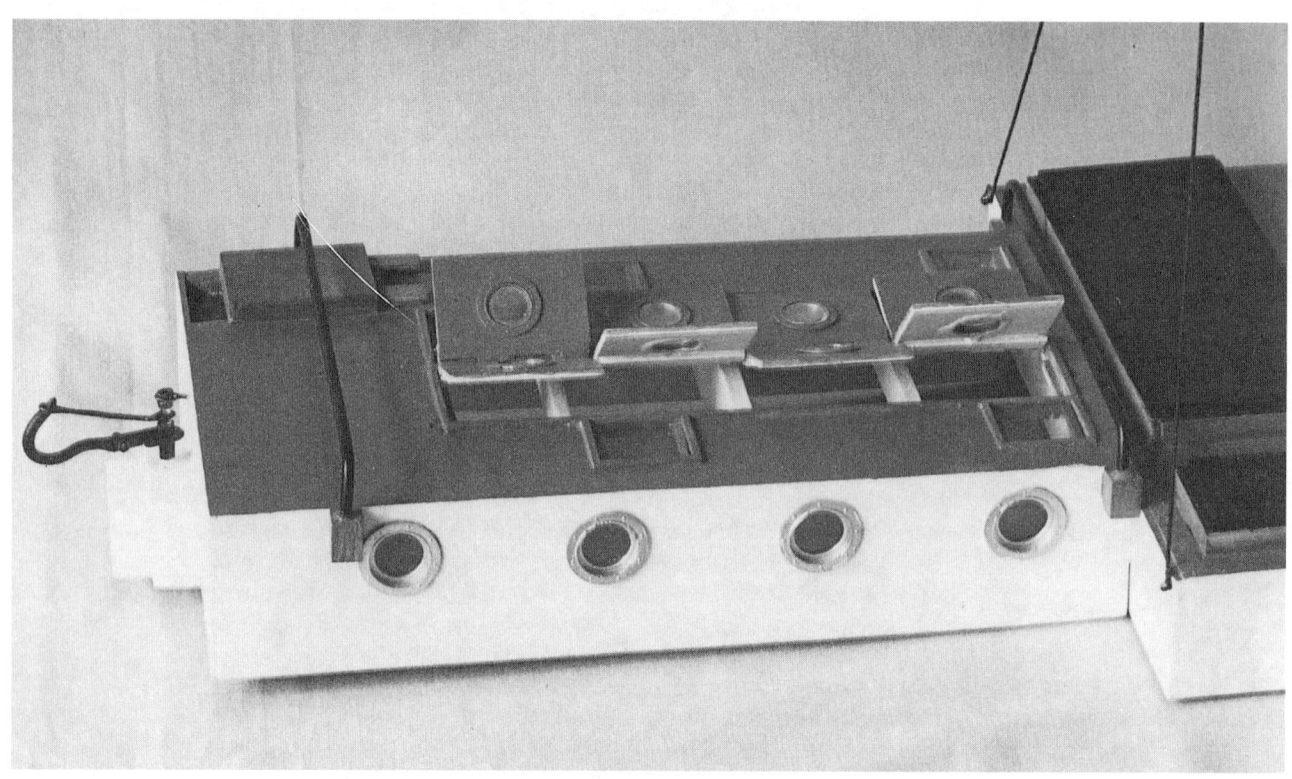

Fig. 227 Engine room skylight for model of the steam driven tug GONDIA.

STEERING GEAR

The rudder of the ship, even a fairly small ship, is a heavy item that is difficult to move against the resistance of the water. Even in early times it was realised that the man at the tiller needed to have help particularly in heavy weather. The tiller could be moved more easily using a system of blocks and ropes to allow the rudder to be moved by a single seaman. When the steam engine was installed, at first the steering wheel remained near the stern and was rope worked. Later the wheel was positioned in the wheelhouse on the bridge and the movement of the wheel was transmitted to the quadrant of the rudder by means of gears, chains and rods. This arrangement still required assistance when the weather was heavy as the kick of the rudder could be transmitted through the system. Eventually the telemotor steering system was installed which sent signals to a steam engine mounted near and connected to the rudder from the steering wheel in the wheelhouse.

Today most steering is carried out by means of hydraulic cylinders connected to the rudder and which are moved by electronic signals from the bridge. Some ships still use a steering wheel on the bridge and some ship's masters prefer this but many ships are steered by means of a small joystick. The electro-hydraulic method of steering allows control of the rudder to be done from more than one central position, for example from either bridge wing, giving the officer of the watch a greater degree of accuracy when steering the ship in a confined area.

The model rudder is more easily controlled but in a similar manner by means of the radio controls and a suitable servo unit. Where the rudder is of small size and well balanced it is easy to connect from the servo to a suitable tiller arm on the rudder stock using brass or steel rods and suitable clevis fork connectors **Fig.228**. Where the rudder is larger and thus resistance to turning is greater it is wise to use a closed circuit of rods and clevis forks to connect from servo to rudder **Fig. 229**. It is also possible to operate the rudder from the servo using a flexible-wire-in-tube method but here the outer tube of the system must be very securely fastened to the ship to prevent movement except at the extreme ends of the inner wire. This is known as a Bowden wire system and is not usually needed on scale models except in special places where access to the rudder can be restricted by a low deck or similar obstruction. Where there are twin rudders in line with twin screws then it is necessary to connect the tillers of both rudders and to operated them from a single servo. It is not practical to attempt to steer each rudder separately nor would they be so operated in full size practice **Fig. 230**

Fig. 228   <u>**Single Rod Connection to Rudder**</u>

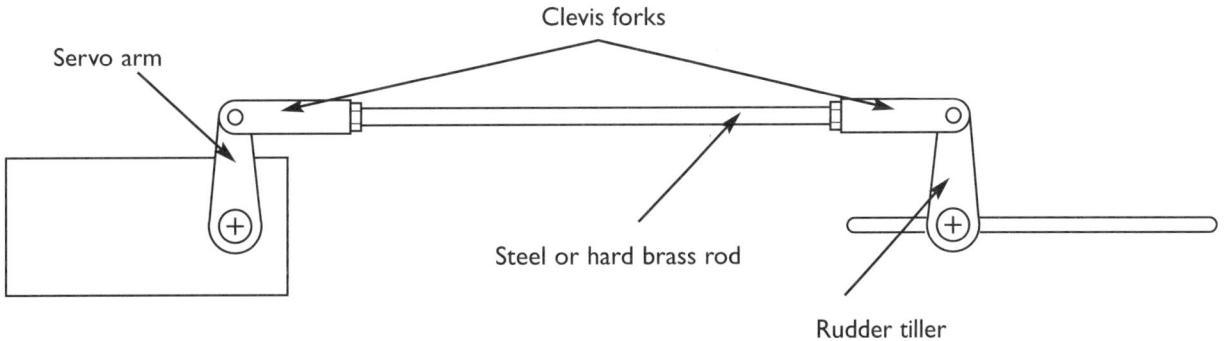

Fig. 229   'Closed Loop' Rod System to Rudder

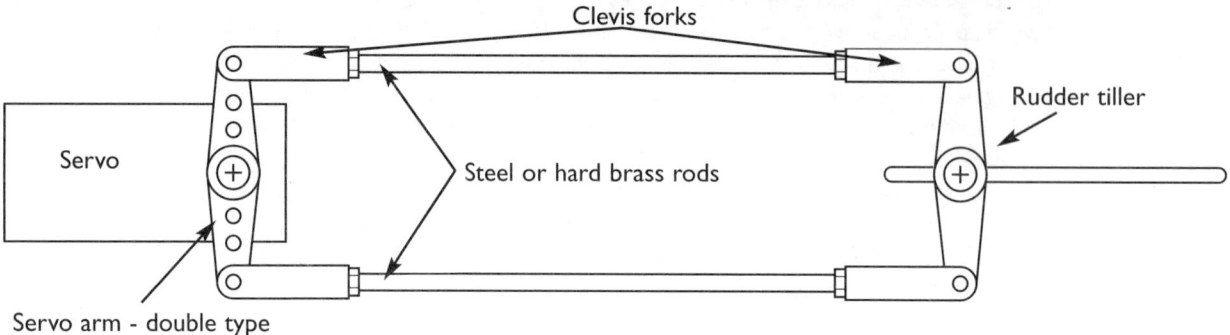

Fig. 231 Navigating bridge of a beautifully made model of the paddle steamer DUCHESS OF FIFE showing wheel, binnacle and four of the five engine room telegraphs.

One particular point that must be born in mind when building the scale model is the question of what may be visible through the windows of the wheelhouse for example. Most steering positions on ships have large windows which on the model show up the interior very clearly unless the model is quite small. Under these circumstances it is necessary to outfit the wheelhouse or bridge unit with details of the equipment that is therein. Some of the older ships had steering positions on top of the wheelhouse and fully visible to any onlooker. In all these cases it is required of the modeller to provide steering wheel(s), steering engine, telegraphs, voice pipes and other items that may be found on the bridge. The modern ship has engine controls, video screens, radar screens, computer units etc. all visible through the large windows. The windows, too, have wipers or, in earlier vessels, clear view screens that revolved at high speed to throw the water away. The modeller must research his/her model for this data so that the bridge, and any other area where there are large windows, can be fitted out inside to give the correct impression.

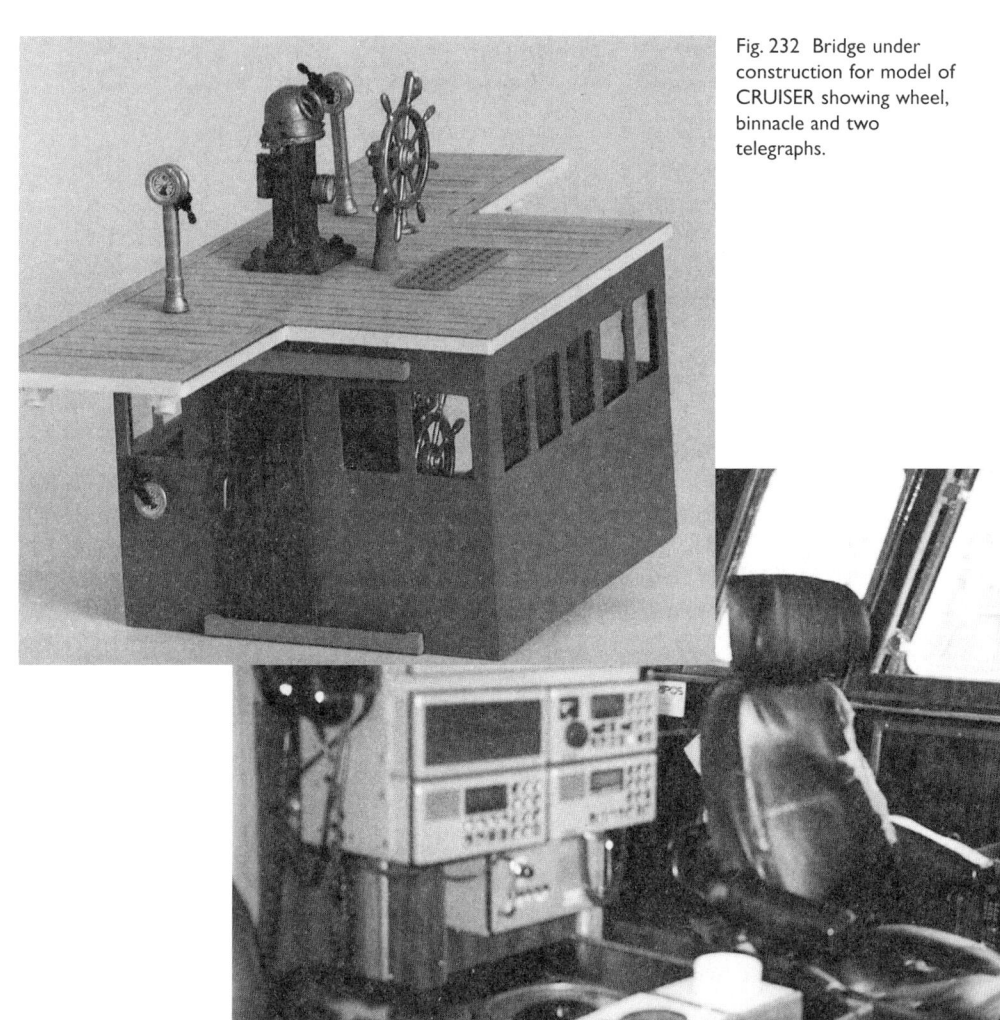

Fig. 232 Bridge under construction for model of CRUISER showing wheel, binnacle and two telegraphs.

Fig. 233 Interior of wheelhouse on motor fishing vessel DENEBULA showing wheel, helmsman's seat and gyro compass.

Fig. 234 Interior of wheelhouse on DENEBULA showing main engine and winch controls.

SUPERSTRUCTURES & DECKHOUSES

Superstructures, in general, refer to the parts of the ship's structure that lie above the main deck and this means accommodation, casings for the engine room or boiler room etc. The general arrangement drawing will usually provide some details of such superstructures which may at first appear complex but when broken down will be found to be a series of box-like structures that are fairly straightforward to produce in miniature. If each level is taken separately and looked at carefully it will be found that, depending upon scale, it is often a simple matter to build the needed replica.

When constructing the superstructures of the ship model bear in mind that the floors must conform to the sheer and camber curves of the ship while the verticals usually are set at right angles to the waterline. Many of the early ships had curved corners and gently curving fronts to accommodation blocks whereas the more modern ship tends to be more angular and thus easier to build in model form. Doors on the external sides of such blocks should be hinged on the forward side to close against the run of the sea washing over the ship from the bow or against the wind when the ship is heading into the wind. External portlights will be visible usually only as rings with a glass insert from the outside as they open internally. Windows, too, will not have very visible frames when in a steel house. Bear in mind that water can enter unglazed window and port openings if the model encounters dirty weather and, unless a free supply of air is needed for a steam outfit, ensure that windows and portlights that are low in the superstructures are well sealed.

Building deckhouses and superstructures for the model is best done using fine quality marine plywood when a steam plant is to be fitted or good quality styrene sheet when the model is fitted with electric motor and is not subject to too much heat or stress. Both materials have their advantages; the plywood will stand up to a great deal more handling than will the styrene but needs filling and rubbing down to a smooth surface to simulate steel sheet. The styrene sheet is smooth as steel and needs little attention before being painted in any but cellulose paint. Cellulose paints will attack the styrene with unpleasant results and thus acrylic paints are best. The styrene construction is not quite so robust as that formed of plywood but it is much easier to work, cut and is almost dust free. It is, of course, necessary to use the appropriate adhesives with these materials; P.V.A. of the aliphatic type is best for the timber or plywood construction and liquid polystyrene cement is best for the styrene sheet. Both materials have their merits and they can be intermixed when necessary.

Method of Driving Twin Rudders

Fig. 219

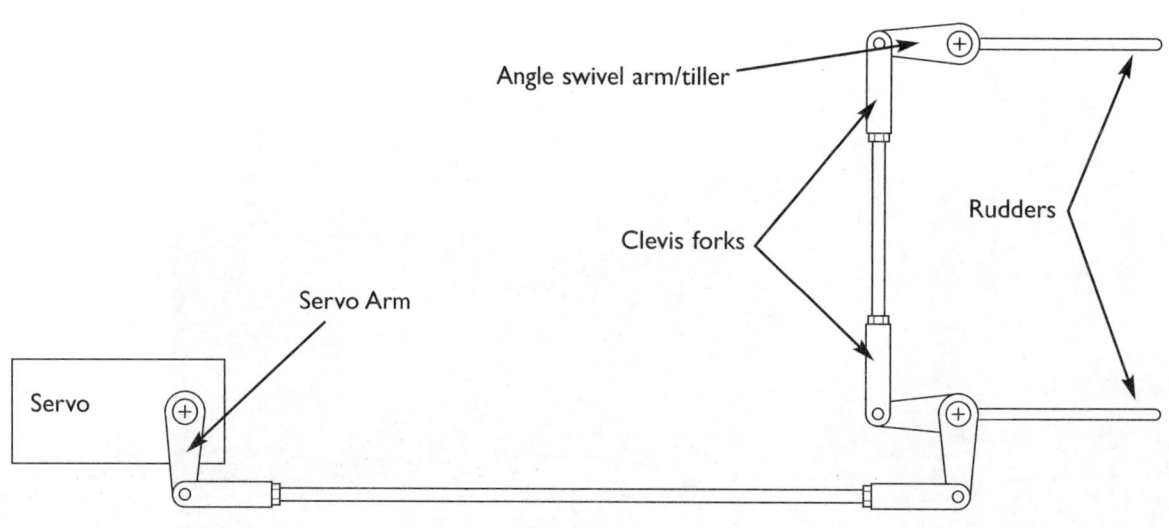

The bridge structure often causes the most problems as it is frequently of open construction with a centrally-placed wheelhouse. However the method of building is much the same as for other structures and the essential point to note is the camber of the bridge and its wings. Very often the bridge deck has a curtain plate beneath it and these plates can be a boon if they are cut carefully and used to brace the curve of the deck. Beams in full size practice brace all bridge structures and it is sensible to build the model bridge in the same way. The bridge support beams should be cut to suit the camber curvature and strengthened with flat pieces to form T or H type sections.

This in styrene makes a particularly strong support beam and, while the exercise can be repeated in thin ply it is not quite such a simple operation unless very fast drying adhesive is used.

Some ships such as the coaster Rovuma illustrated have small deckhouses built fore-and-aft to accommodate specific crew personnel. In the case of Rovuma the deck crew were Chinese and needed to have separate accommodation and cooking facilities, they were thus provided with deckhouses on either side of the ship both forward and aft. Deckhouses are also often erected on the small ship to accommodate a few passengers on short duration voyages. On the tug tender for example there were deckhouses built as saloon accommodation for passengers in transit between port and anchored ship. On the pilot cutter Britannia shown here, the pilots' saloon and entrance to their accommodation was built out forward of the main casing and wheelhouse of the herring drifter from which the cutter was converted. The main saloon and cabins were built within the hold previously used to store the catch of fish.

Access to under-deck facilities is often by way of a companion with a cover and doors on the deck with stairs leading to the space below. Quite often this companion hatch was of fine timber stained, panelled and varnished. The more modern ship today generally has all the accommodation in one block with access within the deckhouse unit. Hatches giving way to spaces below deck for working are usually of steel with covers hinged and fitted with hand wheel or other tightly-closing methods to make them watertight.

Fig. 235 Amidships superstructure of a model of a Union Castle Lines coaster ROVUMA showing cowl ventilators, radio cabin, funnel and stays.

Fig. 236 Main gantry and wheelhouse superstructure on the stern trawler ONWARD CHALLENGER.

Fig. 238 Detail of windows and decoration on the front of the wheelhouse of DENEBULA.

Fig. 237 View of front of main superstructure of a twin screw tug.

Fig. 239 Wheelhouse and main deckhouse of a small fishing vessel under construction.

Fig. 240 Main deckhouse on model of DENEBULA under construction.

143

Fig. 242   Detail of bridge front of motor ship LIZRIX.

Fig. 241   Slender low built engine room casing and forward saloon on model of steam yacht.

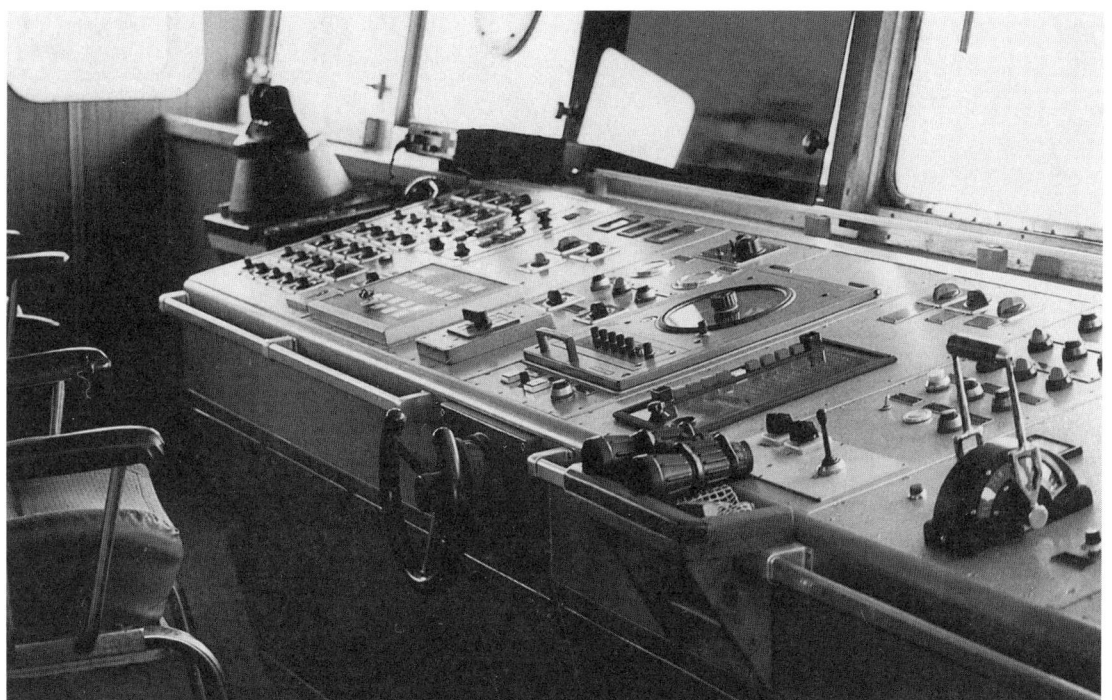

Fig. 243 Interior detail of bridge on motor ship LIZRIX.

Fig. 244 Detail of superstructure on the motor vessel JONRIX.

Fig. 245 Close up of searchlight on superstructure of the motor vessel JONRIX.

Fig. 246 Starboard bridge wing of superstructure of SCOTT GUARDIAN.

TANKS

Here again we are concerned only with those tanks that are visible above decks on the ship. All ships have a fairly large number of tanks built into the hull which are, of course, invisible except that they all have ventilation of one kind or another. The tanks of this section are those that sit on the tops of casings, cabin units, etc. The modern ship has few tanks of any kind visible but the earlier ships quite often carried cylindrical or rectangular tanks high on the tops of the superstructure to provide a gravity supply of water to the baths, galley etc. Fresh water in the modern ship is generally pumped from the deep tanks to a ring serving the various outlets. Small tanks can be seen in the pictures of the earlier ship models shown here. They are a small neat exercise in themselves; each requires an inlet pipe, a vent or overflow pipe and an outlet pipe usually with a shut-off valve.

In the side-fishing trawlers all had a tank located at the stern usually over the rudder quadrant in which was stored the cod liver oil that was a crew perk and pictures of sidewinders will often show this tank quite prominently. **Fig. 247** illustrates a simple water tank with cradle for cabin-top fitting.

<u>Small Water Tank & Fittings</u>

Fig. 247

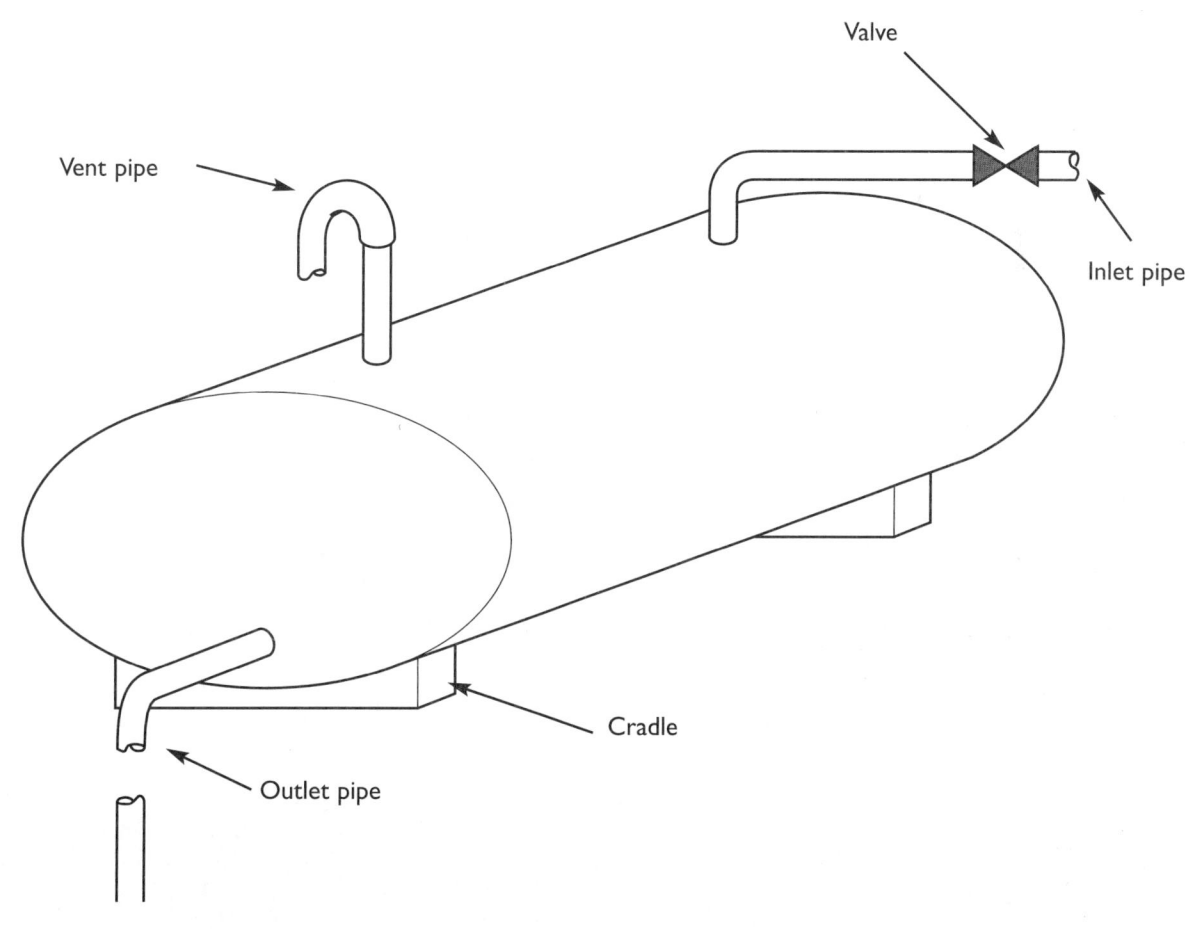

TANKERS

Most modellers will think of tankers as large ships carrying huge quantities of oil and similar fluids but the coastal and bunkering tankers are usually compact ships serving the smaller ports and feeding oil fuel to the large vessels when it is needed. There are no filling stations into which the ship may call for fuel, oil and other supplies so that they are provided by a small ship designed specially for this purpose and known as a bunkering tanker. A number of companies specialising in supplying bunker fuel and oil of all kinds and their ships range from the small self-propelled barge to miniature tank ships capable of short sea voyaging. The Rix Harrier pictured here is just such a ship; she carries heavy fuel in heated tanks and gas oil in others to provide a service to large and small ships on the northeast coast of the UK. The model shown was built by the author and has a total of 76 valve hand wheels visible on the deck together with the connecting pipes and valves. In addition each of the ship's twelve tanks is fitted with a hatch and a contents gauge all located on the tank deck.

The small coastal tanker used for transporting oil and similar liquids between refineries and storage depots on the banks of some of the country's rivers and estuaries has a similar but simpler arrangement of pipes and valves visible on the deck together with a walkway running from the accommodation to the forecastle to allow the crew easy access to the forward machinery.

Both types of ship make attractive models and it is possible to buy small pipes or tubes of brass or styrene from which to form the deck arrangement. Some companies also produce valves and hand wheels that can be used to create the correct configuration. It is, of course, quite a time-consuming task to locate cut, fit and secure all the pipes and fittings needed but there is a great deal of satisfaction in completing such a task on a well-made model.

Fig. 247A Model of the RIX HARRIER a coastal bunkering tanker

TOWING

As previously mentioned the majority of large tugs today use towing winches in preference to the tow hook and a towing winch is illustrated in **Fig. 248**. This winch has a towing capability of 60 tons and, of course, the manufacturers of such winches do build in a range of sizes. There are advantages in using a winch against the simple hook. The winch can shorten or lengthen the towline allowing the tug to be positioned for better control of the tow; short lines for precise movement in confined areas and longer lines for safer towing in open waters. Tugs in the UK and Europe have the superstructure basically forward of amidships leaving a stern deck of about one third of the length of the hull; tugs in the U.S.A. and other countries tend to have the superstructure totally amidships leaving a short stern deck. The tugs in the UK and Europe and most salvage tugs with long stern-deck space have steel and timber towing bows spanning the deck to lift the tow rope clear of aft deck fittings and obstructions. Such towing bows are distinctive parts of the tug and are illustrated in the photographs.

Fig. 248

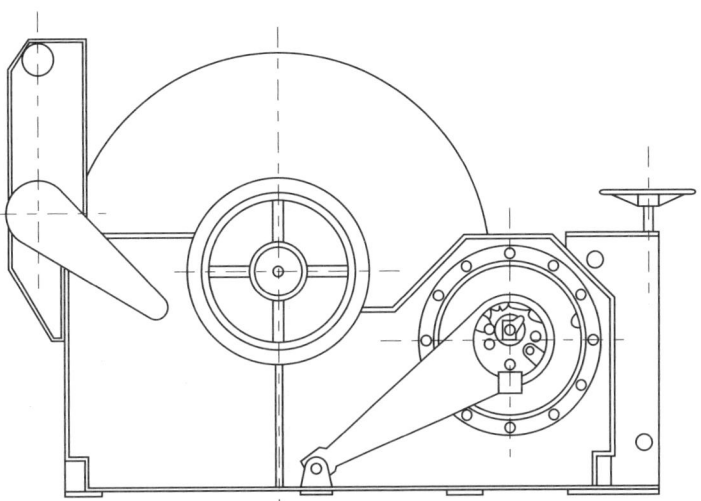

Typical 60 Tons Capacity Hydraulic Towing Winch

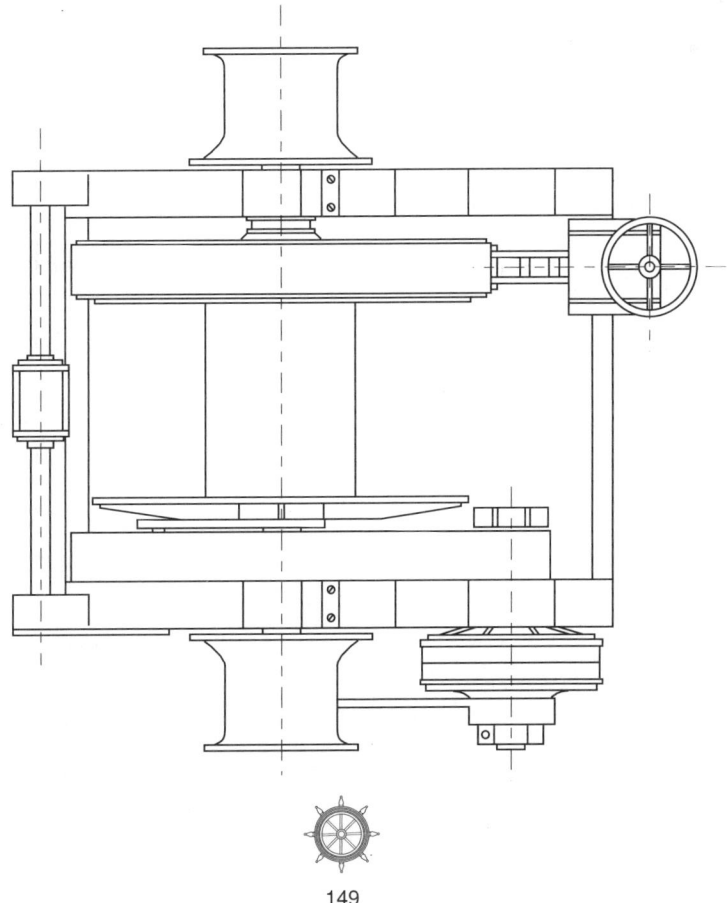

The towing bows shown on the model of the tug Cruiser were made from 6.5mm thick marine plywood cut to the required curve and thickness. To the top face of the bow was glued a length of 0.8mm plywood to represent the hardwood facing and the whole unit was painted black on completion. The additional supports were fashioned from brass rod. On the full size vessels the towing bows are usually made from U-section steel channel curved to suit the span and with heavy hardwood timber fastened into and projecting above the U. The timber serves to prevent the towrope from being worn or chafed as it slides over the bow and, of course, the complete bow is supported from the bulwarks at either end and with stays of steel rod at intervals.

Fig. 254 Stern view of model of tug CRUISER. showing towing bow.

TOW HOOKS

No volume of this type would be complete without some data on the tow hooks used on the variety of tugs to be found round the coasts of this and other countries. There is a tendency today for the tug to use a towing winch in preference to a tow hook and in some countries the tow is connected to bitts mounted firmly through the deck. In the UK and Europe the tow hook reigned supreme for many years and few tug models would be correct without a model tow hook.

In general three types of tow hook were to be found on tugs in this country; they are illustrated here **Figs. 249, 250 & 251**. The main difference in most cases lay in the method of shock absorbing that was built into the tow hook arrangement. Some had a simple box containing a heavy spring that compressed as load was applied and that absorbed the shocks. Others had a system of levers that operated to a connecting spring that in turn absorbed shocks while a third system used a spring which was connected to the draw bar of the hook in such a manner as to absorb shocks. The most modern of tow hooks has a hydraulic shock-absorbing system connected to the hook. In all cases the tow hook(s) is connected to a heavily reinforced part of the tug's superstructure.

Fig. 249

Liverpool Pattern Tow Hook

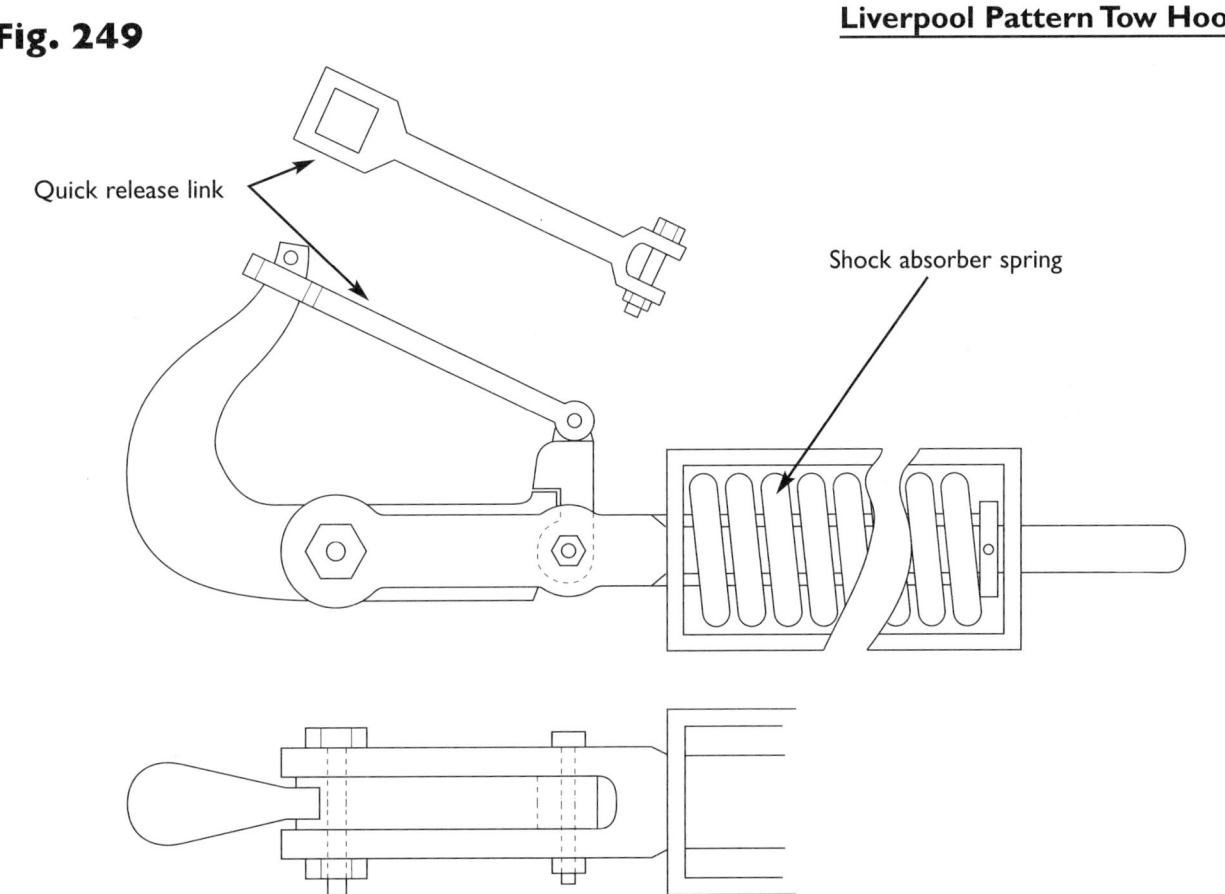

Most model tow hooks made from hard plastics or cast in white metal are very accurate representations of the full size counterparts but they are not suitable for actual use as towing hooks. The model ship builder who desires to have his model tug tow a larger vessel or a number of barges must provide a substantial mounting on his model to which to attach the tow rope.

Fig. 250

Circular Pattern Tow Hook

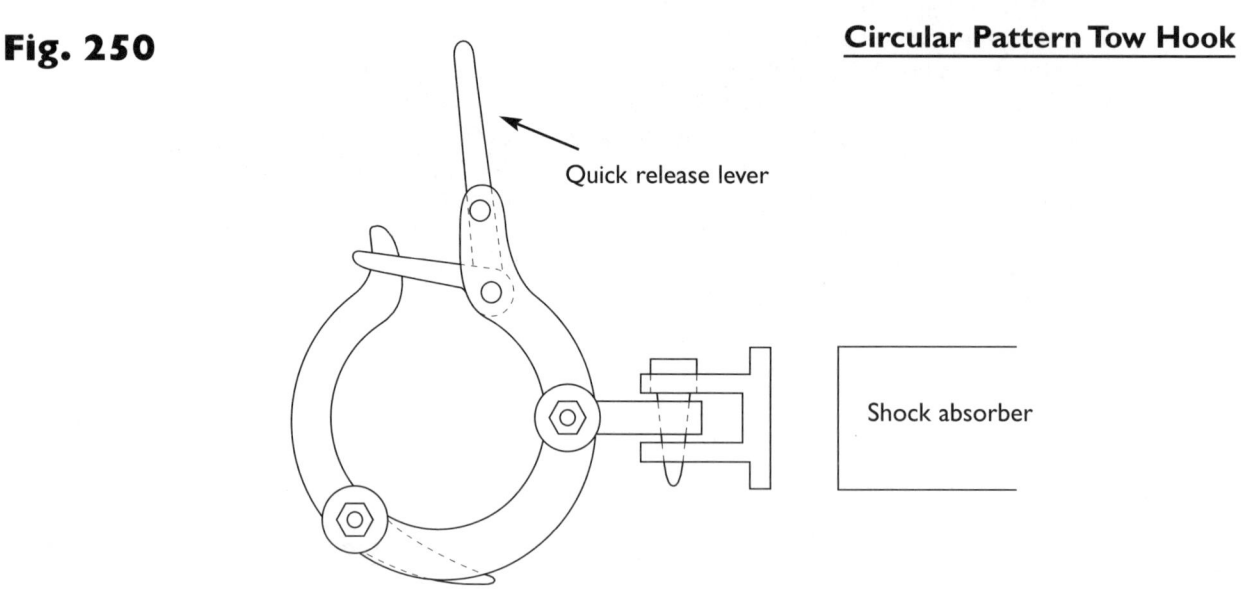

'Monarch' Pattern Tow Hook

Fig. 251

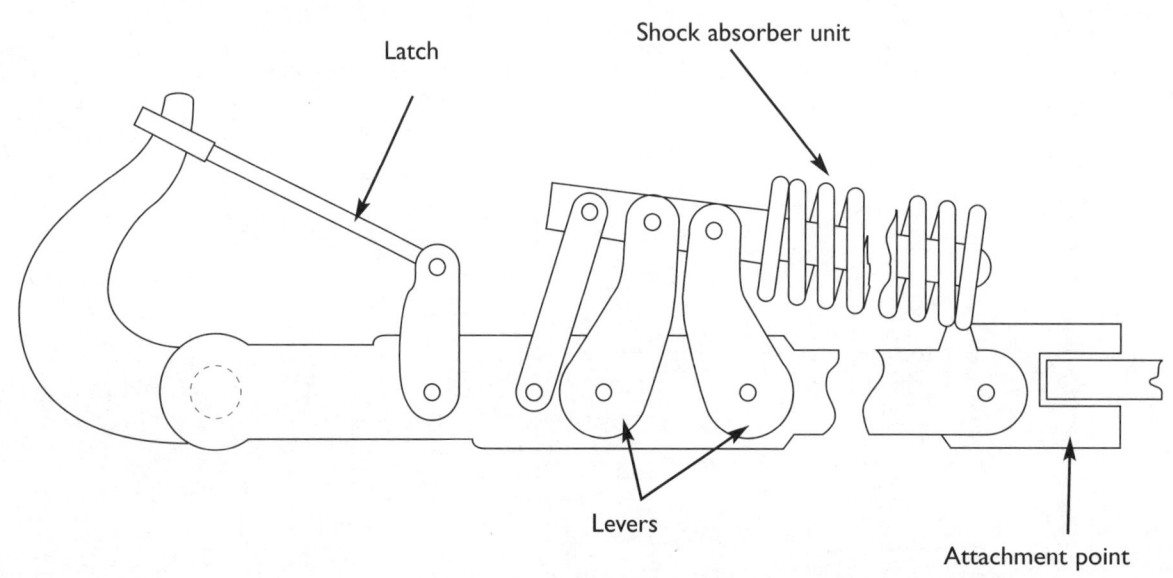

Fig. 252 Tow hook on model of tug CRUISER.

Fig. 253 Tow hook on Envoy class steam tug circa 1944. (Photo courtesy of Mr. Eric Hammal).

VENTS & VENTILATION

Possibly the least noticed of fittings found round the decks of the ship are the tank vents. These are units required to allow air to escape or enter a tank when it is being filled or emptied and are generally pipes terminating, above deck, in a variety of ways. The double bottom of the steel ship is divided up into deep tanks that are used for various means, storing fresh water, storing fuel oil for the drive equipment and for filling with sea water to provide ballast. Obviously the tanks need to be fairly small, as otherwise liquid swilling about would upset the balance of the ship. Each tank will have at least one vent pipe and possibly also a pipe used to permit the level of fluid to be observed by use of a dip rod. The more modern ship will, of course, have electronic content gauges reading quantities on the bridge or in the engine room.

Gooseneck Tank Vents **Fig. 255**

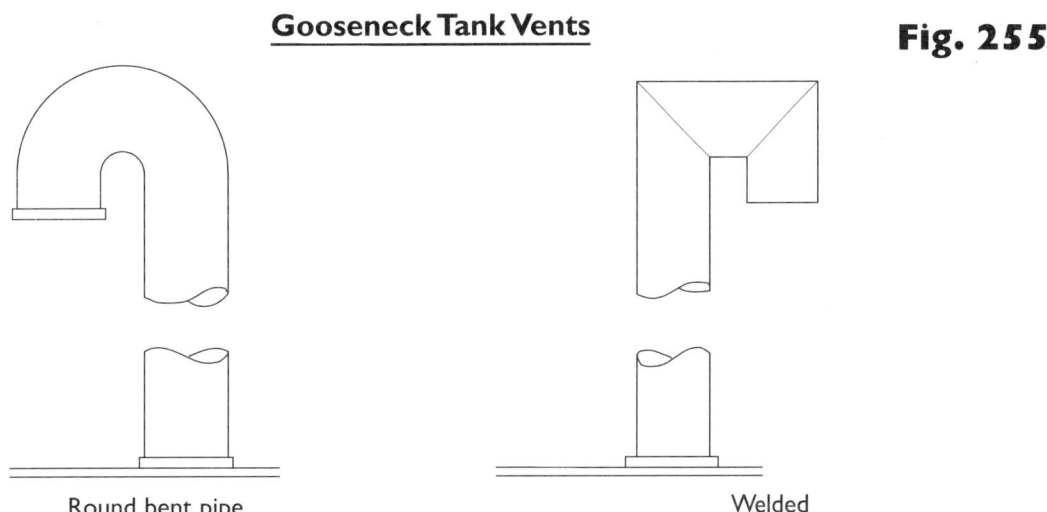

Round bent pipe

Welded

Fig. 256 **Patented Top Tank Vents**

Fig. 261

'Fyffe' Pattern
Extraction
Ventilator

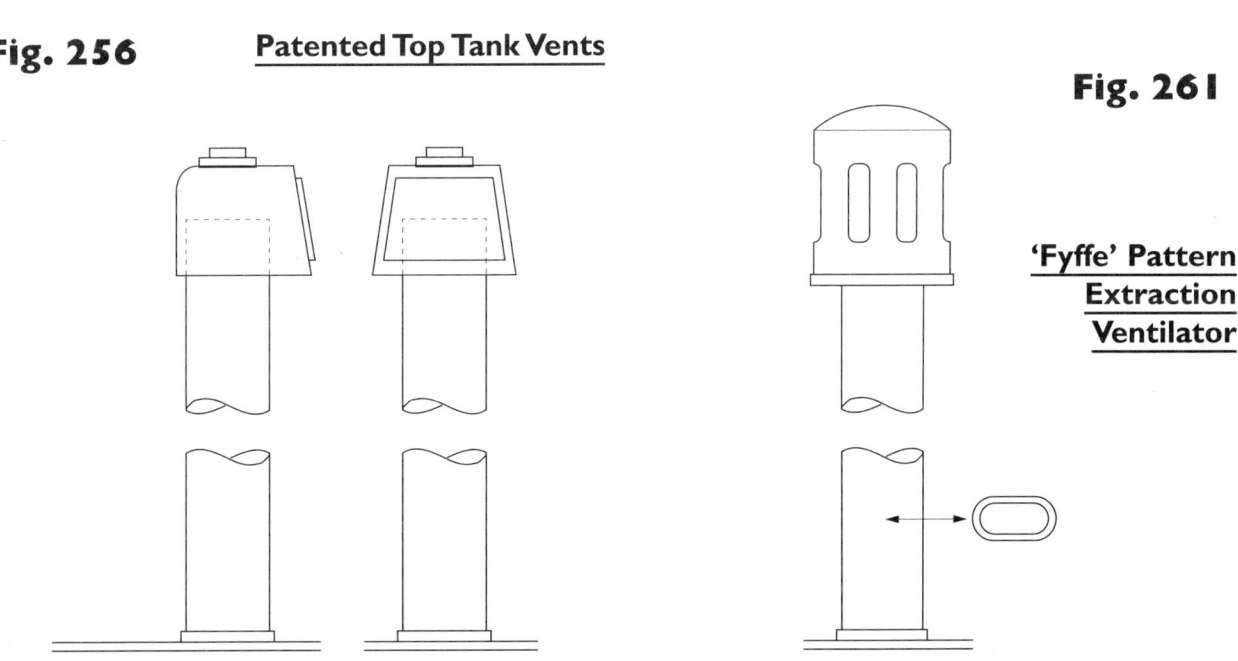

155

In addition to the deep tanks many ships also have tanks built into the hull sides close to the boiler or engine rooms for containing the daily fuel supplies, lubricating oil and other liquids. These tanks, too, have vent pipes and fill lines; all are connected to the various pumps within the machinery spaces of the ship. Many vent pipes terminate in simple goose or swan-neck bends as seen in **Fig. 255** such bends being made on a pipe-bending machine or welded up from short pieces of tube. Most will have a stopper of some kind often in the form of a simple sliding or swivelling lid. Many vents will be fitted with patent tops that allow air to escape but serve other duties, too, **Fig. 256**. The modern ship will have a fair number of such vents. I counted more than fifty fitted to an oilrig standby vessel, virtually all of which were located against the bulwarks with a few close to superstructure sides.

Such small units are easily fashioned from styrene tube and sheet or made from brass rod and tube. Where a large number is needed it would be wise to make a master and cast the required number in white metal or even in resin. Make certain that the locations are correct and that each one is accessible as it would be on the full size ship.

Ventilators and ventilation of the ship is another matter. The earlier ships had ventilators serving the boiler and engine rooms of the cowl pattern as shown in **Fig. 258**. Some had mushroom pattern ventilators allowing air into the cabins of the accommodation, very few had forced air ventilation. Progressively as the ship and machinery developed, ventilation of the accommodation was carried out using fans usually sited on deck with trunking leading to the required areas although the engine and boiler rooms still relied upon the cowl ventilator. The cowl ventilator could be turned to allow the cowl to face into the wind and thus direct air into the space beneath, or it could be turned away from the wind when it effectively extracted air from the space beneath. In some places, such as the galley, ventilators such as the Fyffe type **Fig.261** would be used to release steam and heat from the cooking.

Cowl Pattern Ventilator

Fig. 258

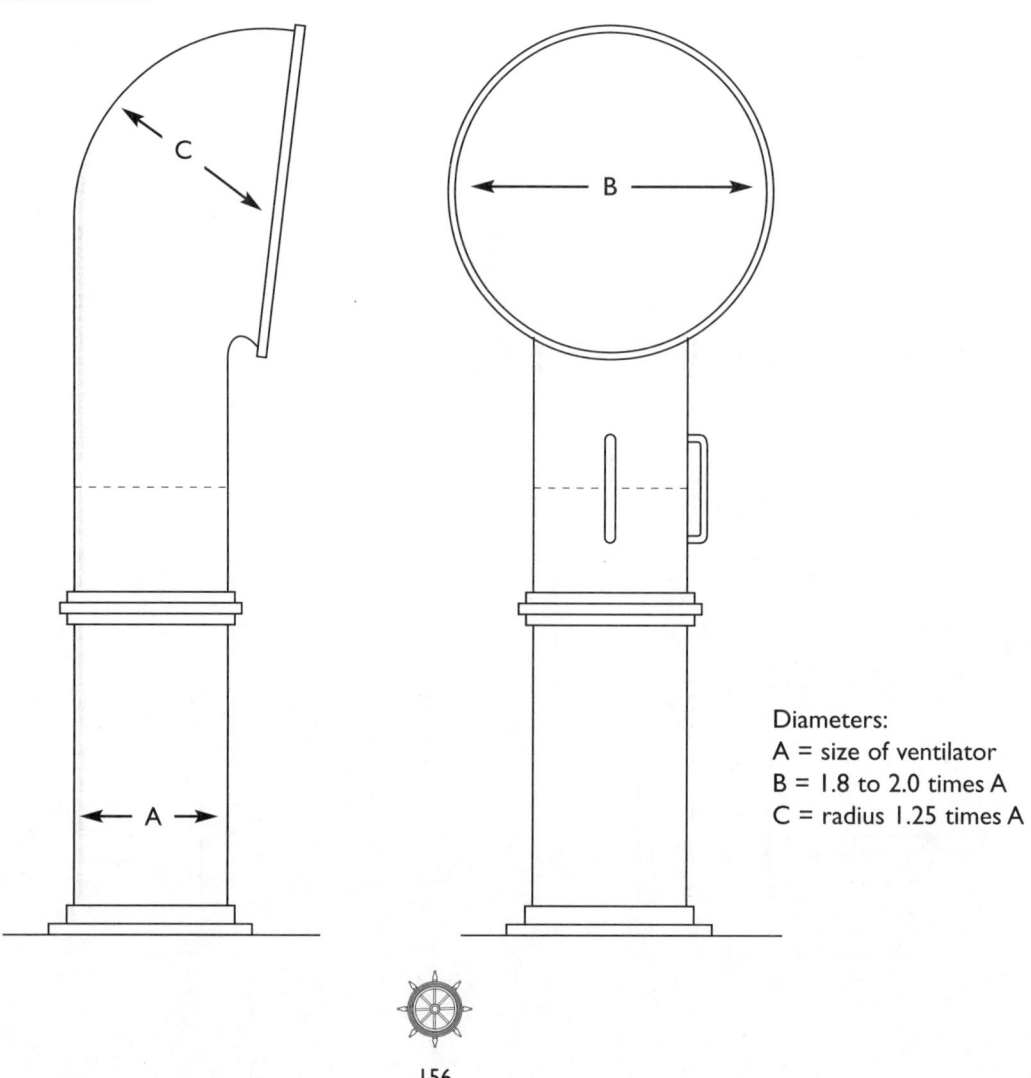

Diameters:
A = size of ventilator
B = 1.8 to 2.0 times A
C = radius 1.25 times A

Ventilation fans take many shapes and can be seen on the decks of many ships although today, most ships have their accommodation ventilated, cooled and heated from a forced ventilation system with the fans for both infeed and extraction contained in a special room usually called the Thermotank room. In this respect the word 'Thermotank', used in the same way as 'Hoover', is indicative of a vacuum cleaner both being the names of the inventors or designers. The Thermotank Company was the first to install such ventilation systems in ships. A Thermotank room is shown in the photographs here and the louvres to allow air into and from the fan space are clearly seen. It should be noted that the louvres have doors that can be closed if particularly heavy weather causes water to be a problem. In most cases the ventilation machinery room is located high on the vessel and usually close to the funnel. The funnel of the motor ship does usually have space in which trunking can be fitted and taken down into the accommodation.

Mushroom Pattern Ventilator

With radial type fan inside

Fig. 264

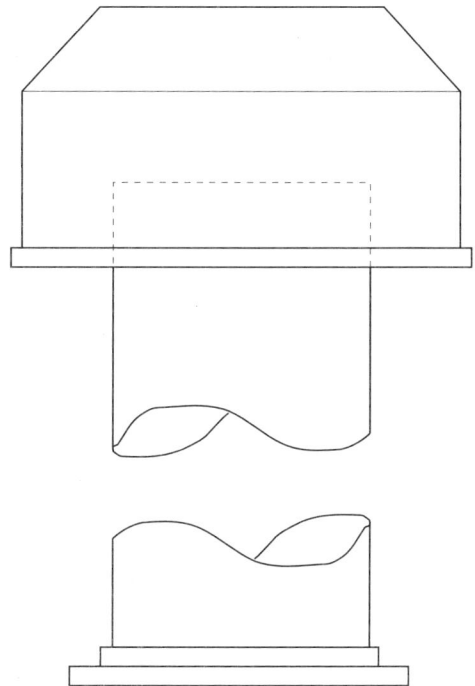

Deck Mounted Powered Ventilation Fan

For feeding air into an accommodation block

Fig. 265

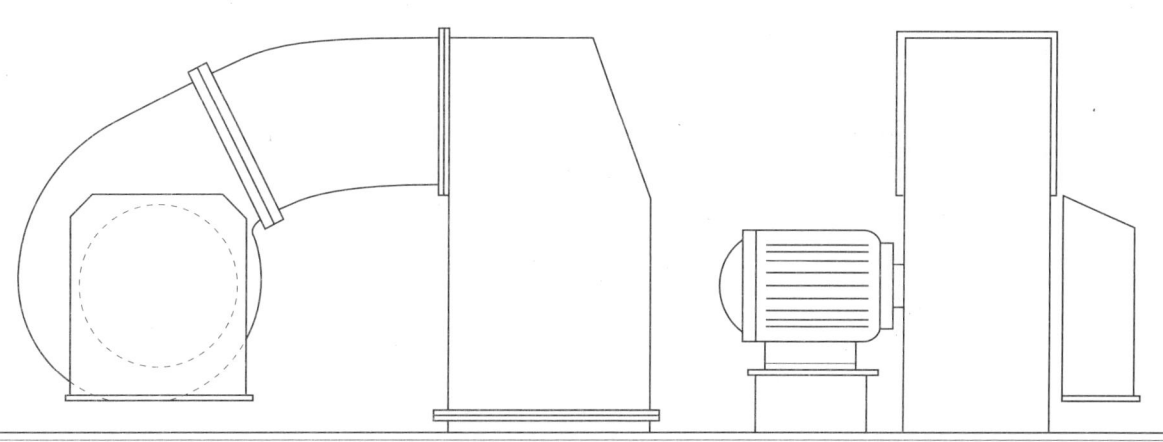

Cowl-type ventilators can be bought from most good model shops; they are produced by a number of manufacturers and vary in quality and size. It is possible to heat-mould the cowl using styrene sheet of about 1.0mm thick. A master must first be made of the dome shape in timber with allowance for the thickness of the sheet. A hole cut in a piece of 6.5mm plywood to accept the dome plug is needed again with allowance for the thickness of the styrene. Next a square of styrene should be taped over the plywood using masking or similar tape then, if the sheet styrene is gently heated with an electric paint stripper until it softens, the dome plug can be pushed into the hole and left until the styrene cools when a suitable cowl will be the result. This can then be attached to a suitably-shaped piece of styrene tube or a length of dowel to form the cowl ventilator.

Ventilation fans and trunking of the type shown in the sketches can be made from scrap pieces of styrene, tube and sheet and suitably painted once completed. There are some ships, particularly tugs in the U.S.A., that use large mushroom pattern ventilators containing radial fans to feed air into the machinery spaces **Fig. 264**. The model of the tug Akron has two such ventilators just aft of the funnel. **Fig. 265** illustrates a type of fan mounted on the decks of a ship and feeding fresh air into an accommodation block. Sometimes the trunking leading from this fan system would have a heater battery to preheat the air in cold weather.

Fig. 257 Gooseneck vent on a short sea trader.

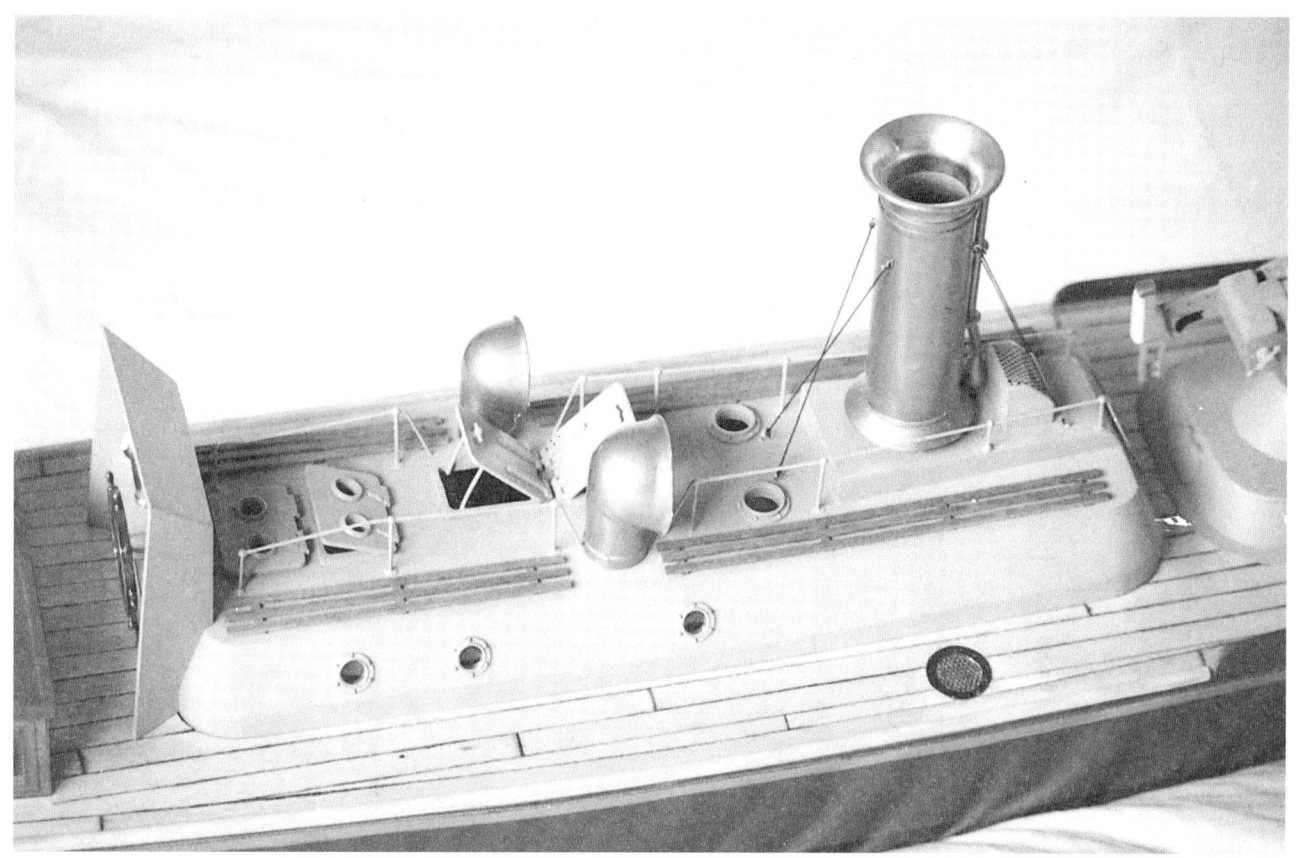
Fig. 259 Large cowl pattern ventilators on a model of a picket boat.

Fig. 260 A number of cowl ventilators on the model coaster ROVUMA.

Fig. 262 The Thermotank room on the motor ship JONRIX.

Fig. 263 Louvered air inlet opening with door to Thermotank room on the JONRIX.

Fig. 266 Three tank vents on a motor coaster.

Fig. 267 A battery of three tank vents, coloured for specific duty, on a motor ship.

WINCHES

Winches and windlasses are often confused by the uninitiated, but they are quite distinctive. A winch has a drum upon which rope is wound for the purpose of lifting or lowering a load and the drum, with its auxiliary parts, can be driven by a steam engine, an electric motor or a hydraulic motor. Small winches are quite often operated by hand. The windlass has a gypsy for

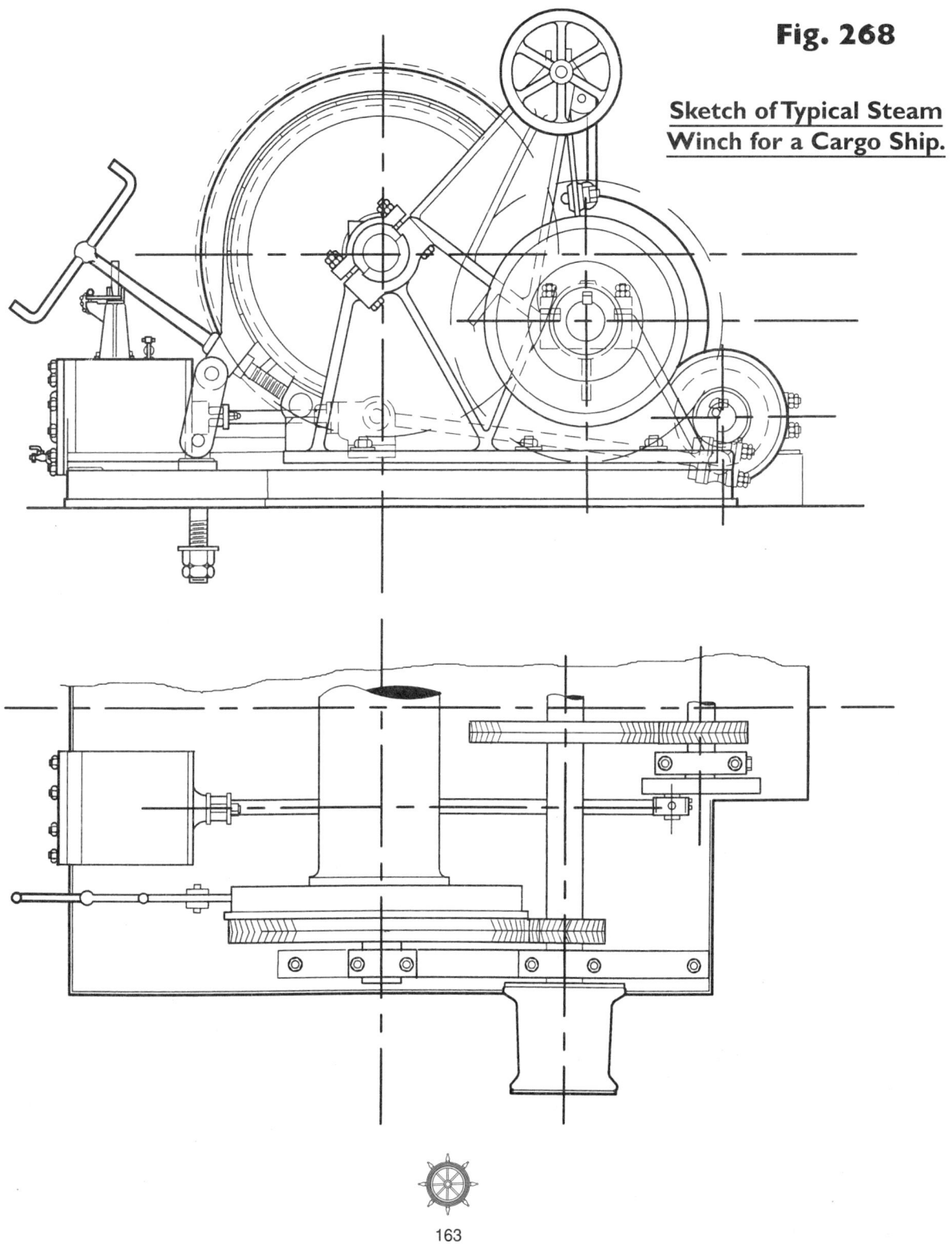

Fig. 268

Sketch of Typical Steam Winch for a Cargo Ship.

the purpose of lifting or lowering an anchor using the anchor cable; it does not have the facility of a drum for rope. In the same way as the winch, the windlass can be steam or motor driven and some small windlasses can be manually operated. Both units may have drums known as warping drums fitted on spindles extending to one or both sides of the unit.

Winches can be found on almost all types of ships. The early steam-driven coaster and cargo ships had steam-driven winches serving almost all the derricks and one type of steam winch is shown in **Fig. 268**. More modern ships were fitted with electric motor-driven winches for cargo handling and one type of such is shown in **Fig. 270**. The fishing vessel of today is almost

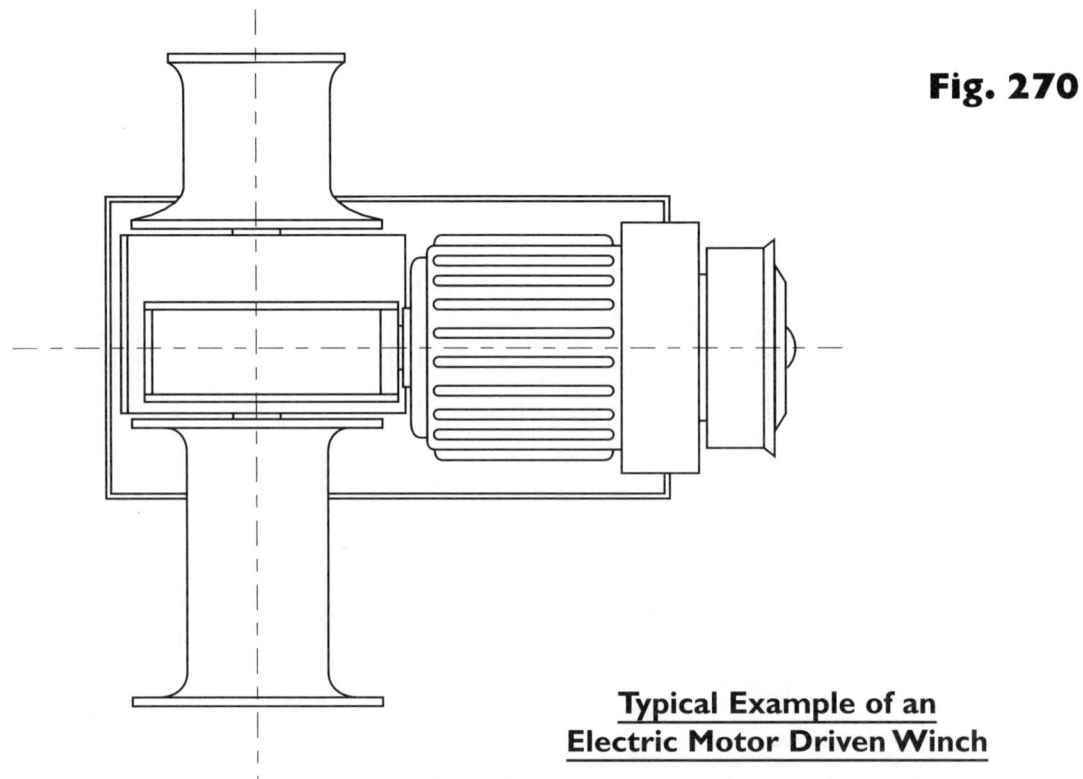

Fig. 270

Typical Example of an Electric Motor Driven Winch

Size is dictated by the haulage capacity in tons.

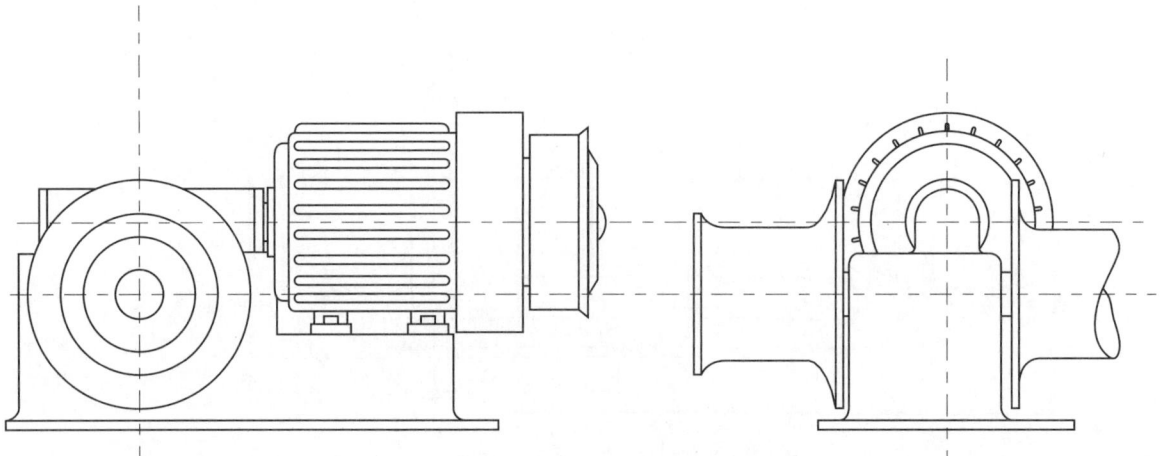

always fitted with winches driven hydraulically, as hydraulic motors are less prone to problems in freezing conditions. Stern trawlers, for example, have a number of winches for different tasks and some of these are shown in the sketches **Fig. 272**.

Several manufacturers produce model winches as miniature kits for different scales; some are of steam outline and others of electric motor outline. Some makers produce complete winches to scale in brass and some in resin or hard plastic. All are fine quality pieces and worth seeking if the scale suits. Making a model winch from scratch is not quite so easy but can be managed if one can use files and abrasives on timber or brass while turning the part in a drill.

Fig. 272
Hydraulically Driven 'Cod End' Winch for a Fishing Vessel

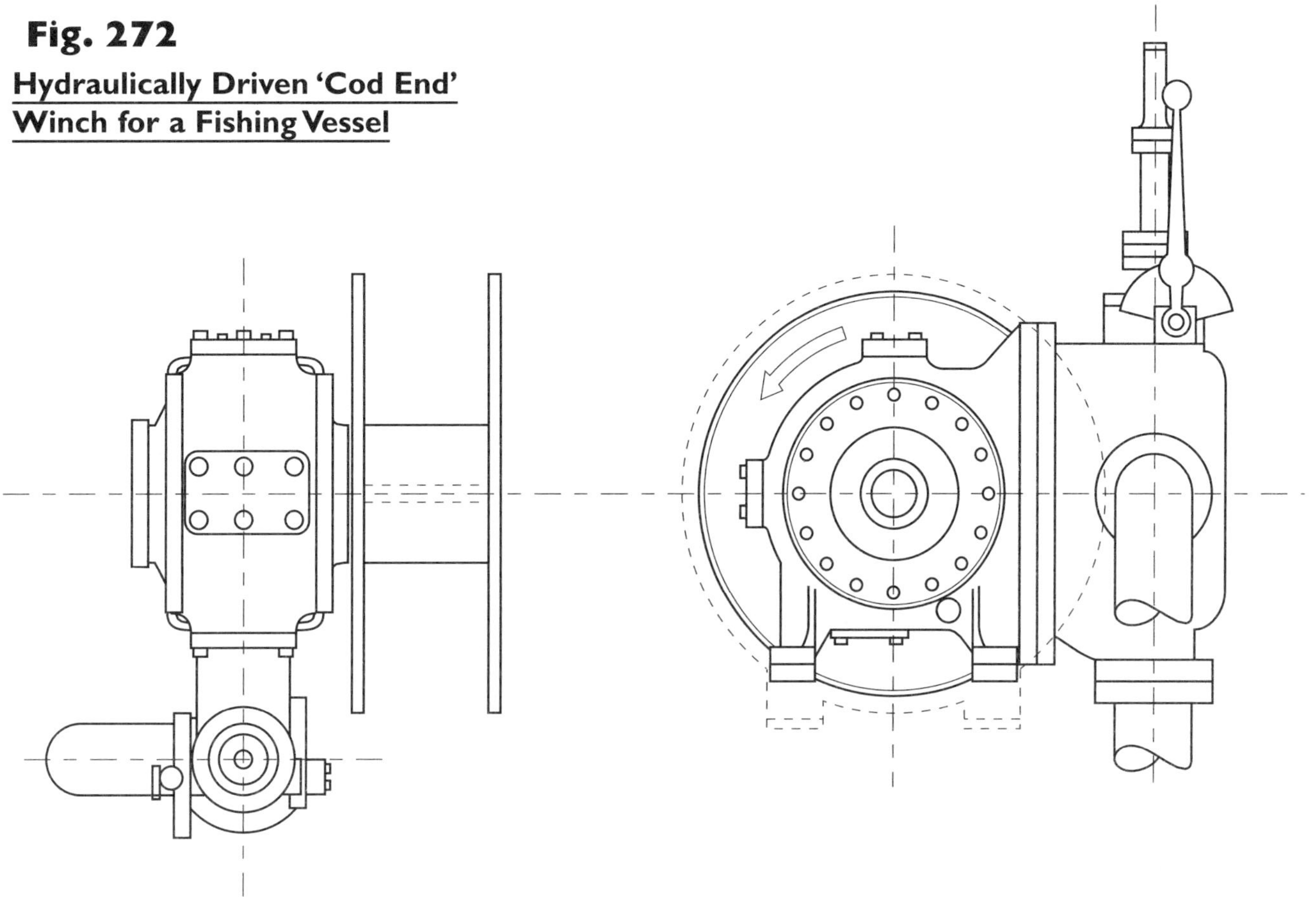

Fig. 271 Electric winches showing on the model of the coaster ARRAN MAIL.

Using a hand drill or an electric drill as a lathe does permit a degree of turning using soft materials and it is astonishing how successful one can be if a modicum of patience is used. Until comparatively recently all my turning was done using an electric drill in an old lathe mounting but I must admit that a lathe is extremely useful if one can justify the expense.

The warping drum of the winch or, for that matter, the windlass is a means of hauling ropes. The rope to be drawn is wrapped twice round the drum, the drum is set to turn and the operator pulls the rope by hand keeping the free end taut, the drum provides the force and draws the rope in. Used mainly to draw the ship to the wharf using the mooring ropes, the warping facility of the winch is easy to use and ideal for the duty. Once the ship is correctly positioned the mooring rope would be fastened over the nearest bollard. The photographs here and in other sections of this volume illustrate both winches and windlasses on a number of vessels. Small winches will be seen serving cranes and fitted to davits to permit the handling of lifeboats, some being power operated and others manually worked. Some winches are used exclusively for handling stores and similar small duties and others will be used for handling the boarding companion or similar ladder. The size and duties of the winch are manifold.

Fig. 274 Cod end winch with hydraulic motor on the stern trawler GLENROSE I.

Fig. 275 Auxiliary winch with hydraulic motor on the stern trawler GLENROSE I.

Fig. 276 Net winch as fitted to GLENROSE I.

Fig. 277 Main trawl winch on the model of the side fishing trawler KINGSTON PERIDOT.

WINDLASSES

As mentioned previously the windlass is used mainly for anchor handling and is designed for this purpose. The warping drums are useful additions to the windlass as a means of handling the mooring ropes at the forecastle. On some ships, although rare to the size considered in this volume, there would be a stern anchor and then a windlass or capstan with a gypsy would be installed on the stern of the vessel. Windlasses come in a variety of sizes obviously to suit the size of anchor carried by the ship. Some ships have twin anchors one on each side of the bows, and the windlass will be fitted with twin gypsies to handle the two anchor cables. Some small ships have only one ready-to-use anchor generally mounted on the port side of the bow and here one would find a windlass with a single gypsy.

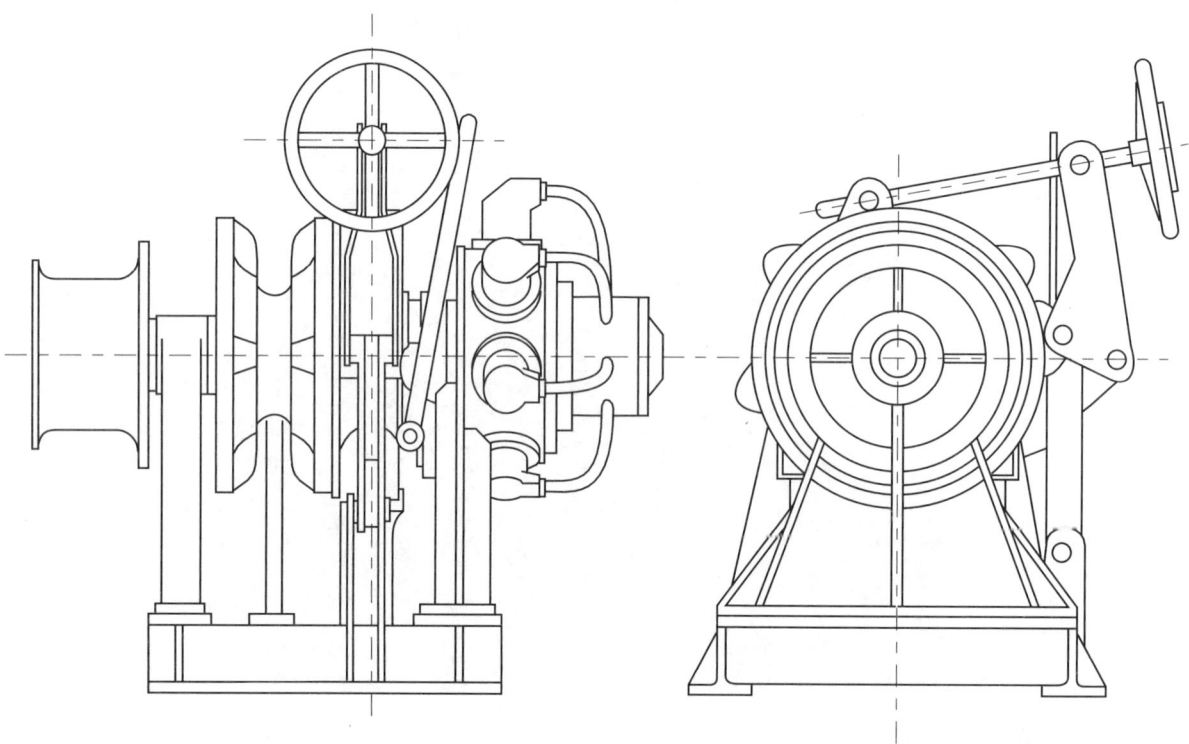

Fig. 278

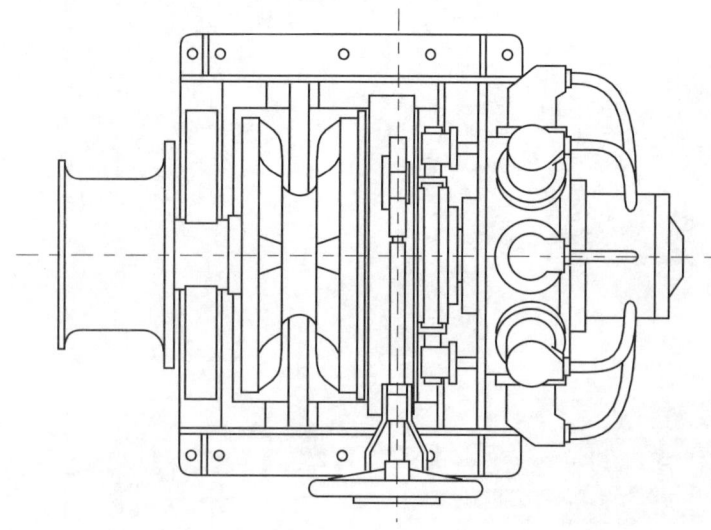

Windlas with Single Gypsy

To handle single anchor cable

In the same way as the winch, the windlass can be powered by a steam engine or by electric or hydraulic motors. The photographs depict some windlasses full size and some in model form, the sketch **Fig. 278** shows a windlass for a single anchor installation and **Fig. 279** shows a standard windlass for twin cables. Both are of the hydraulic-drive type.

However, there are some instances where a windlass is not fitted and where the anchor cable is handled by a capstan fitted with a suitable gypsy. **Figs. 282 & 283** illustrate capstans so fitted; one of which is driven from a motor located below deck and the other by a hydraulic motor inside the drum of the unit. In both cases the anchor cable must have a guided run to the capstan through the chain stopper and thence to the chain locker below decks.

While winches have disappeared from some coasters that are now dependent upon shore facilities for loading and loading, the windlass is still a common item of deck machinery. Anchor capstans, other than those for warping only, are rarely found on small ships of the type included here.

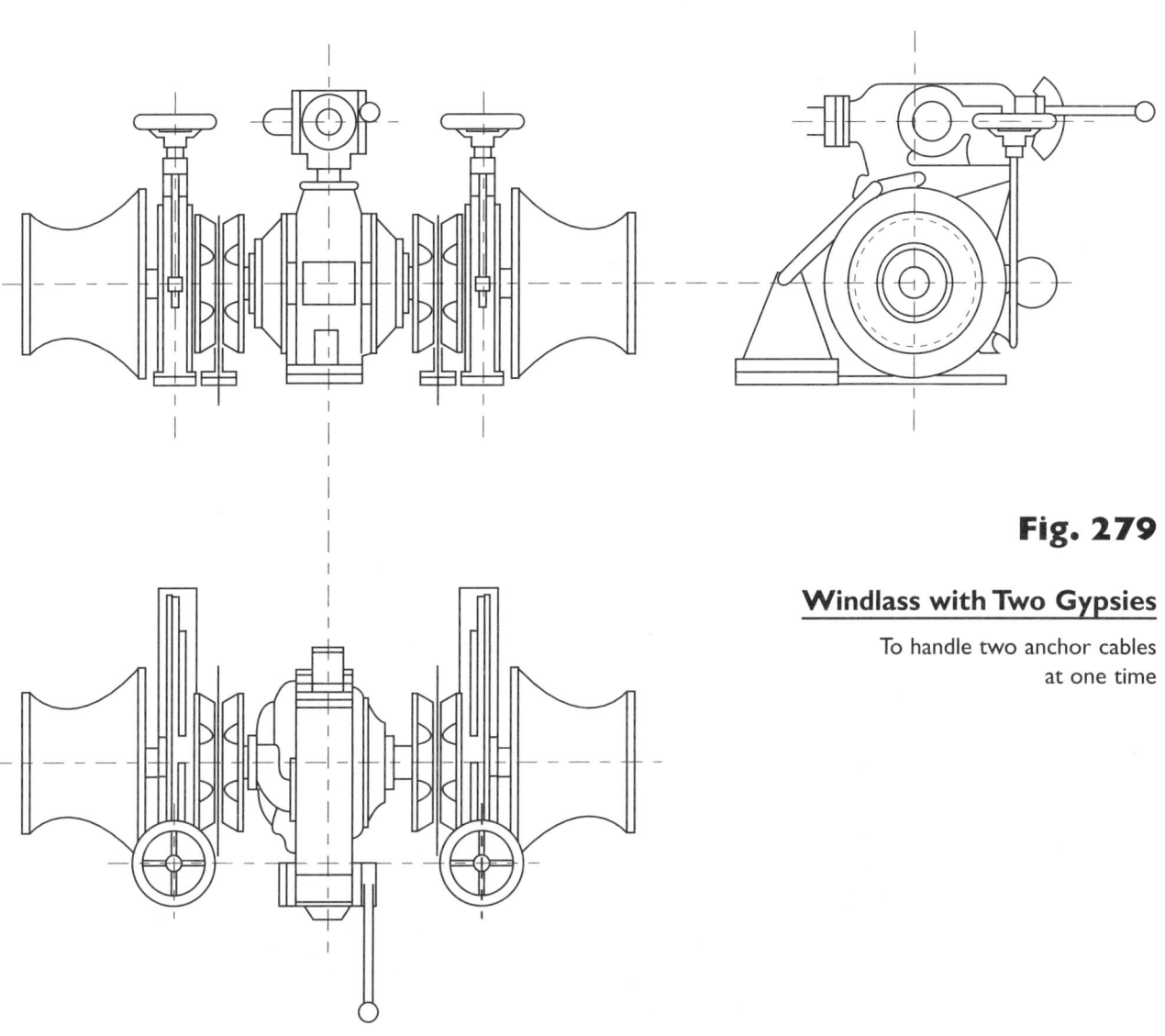

Fig. 279

Windlass with Two Gypsies

To handle two anchor cables at one time

Fig. 280 Windlass on the stern trawler GLENROSE I with single gypsy, warping drum and hydraulic motor.

Fig. 281 Windlass on the bunkering tanker RIX HARRIER with twin gypsies, and warping drums.
Note the guide sheave on the steel pedestal.

Anchor Capstan with Under Deck Drive

Fig. 282

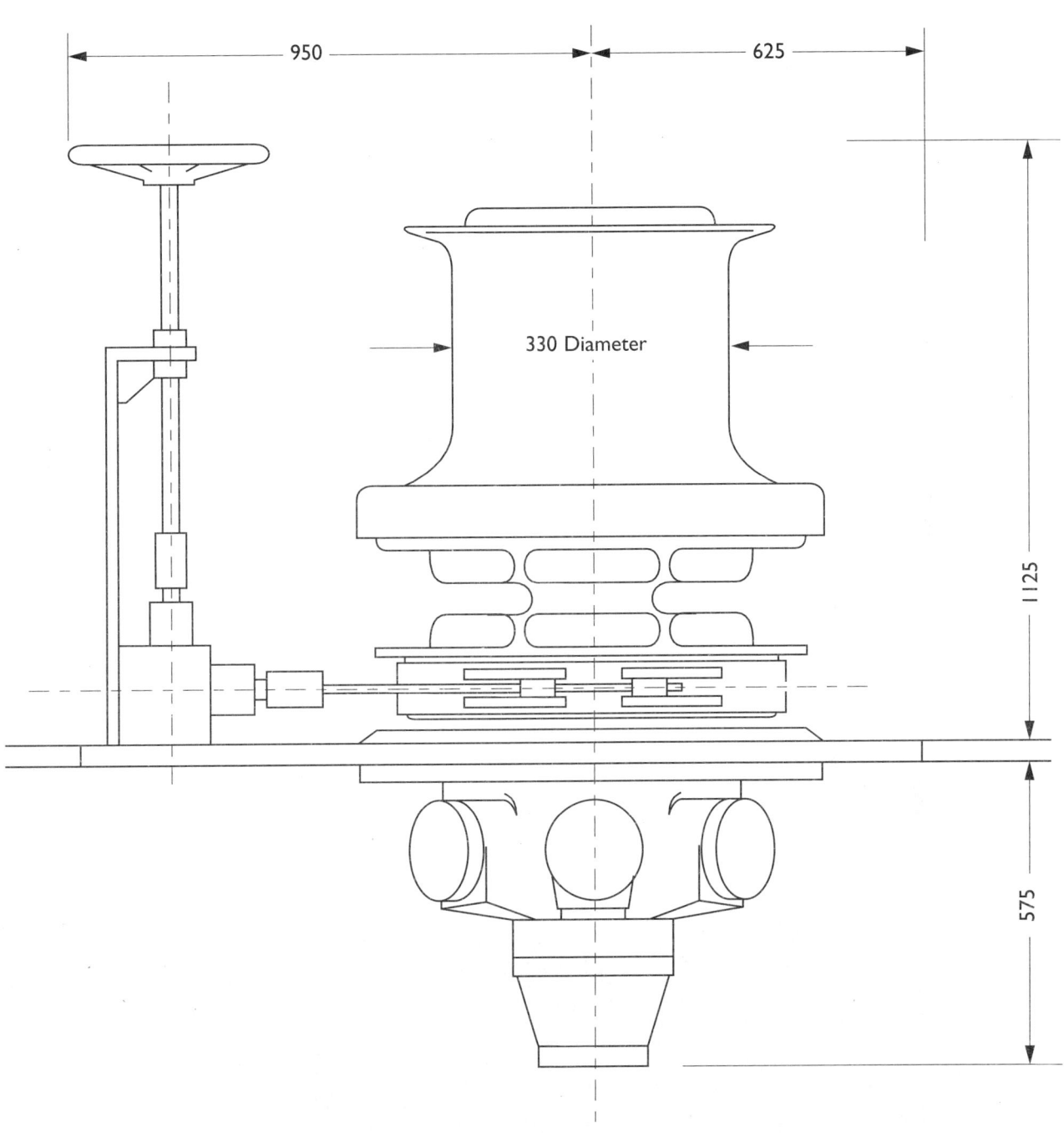

Dimensions in Millimetres

Fig. 283

Anchor Handling Capstan
With internally fitted motor

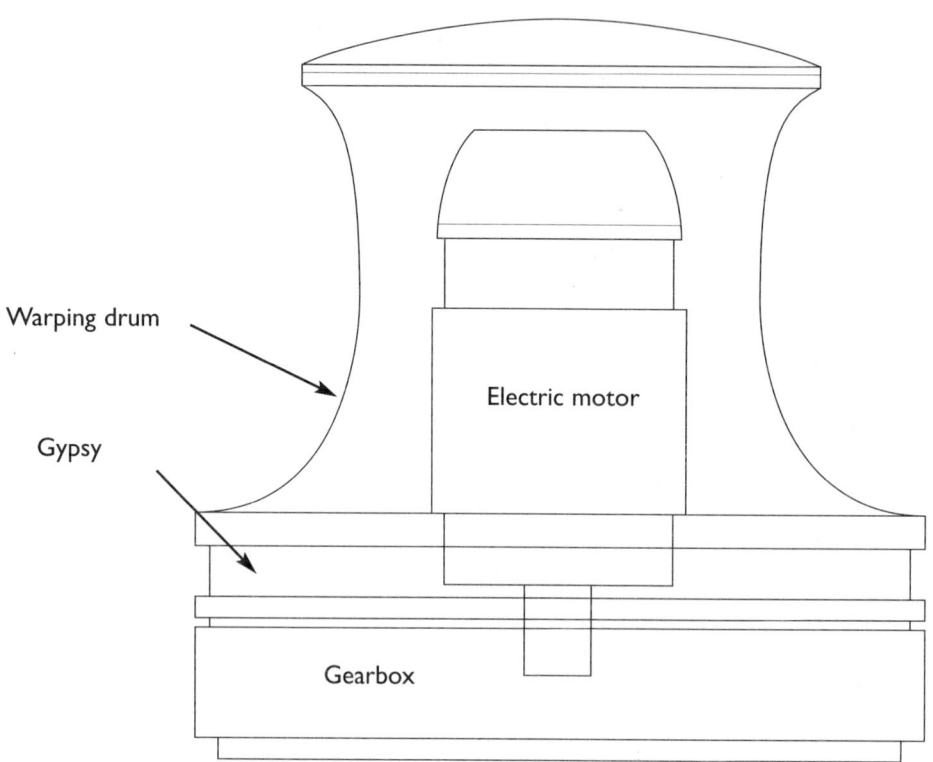

Warping drum

Gypsy

Electric motor

Gearbox

Fig. 2847 Windlass with rope winding drums in addition to warping drums on the motor ship JONRIX.

Fig. 285 JONRIX windlass of Fig.284 from a different view point.

APPENDICES

SOURCES & REFERENCE

British Steam Tugs
Waine Research Publications.
P.N. Thomas

Steam Coasters & Short Sea Traders
Waine Research Publications.
C.V. Waine & R.S. Fenton

From Tree to Sea
Terence Dalton.
Ted Frost

The Golden Age of Shipping
Conway Maritime Press.

Shipping Wonders of the World
Amalgamated Press.
edited by Clarence Winchester

SPECIALIST SUPPLIERS

Shops Specialising in Model Ships - Kits and Materials.

Westbourne Model Centre, 41 Seamoor Road, Westbourne, Bournemouth, Dorset. BH4 9AE.
Tel:- 01202 763480

Bagnalls Models, 18, Salter Street, Stafford, ST16 2JU
Tel:- 01785 223349.

E. Radestock (mail order only) Dept. 1, Government Road, Wirral, CH47 2DB.

The Model Dockyard, (mail order only) 17, Tremorvah Barton, Tregolls Rd, Truro, Cornwall, TR1 1NN
Tel:- 01872 261755.

Midway Models, 157, St. Leonards Road, Leicester, LE2 3BZ
Tel:- 01162 701609.

The Dockyard Model Shop, Ordnance Mews Craft Centre, The Historic Dockyard, Chatham, Kent ME4 4TE
Tel:- 01634 830404.

Manufacturers of Model Ship Kits.

Deans Marine, Conquest Drove, Farcet Fen, Peterborough PE7 3DH.
Tel:- 01733 244166.

Model Slipway, 77, Arundell Drive, Lundwood, Barnsley S71 5LE.
Tel:- 01226 770008.

Mount Fleet Models, Laurel Mount, 79 Holmfirth Road, Meltham, Huddersfield HD7 3D
Tel:- 01484 851569.

Jotika Ltd., Caldercraft, Unit 7, Highgrove Farm, Pinvin, Worcs. WR10 2LF.

R M Marine, Chester House, The Dingle, Colwyn Bay, LL29 7SN.
Tel:- 01492 534347.

Billings - UK Agents - Amerang Ltd., Commerce Way, Lancing, West Sussex BN15 8TE.
Tel:- 01903 765496

Robbe - Robbe Schluter U.K. Unit 53, Hinckley Workspace, Southfield Road, Hinckley, Leicester LE10 2AS.

Graupner - UK Agents, Ripmax Ltd., Ripmax Corner, Green Street, Enfield. EN3 7SJ.

Midwest Products (USA) - UK Agents, J.Perkins Distribution Ltd.,

Artesania Latina - UK Agents, Riko Ltd., Hemel Hempstead.

NOTE:- *Most kits produced by the above can be found in good model shops.*

Specialist Marine Model Equipment.

Electronise Design, 2, Hillside Road, Sutton Coldfield, B74 4DQ
Tel:- 01213 085877.
Electronic speed controllers, motors, switches, etc.

Action, 140 Holme Court Avenue, Biggleswade, Beds. SG18 8PB.
Electronic speed controllers, switches, sound equipment, etc.

James Lane (Display Models), 30, The Broadway, Blyth, Northumberland, NE24 2PP.
Etched rails, stanchions, ladders, etc.

Quaycraft, Harbour Cottage, 2, Quayfield Road, Ilfracombe, North Devon. EX34 9EN.
Tel:- 01271 866837.
Scale model ships boats in various sizes - very high quality.

Precision Controls, 3 Chantry Avenue, Bideford, Devon. EX39 2QW.
Tel:- 01237 476820
Fine scale ships fittings in brass and resin.

Marcle Models, Turnagain, Finch Lane, Amersham, Bucks. HP7 9NE
Tel:-01494 765910
Ship model kits of fine quality card.

Model Marine Steam Plants

Unit Steam Engines, The Coach House, Rose Cottage, London Road, Mickleham, Surrey. RH5 6EH.
Tel:- 01372 378075.

Stour Valley Steam Engines, Applecroft, Watery Lane, Pillerton Hersey, Warwick CV35 0QP.
Tel:- 01789 740371.

Cheddar Models Ltd., Sharpham Road, Cheddar, Somerset. BS27 3DR.
Tel:- 01934 744634.

Propellers and Shafts

The Prop Shop, Unit 5, Alscot Park Stables, Preston-on-Stour, Warwickshire, CV37 8BL.
Tel:- 01789 450905.

E.Radestock, (see above).

MAGAZINES AND PLANS

Model Boats - magazine . Nexus Special Interests, Nexus House, Azalea Drive, Swanley BR8 8HU.
Also has plans service. Tel:- 01322 660070.

Marine Modelling International - magazine. Traplet Publications Ltd., Traplet House,
Severn Drive, Upton-upon-Severn, Worcs. WR8 0JL
Tel:- 01684 594505.
Also has plans service.

Model Shipwright - magazine, quarterly see model press for latest address and
telephone number.

Jecobin Plans Service, 31, Romans Way, Pyrford, Woking, Surrey. GU22 8TR.

Bow Wave Marine Models, 13, Ludlow Close, Bridgwater TA6 6BZ.
Tel:- 01278 459837.

Modele Reduit De Bateau - French model boat plans.

David Macgregor Plans, 12 Upper Oldfield Park, Bath BA2 3JZ.

Taubman Plans Service International, 11, College Drive, Jersey City, New Jersey. 07305 U.S.A.

LIST OF ILLUSTRATIONS & DRAWINGS

Fig. I	ACADEMUS a scallop dredging fishing vessel built in 1998.	vi
Fig. II	Model of the scallop dredger ACADEMUS built for presentation to the owner.	vii
Fig. III	Working model of the stern trawler GLENROSE I.	vii
Fig. IV	Steam driven model open steam launch MARVON QUEEN.	viii
Fig. V	Model pilot cutter, steam driven. CHIMAERA.	ix
Fig. VI	Model of CHIMAERA completed and ready for testing.	x
Fig. VII	Prize winning working model of the twin screw coaster ARRAN MAIL built by the author.	x
Fig. VIII	Model of SEGUIN under way.	x
Fig. IX	Model of luxury sailing yacht INGA IV.	xi
Fig. X	Model of HM Customs & Excise cutter BADGER in rough water.	xii
Fig. 1	Typical arrangement of single wire radio aerial between masts on early ship.	1
Fig. 2	Typical arrangement of twin wire radio aerial system for increased range of signals.	1
Fig. 3	Main mast of short sea trader showing aerials, radar etc.	2
Fig. 4	Mast and detail of aerials on stern trawler GLENROSE I.	2
Fig. 5	Mast and aerial detail on an inshore fishing vessel.	2
Fig. 6	Sketch of porcelain aerial insulator.	3
Fig. 7	Model of main mast for a small trawler.	3
Fig. 8	Model of main mast for an inshore fishing vessel.	3
Fig. 9	Hall anchor shown drawn snugly into hawse pipe of a cargo vessel.	4
Fig. 10	Spare anchor fitted behind substantial frame on foredeck of cargo ship - note measuring rod.	4
Fig. 11	Sketch of 'Hall' anchor with dimensions etc.	5
Fig. 11A	Some dimensions of 'Hall' anchors.	5
Fig. 12	Spare anchor on foredeck of trawler GLENROSE I.	6
Fig. 13	Sketch of modern high holding power anchor.	6
Fig. 14	Sketch of early common stocked anchor.	6
Fig. 15	Danforth anchor seen frequently on small vessels such as cabin cruisers.	6
Fig. 16	Typical arrangement of anchor davit.	7
Fig. 17	Typical arrangement of anchor crane.	7
Fig. 18	Anchor davit on bow of a model steam yacht.	8
Fig. 19	Binnacle on top of wheelhouse of a small model coaster illustrating weather cover open.	9
Fig. 20	Binnacle with voice pipe and telegraph for fitting into the wheelhouse of a coastal tug model.	9
Fig. 21	Sketch of main towing bitt.	10
Fig. 22	Sketch of forward bitt.	11
Fig. 23	Towing bitts on a model tug where the bitts were added for secure towing.	11
Fig. 24	Sketch of typical double bollard.	12
Fig. 25	Table of sizes for double bollards.	13
Fig. 26	Quadruple bollards on the stern deck of a cargo vessel.	13
Fig. 27	Double bollard unit on a coastal motor ship.	14
Fig. 28	Double bollard on foredeck of short sea trader (Note measuring rod)	14
Fig. 29	Single bollards or mooring posts aft of windlass on model coaster ARRAN MAIL.	14
Fig. 30	Bulbous bow showing on a fishing trawler.	16
Fig. 31	Fishing vessel under construction showing framing for bow bulb.	16
Fig. 32	Bow of coaster showing depth marks in metres and in Arabic script. (Photo courtesy of D.Milton)	16
Fig. 33	Sketch of marks that are placed on or near the bow of a vessel fitted with bulb and bow thruster.	15
Fig. 34	Section of timber bulwarks with capping.	17
Fig. 35.	Section of steel bulwark with timber top rail.	17
Fig. 36	Typical arrangement of self-closing wash port in steel bulwarks.	17
Fig. 37	Bulwarks on a steel ship showing stays, cleats and tank vents.	19
Fig. 38	Starboard side of the LIZRIX showing continuous wash port opening.	18
Fig. 40	Model of American all wood steam tug showing timberheads and bulwark rails.	19
Fig. 41	Timberheads fitted round bulwarks of a model herring drifter prior to fitting timber rail.	20
Fig. 42	Timberheads on the bulwarks of a model herring drifter.	20
Fig. 43	Model of coaster under construction showing bulwark stays and wash ports.	20
Fig. 44	Sketch of typical cable stopper of the drop bar pattern.	21
Fig. 45	Screw pattern cable stopper on a modern coaster - port side.	22
Fig. 46	Screw pattern cable stopper on a modern coaster - starboard side.	22
Fig. 47	Screw pattern cable stopper closed on cable on the stern trawler GLENROSE I.	23
Fig. 48	Typical capstan with anchor cable gypsy for a small ship.	24
Fig. 49	Electric capstan on the stern of a motor coaster.	26
Fig. 50	Model of a steam capstan for a model herring drifter.	25
Fig. 51	Capstan on the stern of an oil rig support ship.	26
Fig. 5	MV TIMRIX in dry dock showing 'Hall' anchor and bow depth marks.	25
Fig. 53	Typical stud link chain cable	27
Fig. 54	Anchor cable on a vehicular ferry.	27
Fig. 55	Sketch of Horn cleat.	28
Fig. 56	Sketch of belaying cleat.	28
Fig. 57	Bulwarks of a model herring drifter showing Cavils.	28
Fig. 58	Model of a small crane for handling a rigid inflatable boat 29(R.I.B.)	29
Fig. 59	Hydraulic crane with net haul on a seine net boat.	29

Fig. 60	Small cargo crane for handling stores etc. on a merchant vessel.	30
Fig. 61.	Base of hydraulic crane for handling fish boxes and baskets on a stern trawler.	30
Fig. 62	Middle section of the same crane.	31
Fig. 63	Top section of the fish handling crane.	31
Fig. 64	Radial davits on a model of the tug SEGUIN.	33
Fig. 65	Radial pattern davits for the lifeboats on the model of ARRAN MAIL.	34
Fig. 66	Quadrant davits on the model steam coaster ROVUMA.	34
Fig. 67	Typical arrangements of quadrant, crescent and 'Lum' davits.	35
Fig. 68	'Caley' davit on the oilrig support ship SCOTT GUARDIAN.	35
Fig. 69	'Caley' davit on the oilrig ship shown prior to loading the rescue boat.	36
Fig. 70	Typical arrangement of Gravity type davits.	36
Fig. 71	Totally enclosed lifeboat stowed on slip of large coaster.	37
Fig. 72	Typical arrangement of enclosed lifeboat on stern slipway	38
Fig. 73	Planked decks of a model pilot cutter showing waterways.	39
Fig. 74	Forecastle deck of a model coaster showing smooth plate finish, windlass, cable stoppers etc.	39
Fig. 75	Sketch showing how deck planks were knibbed at the covering boards or waterways.	40
Fig. 76	Sketch showing the shift of butts in deck planking.	40
Fig. 77	Detail of tank deck on a model coastal bunkering tanker showing array of pipes, valves etc.	41
Fig. 78	Twin sheaved fairlead fitted on a platform in the bulwarks of a motor coaster.	44
Fig. 79	Fairleads on the foredeck of a model stern trawler.	45
Fig. 80	Roller fairlead built into the bulwarks of the motor vessel JONRIX.	45
Fig. 81	Panama pattern fairlead built into the bulwarks of a ferry.	45
Fig. 82	Panama pattern fairlead on a model steam coaster.	46
Fig. 83	Open fairleads on a model of a steam coaster.	46
Fig. 84	Standard pattern open fairlead.	43
Fig. 85	A double sheaved fairlead.	44
Fig. 86	Fire valve and tank vent on a small motor ship.	47
Fig. 87	Range of three fire valves on a short sea trader.	47
Fig. 88	Sketch of a typical fire monitor.	48
Fig. 89	Fire monitor on the bridge top of an oilrig support ship.	49
Fig. 90	Working model fire monitor (Courtesy Graupner)	49
Fig. 91	Fire pipeline and valve on bunkering tanker RIX HARRIER.	50
Fig. 92	Fire monitor on the oilrig support ship SCOTT GUARDIAN.	50
Fig. 93	Funnel on model of steam pilot cutterl.	51
Fig. 94.	Funnel for model of steam tug CRUISER.	52
Fig. 95	The very prominent and almost square funnel of the motor ship LIZRIX.	52
Fig. 96	Typical funnel for a steam ship with guy band and wire stays.	52
Fig. 97	Typical funnel for a motor ship.	53
Fig. 98	A small circular hatch on the forecastle of a coastal motor ship.	56
Fig. 99	Detail of the main hatch with tarpaulin cover and flat steel securing bars on the model of ARRAN MAIL.	56
Fig. 100	A cargo of timber stowed on the steel hatch covers of the motor ship LIZRIX.	56
Fig. 101	Details of the hatch coamings, stays, and covers with chains and pulleys on the LIZRIX.	57
Fig. 102.	Hatches of the MacGregor pattern being drawn open by winch on the LIZRIX.	58
Fig. 103	Winch used for drawing hatch covers open.	58
Fig. 104	Alternative to the winch mounting of Fig.103	58
Fig. 105	After end of hatch on a motor ship showing covers, guide rails and fire pipes.	57
Fig. 106	Sketch of hatch coaming with brackets for securing bars and wedges.	55
Fig. 107	Hawse box with 'Hall' anchor stowed on a stern trawler. Note reinforced edges of the hawse box.	59
Fig. 108	Suggested method of making model hawse pipesl.	59
Fig. 109	Joining two sections of keel together using a scarf joint and trenails.	60
Fig. 110	Fitting stern post to keel.	60
Fig. 111	Stern of the model showing frames and deadwood (4 & 5)	61
Fig. 112	Completed keel and frame assembly - model is a wooden herring drifter.	61
Fig. 113	Method of planking over frames.	62
Fig. 114	Stern of model almost completed and showing fitting of balsa blocks.	62
Fig. 115	Keel and frames of model tug SEGUIN set up and prepared for planking.	63
Fig. 116	Typical lines drawing prepared for a fishing vessel.	65
Fig. 117	Typical General Arrangement drawing of a fishing vessel and prepared for modellers.	66
Fig. 118	Bow of a short sea trader showing welding of plates.	63
Fig. 119	The side of a motor ship showing effects of plate welding.	63
Fig. 120	Portable companion for boarding on a model paddle steamer.	69
Fig. 121	Companion leading from well deck to forecastle on model coaster, treads and risers from Plastruct range	69
Fig. 122	Vertical ladder to wheelhouse roof on model coaster.	69
Fig. 123	Companion on stern of model coaster ARRAN MAIL.	70
Fig. 124	Companion ladders on the stern of the motor vessel JONRIX.	70
Fig. 125	A very substantial welded steel companionway leading down to the cargo deck of a motor ship.	71
Fig. 126	Welded rungs on a post to give access to the post top.	71
Fig. 127	A substantial companion with hand rails on an oilrig support ship.	71
Fig. 128	A GRP lifeboat on the port side of the JONRIX .	73
Fig. 129	Close-up detail of the GRP. lifeboat on the JONRIX.	74
Fig. 130	Detail of one of the winches fitted to the JONRIX for raising and lowering the lifeboats.	75
Fig. 131	A model lifeboat suspended from radial davits on the port side of a model pilot cutter.	74
Fig. 132	Model herring drifter showing dinghy used as a lifeboat	77
Fig. 133	Typical arrangement of lifeboat falls.	76
Fig. 134	Model lifeboat cast in resin and supplied by Quaycraft	77

Fig. 135	Sketch of a typical totally enclosed lifeboat	78
Fig. 136	Model lifeboat under construction.	78
Fig. 137	A chute mounted, 'dayglow' orange lifebuoy with self igniting light on the starboard bridge wing of JONRIX.	79
Fig. 138	Red and white painted lifebuoys on a model tug.	79
Fig. 139	A lifebuoy in a chute on the bridge wing of an oilrig support ship.	80
Fig. 140	Clear stowage of a lifebuoy on a model motor coaster.	80
Fig. 141	A liferaft canister cradle prepared and awaiting the canister to be fitted.	81
Fig. 142	Liferaft canister mounted on the starboard side of a bunkering tanker.	81
Fig. 143	Liferaft canister on a fishing vessel.	82
Fig. 144	Liferaft of timber on the superstructure of the model of the Customs launch BADGER.	82
Fig. 145	A fine view of the motor ship TIMRIX clearly showing lifebuoys, liferafts and lifeboats on the superstructure.	82
Fig. 146	Lights on a motor ship, the upper to indicate towing and the lower is the stern navigation light.	83
Fig. 147	Stern light unit on a motor ship.	83
Fig. 148	Main mast on a fishing vessel with lights.	86
Fig. 149	Sketch of mast of fishing vessel GLENROSE I showing lights with colours and appropriate legend.	84
Fig. 150	Sketch of typical arrangement of lights for an oilrig vessel or large tug.	85
Fig. 151	Starboard light box on model coaster showing both electric and oil pattern lamps	87
Fig. 153	Lights on main mast and gantry of stern trawler ONWARD CHALLENGER.	87
Fig. 154	Sketch of Derrick mountings and swivels.	89
Fig. 155	Samson post with topping blocks and derrick.	90
Fig. 156	Mast, spars and deckhouse for a model pilot cutter.	91
Fig. 157	Main mast and loading derrick for a model steam tug.	91
Fig. 158	Lower section of foremast on a modern motor ship.	91
Fig. 159	Middle section of the mast shown in Fig. 158.	92
Fig. 160	Tripod foremast with derrick and swivel on a fishing vessel under construction.	94
Fig. 161	Samson post with two derricks on the stern trawler DOROTHY GRAY.	92
Fig. 162	Typical blocks for marine duty.	93
Fig. 163	Sketch of typical mooring pipe with sizes.	96
Fig. 164	Mooring pipe in the bulwarks of a large coaster.	95
Fig. 165	Plimsoll line and markings on the side of a small coastal vessel.	95
Fig. 166	Stern deck of the motor ship TIMRIX showing capstan, bollards and mooring pipe at extreme right.	96
Fig. 167	Paddle wheel of a large model showing operating linkage to feathering paddles.	98
Fig. 168	A selection of brass propellers - courtesy of the 'Prop Shop'.	99
Fig. 169	A four-blade propeller fitted to the hull of a model tug.	99
Fig. 170	Four-blade propeller fitted to a model fishing vessel.	101
Fig. 171	Spare propeller fastened to the superstructure of the motor vessel LIZRIX.	100
Fig. 172	Stern of model fishing vessel showing Kort nozzle and propeller.	101
Fig. 173	View of GLENROSE I in dry-dock illustrating Kort nozzle, rudder etc.	102
Fig. 174	Schottel drive unit in model form - courtesy of Graupner.	103
Fig. 175	Two types of water jet units in model form available from Graupner - courtesy of Graupner.	104
Fig. 176	Model hull with two propeller shafts & couplings installed to allow model steam plant.	104
Fig. 177	Some types of electric motor available to the model ship builder.	105
Fig. 178	Electric motor mounted with reduction gearing.	105
Fig. 179	Twin cylinder slide valve steam engine and gas fired boiler.	106
Fig. 180	Steam plant of Maxwell Hemmens manufacture installed in a slender model steam yacht.	107
Fig. 181	Vertical boiler and twin cylinder steam engine in a model open steam launch.	107
Fig. 182	A Cheddar Models 'Proteus' steam outfit in the hull of the model side fishing trawler KINGSTON PERIDOT.	108
Fig. 183	A Stour Valley Steam outfit suitable for installing in a model ship. By courtesy of Stour Valley.	108
Fig. 184	Maxwell Hemmens 'V' four cylinder steam outfit fitted into the hull of a model steam launch.	109
Fig. 185	An azimuth thruster on an oilrig support vessel.	109
Fig. 186	A hand pump with capped outlet on the side of the superstructure of a small fishing boat.	110
Fig. 187	A model water pump for 6 volt DC supply - courtesy Robbe Schluter UK Ltd.	110
Fig. 188	Radar units on the main mast of an oilrig ship.	111
Fig. 189	Radar unit in a casing on a small oil tanker.	111
Fig. 190	Typical guard rails with stanchion. (Ball pattern)	114
Fig. 191	Typical guard rails with stanchion. (Flat bar pattern).	114
Fig. 192	Typical guard rails with timber top rail.	114
Fig. 193	Flat bar stanchions and welded hand rails on a fishing vessel.	112
Fig. 194	Flat bar stanchions and rails on the forecastle of a fishing vessel.	113
Fig. 195.	Rails and stanchions modelled in styrene strip and rod for a small static model fishing boat.	113
Fig. 196	View of large diameter top rail and smaller diameter lower rails on a fishing vessel.	113
Fig. 197	Flat bar stanchions, some with braces, on the fishing vessel DENEBULA.	115
Fig. 198	Rails, stanchions, platforms and companions on an oilrig support ship.	115
Fig. 199	Sketch showing deadeyes and lanyards for tensioning standing rigging.	116
Fig. 200	Sketch showing rigging screw for tensioning standing rigging.	117
Fig. 201	Foremast of model side fishing trawler showing standing rigging with ratlines.	118
Fig. 202	Main mast of model yacht SKEANDHU showing shelf, deadeyes and chainplates.	118
Fig. 203	Bowsprit of model yacht SKEANDHU illustrating standing rigging and decoration.	118
Fig. 204	Foremast of a model stern trawler GLENROSE I.	119
Fig. 205	Standing rigging clearly visible on the model of SKEANDHU.	119
Fig. 206	Sketch to show types of rivets used in ship building.	120
Fig. 207	Sketch of shell plating and rivets.	120
Fig. 208	Sketch of typical rope reel.	122
Fig. 209	Rope reel and other items on the model of the oil rig standby vessel SCOTT GUARDIAN.	122
Fig. 210	Two rope reels on the motor ship LIZRIX.	123

Fig.	Description	Page
Fig. 211	Rope reel on a model oil rig rescue ship SCOTT GUARDIAN	
Fig. 212	Single plate rudder.	125
Fig. 213	Balanced rudder.	125
Fig. 214	Balanced suspended rudder.	125
Fig. 215	Component parts of a single blade balanced rudder for a model steam launch.	126
Fig. 216	Model rudder assembled on steam launch.	126
Fig. 217	Model bow thruster with electric motor - courtesy of Graupner.	127
Fig. 218	Model herring drifter with mizzen sail hoisted.	129
Fig. 219	Sketch of sail and lashings for a model herring drifter.	130
Fig. 220	Typical propeller shaft for a model ship.	131
Fig. 221	Range of couplings for connecting drive unit to propeller shaft - courtesy of Graupner.	132
Fig. 222	Stern of motor ship TIMRIX in dry-dock illustrating projecting tail shaft and rudder.	133
Fig. 223	A very basic skylight over the saloon of the bunkering tanker RIX HARRIER.	134
Fig. 224	Skylight of timber under construction for a model pilot cutter.	135
Fig. 225	Engine room skylight for the model tug CRUISER.	135
Fig. 226	Skylight under construction for model of the Tyne pilot cutter BRITANNIA.	135
Fig. 227	Engine room skylight for model of the steam driven tug GONDIA.	136
Fig. 228	Sketch showing single rod connection between rudder tiller and servo.	137
Fig. 229	Sketch showing `closed loop' rod system between rudder tiller and servo.	138
Fig. 230	Sketch to illustrate connections between twin rudders and single servo.	140
Fig. 231	Navigating bridge of a beautifully made model of the paddle steamer DUCHESS OF FIFE.	138
Fig. 232	Bridge under construction for model of CRUISER showing wheel, binnacle and two telegraphs.	139
Fig. 233	Interior of wheelhouse on motor fishing vessel DENEBULA showing wheel, helmsman's seat and gyro compass.	139
Fig. 234	Interior of wheelhouse on DENEBULA showing main engine and winch controls.	139
Fig. 235	Amidships superstructure of a model of a Union Castle Lines coaster ROVUMA.	141
Fig. 236	Main gantry and wheelhouse superstructure on the stern trawler ONWARD CHALLENGER.	142
Fig. 237	View of front of main superstructure of a twin screw tug.	142
Fig. 238	Detail of windows and decoration on the front of the wheelhouse of DENEBULA.	142
Fig. 239	Wheelhouse and main deckhouse of a small fishing vessel under construction.	143
Fig. 240	Main deckhouse on model of DENEBULA under construction.	143
Fig. 241	Slender low built engine room casing and forward saloon on model of steam yacht.	144
Fig. 242	Detail of bridge front of motor ship LIZRIX.	144
Fig. 243	Interior detail of bridge on motor ship LIZRIX.	145
Fig. 244	Detail of superstructure on the motor vessel JONRIX.	145
Fig. 245	Close up of searchlight on superstructure of the motor vessel JONRIX.	146
Fig. 246	Starboard bridge wing of superstructure of SCOTT GUARDIAN.	146
Fig. 247	Sketch of small water tank, cradle, connecting pipes and valve.	147
Fig. 247A	Model of the bunkering tanker RIX HARRIER.	148
Fig. 248	Typical 60 ton towing winch.	149
Fig. 249	Liverpool pattern tow hook.	151
Fig. 250	Circular pattern tow hook.	152
Fig. 251	Monarch tow hook with lever system to shock absorbing spring.	152
Fig. 252	Tow hook on model of tug CRUISER.	153
Fig. 253	Tow hook on Envoy class steam tug circa 1944. Photo courtesy of Mr. Eric Hammal.	153
Fig. 254	Stern view of model of tug CRUISER. showing towing bow.	150
Fig. 255	Simple gooseneck vents of two constructions.	155
Fig. 256	Tank vent with patented top.	155
Fig. 257	Gooseneck vent on a short sea trader.	158
Fig. 258	Sketch of Cowl pattern ventilator with dimensions.	156
Fig. 259	Large cowl pattern ventilators on model picket boat.	159
Fig. 260	A number of cowl ventilators on the model coaster ROVUMA.	159
Fig. 261	`Fyffe' pattern extraction ventilator.	155
Fig. 262	The `Thermotank' room on the motor ship JONRIX.	160
Fig. 263	Louvered air inlet opening with door to Thermotank room on the JONRIX.	160
Fig. 264	Mushroom pattern ventilator with radial pattern fan inside, replacement for the cowl pattern ventilator.	157
Fig. 265	Deck mounted, powered ventilation fan for feeding air into an accommodation block.	157
Fig. 266	Three tank vents on a motor coaster.	161
Fig. 267	A battery of three tank vents, coloured for specific duty, on a motor ship.	161
Fig. 268	Sketch of typical steam winch for a cargo ship.	163
Fig. 269	Two steam winches on a model steam coaster.	
Fig. 270	Typical electric motor driven cargo handling winch.	164
Fig. 271	Electric winches showing on the model of the coaster ARRAN MAIL.	165
Fig. 272	Hydraulic cod end winch for a fishing vessel.	165
Fig. 274	Cod end winch with hydraulic motor on the stern trawler GLENROSE I.	166
Fig. 275	Auxiliary winch with hydraulic motor on the stern trawler GLENROSE I.	166
Fig. 276	Net winch as fitted to GLENROSE I.	167
Fig. 277	Main trawl winch on the model of the side fishing trawler KINGSTON PERIDOT.	167
Fig. 278	Windlass with single gypsy for handling one anchor.	168
Fig. 279	Windlass with two gypsies for handling two anchors.	169
Fig. 280	Windlass on the stern trawler GLENROSE I with single gypsy, warping drum and hydraulic motor.	170
Fig. 281	Windlass on the bunkering tanker RIX HARRIER with twin gypsies, and warping drums. Note the guide sheave on the steel pedestal.	170
Fig. 282	Anchor handling capstan with hydraulic drive motor below deck.	171
Fig. 283	Anchor handling capstan with motor fitted inside the rotating drum.	172
Fig. 284	Windlass with rope winding drums in addition to warping drums on the motor ship JONRIX.	172
Fig. 285	The windlass of Fig.284 from a different view point.	173